Mary Schafer,
American Quilt Maker

Mary Schafer,

American Quilt Maker

GWEN MARSTON

THE UNIVERSITY OF MICHIGAN PRESS   ANN ARBOR

Copyright © by the University of Michigan 2004
All rights reserved
Published in the United States of America by
The University of Michigan Press
Manufactured in Singapore
∞ Printed on acid-free paper

2007   2006   2005   2004   4   3   2   1

A CIP catalog record for this book is available from the British Library.

Library of Congress Cataloging-in-Publication Data

Marston, Gwen.
        Mary Schafer, American quilt maker/ Gwen Marston.
            p.   cm.
        Includes bibliographical references.
        ISBN 0-472-09855-1 (Cloth : alk. paper) ISBN 0-472-06855-5
(Paper : alk. paper)
        1. Schafer, Mary, 1910–   . 2. Quiltmakers—Michigan—Biography. I.
Title.
    NK9198.S33 M368 2004
    746.46'092—dc22   2003018071

3364 2934   11/05

I dedicate this book to the memory of my friend Sally Goodin. Sally was a brilliant quilt maker and a woman who lived life with zest, courage, and good humor.

Preface: Mary and Gwen, Quilting Friends

 IT WAS LOVE AT FIRST SIGHT. FROM OUR VERY FIRST VISIT, Mary and I both felt we had found a special friendship. Here is how fate brought us together.

In 1977, I gave a quilt lecture to a women's group at the University of Michigan. A follow-up article in the *Flint Journal* mentioned that I'd spent the previous year working with Mennonite quilters in Oregon, and that my particular interest was in traditional quilts. Mary, who never missed anything about quilts in the news, called me the next day and introduced herself. After a brief conversation, we made arrangements for me to visit her the following day.

At the time, I lived in Flint, Michigan, an industrial city sixty miles north of Detroit. Mary's home was in Flushing, an adjacent suburb, just a fifteen-minute drive for me. I had no idea what to expect that first day as I waited for someone to answer the doorbell. The door opened, and Mary, all 5′1″ of her, with a warm smile and a twinkle in her eye, entered my life.

I was astonished at the number of quilts Mary had stored in her "finished" basement. They were folded four or five to the box—not just any kind of box but the egg boxes she liberated from the grocery store. Later, when the boxes began to show wear after years of hauling them up and down the stairs, I asked Mary if she might want to replace them with acid-free boxes. Mary said no, she liked the egg boxes. They were the right size for her to handle and had holes for handgrips on both ends. She wanted to be able to handle her quilts by herself.

With the hum of the dehumidifier ever present, I sat through the grandest show-and-tell I could ever imagine. And then there were the stacks of correspondence, quilt publications, fabrics, blocks, and tops, all carefully organized for reference. Mary herself seemed to be an encyclopedia of quilt information. I was overwhelmed to say the least.

Not all of the quilts were in storage in Mary's basement, however. She and her husband Fred lived in a ranch-style house with a full-size bed in each of the two bedrooms. Later I realized that Mary rotated the quilts on these beds and delighted in showing quilts to guests in this way. I remember especially that she was always attentive to Fred's tastes in quilts and made sure that his bed was covered in one of his favorites.

As I left Mary's house that first day, I knew I had experienced something very special. On my way home, I determined to work at making Mary and her quilts known to as many people as possible so that others could enjoy the fruits of her life's work. Within a year, I had applied for a grant to document her collection and had arranged the first in what would be six annual exhibits of Mary's quilts.

It was in that house that I learned, literally at Mary's knee, about the value of studying old quilts. More than any other factor, it is this course of study that has influenced my work. She lent me all of her *Progressive Farmer* and Nancy Cabot patterns collected through the round robins in which she had participated. I faithfully copied them, studied them, and learned the names of hundreds of patterns. Mary taught me to appliqué, and what a gift that was.

From our first meeting, Mary and I talked quilts. We could *really* talk quilts. We would get on a subject and explore every conceivable detail to its final conclusion. Weekly visits were common. Usually I would go out to Mary's. Less often Fred would drive Mary into Flint to see me. Between visits we would talk on the phone. Mary was busy dishing it out, and I was busy taking it in. We bought all the *Quilt Engagement Calendars* published by E. P. Dutton and Company and discussed the quilts in detail. We practically had them memorized.

Over the years, Mary and I discovered that we worked together well. Planning and executing the Whaley Historical House exhibits, for example, kept us both busy for six years. We were trying our level best to make everything work as efficiently and smoothly as possible. These exhibits in the late 1970s and early 1980s were the first to feature large portions of her collections.

But in truth the most enjoyable part of it all was making quilts, talking quilts, and having our regular, private show-and-tells. We couldn't wait to show each other our latest projects. Once I bought a big box chock full of old blocks. I was so excited I could hardly bear it. Before even finding out what treasures were in the box, I called Mary and told her what I had acquired. She

Mary and Gwen talking quilts in Mary's bedroom

was as excited as I was, and so I went directly out to see her. We were like two little girls on Christmas morning. We sat down on the floor and opened the box. We spread the blocks all over the floor, putting them into piles of the same pattern and talking about them as we proceeded. You would have thought we'd won the lottery.

We often played off of each other. Sometimes we got excited about the same idea and made the same quilt at the same time. Two examples are our Morning Star and GIANT TULIP quilts. In 1978, Mary was advising me about the best use for some antique yardage in my collection. I had probably eight yards each of a blue and a black print from before the turn of the twentieth century. Mary suggested it would be perfect for a Morning Star quilt. She drew up the pattern, made one block up for me, and talked me into hand piecing the whole quilt.

My finished Morning Star was 68″ × 83″, and it was the first and last totally hand pieced quilt I ever made. Mary got excited about the project and decided to make one for herself. Her quilt was 81″ × 101″ and was red and black with white stars. This quilt was part of the First Collection, which went to Michigan State University Museum.[1]

With our GIANT TULIPs, it started with a black and white picture of a quilt made in Pennsylvania circa 1820. We found it in *American Quilts and Coverlets* (Safford and Bishop 1974, 194). The old quilt was housed at the Philadelphia Museum of Art. I wrote asking for information about the quilt, particularly about the color. What color is it? A member of the museum staff responded that they no longer had the quilt in their collection and offered no other information. Mary and I continued talking about it each time we spoke, and finally we decided to each make one. We drew up a pattern and went to work. My notes read: 18″ blocks, 3″ striping, 6″ border—longer on top and bottom, 8″ tulip from tip to tip. We wondered what had happened to that wonderful old quilt after it left the Philadelphia Museum of Art. We went with pink and green. Both quilts are quilted all over with triple fans, as was the original.

Our friendship deepened. She borrowed my old FEATHER-EDGED STAR top and copied it. She borrowed my antique BEAR'S PAW and made a copy of it. She borrowed my antique CHERRY BASKET and copied it. I marked the feathers on her ROSE WREATH. One day when we were attending a quilt show together we found two old tops sewn together to make a featherbed coverlet. We both wanted it, so Mary suggested we buy it together, take it apart, and each of us could have one top.[2]

There came a time when I began to write about quilts as well as make them, and naturally I thought this was another way I could promote my friend's work. In both *Sets and Borders* (Marston and Cunningham 1987) and *American Beauties: Rose and Tulip Quilts* (Marston and Cunningham 1988), I was thrilled with the opportunity to display her quilts. *Sets and Borders* featured twenty-nine of Mary's quilts and *American Beauties* included seven blocks and twenty-four of her quilts. As the books were being written, Mary was always eager to share the rare old patterns and wonderful blocks she had collected and to answer any and all questions.

GIANT TULIP
75″ × 86″, 1980. Made by Mary Schafer.

When I moved to Beaver Island in 1983, Mary sent me off with cuttings from her garden: candytuft, violets, iris, ajuga, pachysandra, and lamb's ears. They continue to thrive and delight me, as does our friendship. We continued our communication in the way so familiar to her—letter writing. We wrote long, detailed letters to each other about quilts. And we continued to share quilt materials. The year 2003 marked the twentieth anniversary of my annual Beaver Island Quilt Retreats. Each year I have a different theme, and Mary has always shown an interest in whatever the chosen subject is. She sends quilt patterns, quilt blocks, and quilts to Beaver Island to use as examples.

Mary visited me several times on Beaver Island. Being a real nature buff, she loved taking long walks and identifying the wild flowers that grow in abundance there. I can still remember how agile she was "in the bush" and how she kept up a brisk pace on some very long hikes.

When Fred died on December 8, 1988, he was cremated, and Mary knew exactly where she wanted to scatter his ashes. In the spring of 1989, she brought Fred's ashes to Beaver Island. Her daughter-in-law, Esther, accompanied her on this trip. Mary remembered a lovely wooded area where the trillium are thick. She and I trudged off along a dirt road with Mary holding the urn. I stood close by and watched as she scattered his ashes among the trillium. Then we walked back to the house. I pass that way often on my walks and always have a reason to remember Fred.

Today the telephone may ring, and I may hear Mary's cheery voice saying, "Hello Dear." After all these years, we still have a lot to talk about, and much of what we talk about is quilts. I have never tired of asking her about or reading her correspondence with Benberry, Peto, Craddock, Bannister, and the others. This is another wonderful gift Mary gave me. Through her, I feel connected to these old quilting friends of another generation.

When I began thinking about this book, about my friend Mary Schafer, I started pulling together all my materials. When you have a close friendship that spans more than two decades, it's not unusual to accumulate materials in the way of letters and small gifts. But in Mary's case there are quilt patterns, quilting designs, blocks, fabric samples, cardboard templates, show notices, and catalogs . . . , I seem to have saved everything. But not foreseeing that I would be writing this book I hadn't saved them in any particular order.

When I began to gather the materials for this book, I was shocked at just how much I had. I didn't need to be reminded about how much Mary had guided me, and how much she meant to me; but until I organized these materials for publication I didn't know just how much she had shared, and continues to share, with me. It's as if one day I woke up and found myself in possession, all at once, of priceless holdings.

Because I've known Mary for many years, I thought working on this book would be a walk in the park. But once I tapped the surface, I realized how large her world is and that I had my work cut out for me. As work proceeded on the book, a semicircle of Mary's letters, patterns, and associated books grew outward from my desk, like the concentric fans in an old quilt or round robin of old friends.

The Mary Schafer story is the story of a little immigrant girl who learned to use a needle. With her needle, she stitched a life for herself and made piles and piles of beautiful quilts as well.

*A*cknowledgments

SPECIAL THANKS TO VI GRAVES, WHO EDITED MY ORIGINAL text. Her encouragement and professional advice at the beginning of this book guided me in the right direction. I regret that Vi passed away before she could see this book in print.

My friend Valerie Clarke, whom I've known for twenty-nine years, and my daughter Brenda Marston, whom I've known all her life, also read for me. Carol Spaly helped with the research, made several trips to see Mary on my behalf, and allowed me to include in this book two Schafer quilts in her own collection. Carol Grossman was always available to obtain information I needed for the book.

Cuesta Benberry and the late Dolores Hinson were enthusiastic in helping me to reconstruct events in the late 1950s and early 1960s. I thank Cuesta Benberry for allowing me to quote her extensively and for answering all of my questions completely and promptly. Suellen Meyer generously gave me photographs of some of Betty Harriman's quilts and dolls. Hazel Carter provided me with information regarding Cuesta Benberry's donation of her Mary Schafer blocks to the Quilters Hall of Fame. Virginia Anderson drafted all of the patterns for this book. More than that, Virginia has been a friend and a help to me and to Mary.

The photography was done by Valerie Clarke and Ken Hannon of the KEVA Partnership, unless otherwise credited. Alan Zinn and Suellen Meyer also contributed photographs to this book.

$\mathscr{C}$ontents

Illustrations

Quilts illustrated in this book are indicated by capital letters.

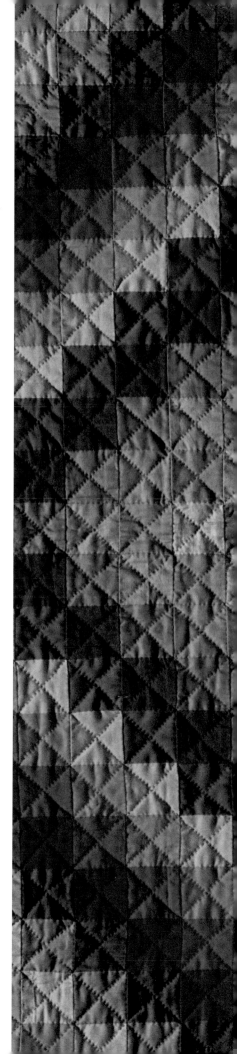

Part One

Laying the Groundwork

An Overview of the Quilt Revival in the Twentieth Century

Today's quilting world did not just spring from the head of Zeus.
—*Cuesta Benberry and Joyce Gross*

 DURING A REVIVAL, EVERYONE GETS SAVED. When quilting is enjoying one of its revivals, many become interested and tag along for the ride because it's the thing to do. Joiners tinker at it because of its current popularity. A case can be made for one revival beginning around the time of the country's centennial and fading out in the 1940s and a second revival beginning around the time of the bicentennial and continuing to this day.

The first revival of the twentieth century actually began in the nineteenth as the country prepared for its first centennial. Interest in all things American prompted renewed attention to quilt making. Articles began to appear in women's magazines encouraging readers to return to the home arts that, even then, represented quilts as artifacts from "the good old days."

The Newark Museum had the first museum-sponsored quilt exhibit in 1914 and bought its first quilt for the permanent collection in 1918. Things were beginning to change. With museums leading the way, art historians became interested, quilt scholars clocked in, and quilt shows began to pop up around the country. In 1915, Marie Webster published the first quilt book, *Quilts, Their Story and How to Make Them.* In 1924, the Metropolitan Museum of Art in New York City opened its new American wing to house colonial arts and crafts. Interest surged as the whole country renewed its appreciation of colonial arts and crafts.[1]

With political suffrage and an increasing presence in the world outside the home, some women grew sentimental for what was perceived as a more simple past. They began to decorate their homes in the "colonial revival" style, which of course included quilts. A renewed interest in quilt making ensued as the modern homemaker, intent on achieving the colonial American look, sought to cover the beds in her house with quilts, even if it meant she had to make them herself. Quilts were just the right complement to the early American reproduction furnishings being touted by women's magazines and other commercial ventures of the times.

While the Roaring Twenties was a time when the nation could afford to indulge in such extravagances as home decorating, the Depression quickly replaced lavishness with clear realism and frugality. Hard times brought on by the Great Depression were reason enough to keep women making quilts. The Chicago World's Fair of 1933 caught the nation's attention. Sears, Roebuck, and Company caught the attention of the nation's quilters by sponsoring a contest in conjunction with the World's Fair. The contest received more than twenty-four thousand entries.[2]

Although general interest was fading by the late 1930s, some important events occurred. Ruth Finley published *Old Patchwork Quilts* in 1929, in 1935 Carrie Hall and Rose Kretsinger published *The Romance of the Patchwork Quilt in America,* and Florence Peto published *Historic Quilts* in 1939. These three seminal books on quilt history remained a major influence well into the 1970s.

In addition, several significant exhibits set the stage for taking quilts off the beds and hanging them on the walls. In 1939, Rose Kretsinger had a one-woman show at the Muehback Hotel in Kansas City. The Chicago Art Institute exhibited quilts made by Bertha Stenge in 1943, and in 1948 the New York Historical Society presented an exhibit of Florence Peto's quilts.[3]

World War II, however, demanded that the country shift its attention to the war effort. Rosie the Riveter was not making quilts, she was making planes.

After the war, the desire for new manufactured goods took center stage. No one wanted the handmade, and that included bread, clothing, and bedcoverings. While some women, especially in rural areas, continued to make quilts, the next great quilt revival would not arrive until the country began planning another birthday party, the bicentennial.

During the period between quilt revivals, the craft was kept alive by dedicated women such as Mary Schafer, wife, mother, and homemaker, who in time would become a national figure in the quilt world. Not only did quilting stay alive, it flourished, though not in a public way. Quietly, attracting little or no attention, women across the nation began to network for the purpose of studying quilts—how they were made, what their names were, what region they hailed from. They documented their findings by circulating detailed reports among themselves and by submitting articles to home-produced newsletters whose popularity grew by word-of-mouth. By doing so, these dedicated and intrepid quilt enthusiasts bridged the revivals and laid the foundation for today's quilt scholarship.

The study of quilting by Mary Schafer and her far-flung circle of friends was done for its own sake. In the 1940s, 1950s, and 1960s, it was not possible to make a national name for oneself in quilting. It wasn't a profession a woman could choose in hopes of paying the rent. There were no quilt "stars" in the way there are today, and that's the glory of it all. The stitches that held the quilt world together were supplied by women consumed not with the promise of fame or fortune but with a passion for their own history and an insatiable appetite for all things quilt.

By the time Mary made her first quilt in 1952, interest in unearthing and recording quilt history was rekindling. Hungry for more quilt information than what was then available in mainstream society, women began a determined search. They traveled. They asked questions. They collected and traded patterns. They traced the history of patterns. They collected antique quilts, old blocks, and historical fabrics. And, most importantly, they shared.

My dear friend Mary Katherine Jarrell remembers these times as if they were yesterday. Mary Katherine has spent the better part of sixty years making quilts, collecting and researching quilts, and teaching and lecturing about quilts. She told me about a collector who traveled the back roads with a trunk full of blankets to trade for old quilts. There was a time when this would have worked. Today you would have to travel with a trunk full of cash.

A native of West Virginia, Mary Katherine traces her lifetime interest in quilts to her youth in Appalachia, where quilts were both useful and decorative. She maintained her interest as a graduate home economist by teaching sewing. She has enjoyed a long and illustrious career as a quilt teacher, lecturer, and distinguished authority on quilts. She now lives in Charlotte, North Carolina.

Her interest in quilts from Appalachia prompted her to scour the rural countryside for antique quilts, and sometimes she found them. In *Uncoverings 1981,* she wrote about some of her experiences searching for quilts.

> *In my quest for quilts in Appalachia, I have traveled up the hollows and mountain sides, climbed into barn lofts, explored dusty attics and dank cellars, and found disappointment more often than treasures. But the treasures have been sufficient to keep me following every lead. Many of my treasures were abandoned long ago to rot in dirt and neglect. Often I can learn nothing of the maker.*[4]

Quilt enthusiasts found each other across the divide of geography, education, and social class. They introduced each other through letters and built networks operated by the U.S. mail through which they shared information about quilt patterns, antique fabrics, and quilt history. Mary was in the thick of it. She reveled in it. She was like a one-woman letter-writing factory. There was little public awareness of quilts in the 1960s, but for Mary quilts occupied every free moment. It's hard to imagine how she carried on such a prolific correspondence, made so many quilts, and managed her house and gardens with such efficiency.

In the early 1970s, the approaching bicentennial and the "back to the land" movement once again turned the country's attention to early American arts and crafts. Because quilts embody the creative spirit of American women more than any other art form, it continued to be a natural response for women to pick up their needles. Even though there have been long periods in which interest in quilting waned, it has never been forgotten. The bicentennial spurred a quilt revival that as yet shows no sign of slowing down.

Two major quilt shows furthered the notion of quilting as a dynamic activity: the 1971 groundbreaking exhibit at the Whitney Museum of American Art in New York City and the 1972 American Pieced Quilts exhibit at the Smithsonian Institution in Washington, D.C. Quilts were beginning to be appreciated both as art and as historical artifacts.

Quilt guilds formed from coast to coast, and most are still active today. Weekend quilt shows began popping up in every region at small country churches. Cardboard signs placed at strategic places along the roadside brought people in to view locally made quilts draped over the backs of pews. No longer did one have to wait for the annual county fair to see quilts on public display.

When the bicentennial arrived, Mary Schafer was ready. She had made six full-size quilts with bicentennial themes. She was now a nationally recognized quilter, having earned two blue ribbons in the 1970 National Quilting Association competition; one for Best Pieced Quilt and one for Viewers' Choice. Mary had arrived.

In the 1980s, quilting went commercial. The emergence of huge regional quilt shows and competitions around the country both capitalized on and heightened the popularity of quilting in mainstream America. These events put hundreds of quilts on display and sponsored a variety of how-to workshops. Funded by revenues from ticket sales, workshop and vendor fees, and corporate sponsorships, organizers were able to offer large prize monies for top winners in the competitions. Vendor "malls" offering notions, fabrics, and books for sale were developed solely for the emerging, affluent quilt market. Trade and consumer magazines proliferated, featuring glossy issues full of advertising. Indeed, quilting and quilters had become a "market," to use the terminology of business, worth 1.5 billion dollars according to a report published by Leman Publications in 1995.

Never influenced by the public's waxing and waning interest in quilting, Mary spent the 1980s studying quilts, especially traditional Amish and "doll" quilts, making more quilts, cataloging her vast collection, and responding to the growing number of requests that she show her quilts in galleries and museums.

When the Museum of the American Quilter's Society (MAQS) opened in Paducah, Kentucky, in 1991, the featured event was an exhibit of Schafer quilts. In 1997, MAQS presented an exhibit called 20th Century Quilts, 1900–1970: Women Make Their Mark. This exhibit honored the best of the century, and Mary was included.

Marsha MacDowell, Curator of Folk Arts at the Michigan State University Museum, has written that "Two individuals—Marie Webster of Marian, Indiana and Mary Schafer of Flushing, Michigan—are known nationally for their pioneering efforts in collecting quilt history."[5] With a substantial collection of her quilts residing permanently at the Michigan State University Museum, Mary Schafer has joined quilt legends Charlotte Jane Whitehill and Rose Kretsinger as women who have their quilt collections housed in museums.

The Michigan State University Museum presented an exhibit of Mary's quilts in 2001. The title of the exhibit says it all: The Mary Schafer Collection: A Legacy of Quilt History.

Influences: Early Quilt Magazines

THE QUILT PUBLICATIONS THAT EMERGED CIRCA 1960 PLAYED A critical role in influencing the direction the quilt world would take. With few books on the subject and no counterpart in the marketplace, these home-produced newsletters were principal players in motivating quilters to research, identify, and preserve old quilts and quilt-related materials. They were responsible for linking quilters across vast distances in geography and culture. Once women were in touch with each other on the basis of their shared interest, the formal work of collecting and documenting quilt history began in earnest. To fully comprehend the enormous role Mary Schafer and her quilting correspondents played in the current quilt revival requires a peek at these pioneering quilt magazines.

The first quilt magazine Mary subscribed to was *Aunt Kate's Quilting Bee,* published by Glenna Boyd in Oklahoma from 1962 to 1980. *Aunt Kate's* listed other quilt publications, and Mary subscribed to them, too: Joy Craddock's *4 J's,* Claudine Moffat's *Jay Bees,* and Betty Flack's *Little 'n Big.*

Compared to today's slick quilting periodicals composed on sophisticated computers by highly trained designers and printed on high-speed, fully automated, four-color presses, the early publications seem crude. Along with typewritten commentary, patterns were hand drawn on master templates, which were hand inked and hand rolled sheet by wobbly sheet. But appearances in this case would deceive. What Glenna Boyd, Joy Craddock, Claudine Moffat, and Betty Flack were aesthetically unable to achieve in their basements was more than made up for by the refinement of the information they broadcast. Cuesta Benberry, who would become one of the most respected quilt historians of the twentieth century, remembers:

> *In the 1960s there were a lot of little quilt magazines—not magazines by today's standards but rather little mimeographed journals which were basically pattern books. They also had lists of names of people who were interested in pattern collecting, quilt making or exchanging friendship blocks. The magazines served as sort of a coalescing agent to gather in quilt people. I got to know there were a number of people all over the U.S. who were interested in quilts.*
>
> *There were several publications none of which lasted very long. What they did was to try to feature old patterns that were long since forgotten or had not been used in recent times. Those women were really very good at uncovering information about old quilts and old quilt patterns from old sources—old newspapers and magazines. They also sponsored Round Robins.*[1]

The magazines offered Mary an opportunity to learn about a tradition to which she felt drawn but of which she had little knowledge. In addition, she was able to connect with like-minded women and engage in a wide, long-lived and lively exchange. Letters and parcels of hand-colored patterns and carefully pressed blocks flew from mailbox to mailbox as the women shared their discoveries and their work and engaged in round robins. That many of Mary's long-distance colleagues—Florence Peto, Cuesta Benberry, Barbara Bannister, Lenice Bacon, and others—became known as leaders in the quilting field is a testimonial to the value of these early magazines.

In 1969, Mary added a new quarterly publication called *Nimble Needle Treasures* to her growing cache of quilt-related items. *Treasures* was published in Oklahoma by Pat Almy until 1975. It featured a regular roster of writers earning their reputations in the field: Dolores Hinson, Cuesta Benberry, and Maxine Teele. Like its sister publica-

NORTH CAROLINA LILY
79″ × 96″, 1971. Made by Mary Schafer. (Collection of the Michigan State University Museum, Mary Schafer Collection. Photo by Alan Zinn.)

tions, it not only offered patterns but provided an outlet for women to share their findings and feelings about everything quilt.

Mary submitted an item to *Nimble Needle Treasures* for the 1972 fall issue. In "100 Years of the North Carolina Lily," she showed two quilts, one of her own making and an antique owned by Robert May of Detroit from which Mary took inspiration. From the beginning, Mary understood the importance of crediting her sources, always recording as much information about a quilt as she could. She described her NORTH CAROLINA LILY as follows.

Made by Mary Schafer. Pattern adapted from Mr. May's version. Border is original of Mary Schafer. Mary used 12 blocks in her version, there are 16 in Mr. May's quilt.[2]

Mary's caption is typical of her care and steadfast determination to credit design sources and provide documentation that is as complete as possible. The caption also illustrates the influence the magazines had on the formal characteristics of Mary's quilts. Because many of her early quilts had to be imagined from line drawings or black and white photographs of quilts, Mary had to trust her own understanding of historically appropriate color and print combinations. As a result, even when she reproduced quilts directly from the originals, as was the case with Mr. May's quilt, Mary gave herself the freedom to stay within the spirit of the original—its purpose, its era, its ideas—without becoming a slave to its every detail.

To get an inkling of how this works, pretend it's 1970 and you are reading an article about Betty Harriman's exquisite quilts illustrated with these photographs: FLOWERING ALMOND, WASHINGTON PLUME, and MISSOURI ROSE TREE. To honor Betty and her work, you decide to make a copy of one of them. The article includes a description of the colors and prints, for example, light blue or small floral. What colors and prints do you choose at the fabric store to attempt a re-creation of Betty's work?

In September 1969, another little magazine made its debut: *Quilter's Newsletter* (later *Quilter's Newsletter Magazine,* QNM). Looking very much like its predecessors, it was destined to become the one that would live long and prosper into the twenty-first century. The maiden issue trumpeted its corporate goal on the cover: "*The* magazine for quilt lovers." Published monthly, except for July and August (a combined summer issue), the cost for a single issue was forty cents.

Bonnie Leman, the founder and managing editor until 1996, also started a business, selling reproductions of *Kansas City Star* newspaper patterns she had inherited from her mother.[3] In addition, as the magazine and pattern business fed off each other, keeping pace with a growing national quilting audience, she and her husband expanded into templates. In her 1971 Heirloom Plastics Catalog, Bonnie wrote:

FLOWERING ALMOND
85″ × 99″. Begun by Betty Harriman, ca. 1968, finished by Mary Schafer, 1979. (Collection of the Michigan State University Museum, Mary Schafer Collection.)

WASHINGTON PLUME
88″ × 96″. Begun by Betty Harriman, ca. 1965, finished by Mary Schafer, 1980. This is one of the quilts the Michigan State University Museum sold at auction in 1998. (Collection of April Yorks.)

MISSOURI ROSE TREE
89″ × 92″. Begun by Betty Harriman, ca. 1966, finished by Mary Schafer, 1973. (Collection of the Michigan State University Museum, Mary Schafer Collection.)

In colonial times, when paper was scarce, ladies who could afford it had their quilt patterns cut from metal by the local blacksmith. These metal templates would not wear out and could be passed on to neighbors, friends, and relatives. Heirloom Plastics was started with the idea that modern day quilters would like these long-lasting templates also, if they could be made available at reasonable prices.[4]

Plastics! The times were truly changing, but the winning formula of QNM changed little over the years. Like the earlier magazines from which it evolved, the patterns, the techniques, the emphasis on careful documentation, and the exchange of news and views from rank-and-file quilters remained both the cause and effect of its popularity. Black and white photographs and illustrations were replaced with color in 1975. Today, QNM is available on newsstands everywhere, sustained by an international pool of readers, writers, and advertisers.

Quilt making in the United States is a series of hills and valleys. Mary came to quilting in a valley. Early in her quest for quilt education, she found a handful of homemade publications produced by and for women like herself: inquisitive, determined, and talented. Several became lifelong correspondents, collaborators, and friends. Some were destined to become leading quilt historians such as Florence Peto and Cuesta Benberry; others became unparalleled quilt makers such as Betty Harriman and Mary herself. Together their words, their work, and their influence spread.

In a scenario as American as patchwork, this small group of talented, intrepid quilt colleagues, using the best technology available to them, helped each other climb to the top of the hill. On the way, they called to a new generation of quilters, one pattern at a time.

Quilt Study

THE EARLY QUILTING MAGAZINES NOT ONLY UNITED AMATEUR quilt sleuths from coast to coast, they connected antique quilt dealers to a ready audience. Owning quilts, of course, is a fine way to study them. Mary bought her first quilt in 1967, a Feather-Edged Star, circa 1850, for fifteen dollars.[1] Mary's early forays into collecting had been limited to her home state. But as her zeal for the craft grew she and her husband Fred spent several summer vacations on the road in search of quilts. Thus, they made trips through Pennsylvania and down to the southern states. Mary bought what took her fancy and what she could afford.

Betty Harriman, a pen pal from Bunceton, Missouri, who would over time become the dearest of friends and collaborators, sold Mary several significant quilts: SUNBURST, circa 1825; FOUR PATCH, circa 1800–1825; FRAMED SQUARE, circa 1800–1825; MARINER'S COMPASS, circa 1830–50;[2] and an exquisite, all white quilt, circa 1800–1810. The last quilt Mary bought was a Midwest Amish CUPS AND SAUCERS for three hundred dollars in the 1980s.

There were few books available when Mary Schafer began studying quilts. Every woman serious about quilt scholarship, including Mary, owned *Quilts: Their Story and How to Make Them* (Webster 1915), *Old Patchwork Quilts* (Finley 1929), *The Romance of the Patchwork Quilt in America* (Hall and Kretsinger 1935), *Historic Quilts* (Peto 1939), *American Quilts and Coverlets* (Peto 1949) and *Old Quilts*

(Dunton 1946). Important as these first books were, together they hardly nick the tail of the tradition. To fill in the cavernous gaps, indeed, to discover the parameters of the craft, women would have to scour the backwoods and hollows of their regions to find quilts, record data, and take oral histories. Joy Craddock wrote to Mary in 1965 about just such a quilt hunt.

I was so far behind [in my work] I thought I was ahead, so took off to Arkansas after some quilt samples and patterns. You remember the drawings of Wind Blown Tulip I sent in [in a round robin]. I didn't have the pattern but thought I knew where I could get it as I saw it on a bed in one of the homes I visited last summer. So, wrote to ask the lady for it. It had been given to her and she didn't know how to go about taking the pattern off; [she] told me if I came over I could. . . . Then when I got there, she was gone, but a neighbor told me the name and address of the lady who made the quilt. I had met and talked with Mrs. Williams one evening late, should have realized that was where Clariece had gotten the quilts as she was the one who sent us to see Mrs. Williams about buying her place. To make a long story short, I arrived late at night and forgetting about having to ford the creek, I drove on out. Got to the creek and it was a bit high. Anyhow, I couldn't turn around and wouldn't attempt to back down the icy mountain road at night. So I spent the rest of the night there on the blasted cold mountainside. Thank heavens I had about six quilts in the car. By morning the water had gone down enough for me to cross. I got the pattern alright and six more from some old quilts of the Williams family, has been in the family for over 163 years and they had every kind of document under the sun to prove it. That is the only one she was to make and sell quilts from. Took me all day to talk her into letting me photograph the quilt and make patterns from it. Had to pay her $2.00 per pattern for them and do the work myself.[3]

CUPS AND SAUCERS
69″ × 80¼″, ca. 1920–30. Midwest Amish. (Collection of Mary Schafer.)

The search was on for finding and rescuing old quilts, old patterns, and anything that pertained to quilts. Collecting patterns and researching their origins ran through the quilt world like a fever. These women laid the groundwork for the quilt world we know today. I think of it as a little underground movement of women from all over the country connected through the mail. Friendships grew; women shared information, formed little study groups, and cranked out quilt publications in their basements on mimeograph machines. Imagine . . . they did it all without e-mail too.

Dolores Hinson, in her effort to uncover quilt history, employed a scatter-shot technique.

> *I decided the information still had to be in quilters' brains and I asked everyone if they knew a quilter. Did they ever. In an era when the craft was supposedly dead— everyone knew at least one quilter. Would they talk to me? They were delighted to.*[4]

Some quilt hunters in Mary's group poached in lands far afield. Maxine Teele, for instance, had spotted a story about Gypsy Rose Lee in the St. Louis *Post Dispatch* of April 5, 1959. The story told of quilting parties hosted by Miss Lee in her elegant New York apartment. Regular guests included Miss Lee's sister, June Havoc; Bonnie Cashin, fashion designer; Faye Emerson, actress; Hedda Hopper, columnist; Jane Ashley, interior designer; and Celeste Holm, actress. What a guest list!

Maxine dashed off a quick letter to Miss Lee, even though she didn't have a complete address. Maxine said: "Evidently the postal authorities of New York City had heard of her because my letter reached her and I had an answer." Apparently Miss Lee continued to make quilts because Maxine ran across another publication in 1969 describing a recent quilt made by Gypsy Rose Lee.[5]

Maxine followed her leads no matter where they led. Once, when she found a reference to a quilt in James Pope-Hennessey's *Queen Mary*, she wrote to Queen Elizabeth II asking if she knew its whereabouts. Her query was answered in a letter from Buckingham Palace signed by a lady-in-waiting. Alas, a dead end. No one had any information about the quilt.[6]

Patterns, of course, could dominate the discourse at the drop of a block, each one its own journey of discovery. Dolores Hinson explains.

> *One of the blocks had the darndest red applique on white. I could not decide on the symbolism except—it looked for all the world like a depiction of a circular saw blade. Well, I started with Chesapeake Bay histories, nothing (the blocks were made on the Md. Eastern shore). I finally wound up reading books on Engineering history. In 1841 one of the three first sawmills to install the brand new circular saws opened on the Eastern shore. Can't you just see folks flocking to the mill to sight-see. And one devised this pattern. The mill was south and east of Havre' De' Grace, Md. within 30 miles of the family home of the bride. How's that for documentation (fun!)*[7]

In 1974, Cuesta Benberry published an insider's account of a typical early research project in *Nimble Needle Treasures.*

Most quilt pattern collectors will agree, I'm sure, that it takes very little to get us started on a project. The project about which I'm reporting is not a recent project. We started it quite a few years ago. One day, just as quilt pattern collectors love to do, I was enjoying myself reading a group of Nancy Cabot quilt clippings. They read better than any novel. I picked up one—"Iowa Rose."

It stated, "Every state in the union has contributed to the quilt album with a rose pattern bearing its name."

Well, that did it! If as the clipping stated, there are those quilt patterns for each state, why not try to find them? There were 48 states when the clipping was printed, so that meant looking for 48 patterns of state roses. Out came the pattern lists, the boxes of patterns, the books, the magazines, the scrapbooks, and the usual paraphernalia quilt pattern collectors use.

First, I'd see how many state rose quilt patterns I already had. After an hour or so of searching, I had mixed feelings about this proposed project. I had located some of the patterns, but at least a half-dozen or so were versions and variations of rose patterns for the same state—the Ohio Rose!

Now, I know that the quilt pattern collectors among you are way ahead of me. They know, without my saying, what the next step will be. They're right! I fired off letters to my quilt patterns collecting friends for help. From that beginning, we were off on a state rose quilt pattern safari. And no big game hunter's safari in the wilds of Africa was more fun than our state rose quilt pattern one here in the U.S. It was an enjoyable, though incomplete project. We got for some states several versions or variations; for other states, we didn't find one. Ohio kept its lead in the number of variations with Kentucky as a close second.

Some patterns came from familiar sources, others came from unknown sources. We found more than the 48 we originally looked for but, of course, the number was inflated by the multiple versions we found. I think the crowning point of the project came when Ruth Snyder of Independence, Kansas, shared an old Ohio Rose version that had come from a radio station as a premium in the early days of radio broadcasting in the first quarter of the 1900's. A radio source is a rare source, if I've ever heard of one.

We got multiple versions of rose patterns from many states, including Texas, Indiana, Iowa, Pennsylvania, California, North Carolina, Missouri, New Jersey, Louisiana, North Dakota, Tennessee among others. For states, such as Alabama, Arkansas, Kansas, Delaware, Georgia, Illinois and Wisconsin we scraped by with a single version of a state rose quilt pattern. The states that eluded us completely, and we were unable to locate even one state rose quilt pattern for included New Hampshire, Montana and Minnesota.

Often, we'd find later versions of states having rose quilt patterns named for them. However, the original "Iowa Rose" Nancy Cabot clipping, that got us started on the project, was published in the 1930's. So we decided on an arbitrary cut-off date, not later than the publication date of the Nancy Cabot clipping. The pattern had to be a *quilt known to be in existence prior to this time. For our project could not be considered authentic if we included patterns of quilts known to have been made after Nancy Cabot reported they were already in existence. We were looking for quilts that had been made from the beginning of quiltmaking in the U.S. to the 1930's that had a state rose quilt design.*

We were never able to determine which was the oldest state rose quilt pattern. We found several that were of early 1800's origin. We could not date any back to the late 1700's as we had hoped to do.

One little interesting fact we found was that in the really old versions (1800's origin), the name "Beauty" was sometimes, but not always used interchangeably for state rose quilt patterns. An old version of the Ohio Rose was also called Ohio Beauty: an old Iowa Rose was called Iowa Beauty, too. Likewise for Missouri Beauty, among others. Two notable exceptions to this are New York Beauty and Alabama Beauty, which are not rose patterns at all. However, the synonymous names occurred frequently enough so that if we located an old rose pattern name for a state with Beauty in the title, and from an obscure source, we would double check to see if this pattern also carried just the state name coupled with the word "rose."

Most of the state rose quilt patterns were applique designs, with a number of the 20th century ones being embroidery designs. There were a few pieced ones in the group.

As usual, we claim no originality for the idea of this project. For as any veteran quilt pattern collector knows, just mention any project, and there's always someone who has done it before you ever thought of it. Original project? I doubt it. Fun project? But definitely! And will someone please tell me what the Montana Rose quilt pattern looks like?[8]

Cuesta remembers another pattern search project in which she and Mary were engaged.

I remember our tracing the "Horn of Plenty" design back to the days of the Holy Roman Empire. Although we ended the search for that specific design, both of us believed that with additional effort we probably could have traced it even farther back in time.[9]

Fabrics also occupied the quest. Mary, Dolores Hinson, and Maxine Teele were especially interested in fabrics. In fact, Maxine described herself as "hooked on old fabrics."[10] Twenty years after the fact, Mary, in a private show-and-tell of antique fabrics with Gwen Marston, remembered that Florence Peto had sent "considerable" amounts of fabric to Maxine and sent documented antique fabrics to Mary herself.

Quilters often wrote lengthy, in-depth letters about various aspects of quilt research, and Mary was no exception. In 1986, she responded to an idea Gwen Marston had concerning a book on dating fabric illustrated with examples from their joint collection of antique fabrics. Mary replied:

Dear Gwen,

Your proposed new project to put together a book of fabric samples with dates and information is commendable. It has put my thought processes in motion. I might just as well write as think about all or some of what it entails.

I began with trying to date that "Linden Mill" quilt, the old one found in Ronnie's car. To name it was easy, to date it was something else. I didn't think seriously about the date until the manuscript was written for the collection book. When I got the Finley book I read and re-read it many times (I still do). Chapters 14 and 15 were helpful as were the pictures with dates in the text. Another book I recommend is Printed Textiles: English and American Cottons and Linens 1700–1850, by Florence M. Montgomery. I got the book from the library. I have two pieces shown in that book: Figure 332—Flowers on fancy machine ground about 1830, roller printed and Figure 397—English Roller print with American subject (Eagle) Eagle Shield from Seal of United States, surrounded by Floral Wreath in Palmate vignette. Roller printed 1825–1839, Manchester 163. Don't know what the 163 means. This last piece I got from Florence Peto. The eagles are cut out—used in quilts she made. The first piece from Ruth Parr—it is chintz. The Montgomery book is helpful in dating early and antique materials. The cut off date is 1850, chances are if it isn't listed in the book, materials not shown are probably later than 1850. However I must say there is much over lapping. Scraps were saved over a long period. There could be a span of 10–20 or more years of manufactured goods in a given quilt. A random look through the Orlofsky book quilts are dated Fig. 102 copperplate print 1780–1790. Fig. 70 cotton 3rd quarter nineteenth century, Fig. 37 cotton Mid nineteenth century.

I've noticed in several books quilts were dated by quarter century, by experts.

I believe the best way to date material is by comparison and example. Comparing material in dated quilts with pieces to be dated. The Album quilt I have is dated 1856—I believe it is safe to say all the material used, front and back is dated 1856. The red prints are the same tone and the brown print of the back is 1856 vintage. I must confess that if I was shown a piece of the blue print border alone, I would probably date it around 1900. That's almost a 50 year difference. I must say it is difficult to date material, these days, with more than an educated guess.

I have not been challenged by anyone about the dates given in the collection book [Marston 1980] in other words the dates are acceptable. I did the best I could but I'm not sure they are accurate. The fact I wasn't challenged indicates to me that educated guesses today are acceptable. And I wonder why that is so. I accept dates for quilts printed in the books. I've come to the conclusion there is only limited information available to correctly date material. Then too, interest is lacking.

For your small quilt study group I think materials beginning with 1920s would be the type they could relate to. Perhaps they have family quilts from that date and later.

In the 1920's pastels were popular for quilts—material cotton and sateens.

I believe in the 1930s rayon began to appear. Rayon is not a very good substantial material, wears out quickly, although you see it occasionally in 1930 Amish quilts.

In the 1940s (early) I believe was the time nylon was first used in the making of women's hosiery.

World War II parachutes were made of nylon. Cotton goods were always popular and plentiful. In addition there was linen and wool too.

As you know about the mid 1960s cotton became less plentiful. Nylon was used in the manufacture of yard goods. Many articles of clothing were made of 100% nylon. Nylon wears well but many people didn't like it—it is hot in high temperature and cold in low. It is non absorbent. So now we have blends. I don't like it—nuff said.

Here is an idea—you may start your book with dating the box of fabric materials you got from the antique dealer you knew on Court St. Then too, you have old quilts you could date. That much may be adequate for your purposes.

Materials I bought from Florence Peto are not dated. I asked her to identify and date the materials and her answer was new manufactures would discard old records so information was not available. I have some pieces from Betty that are identified and dated.

Copper plate print

Old blue resist

Oil boiled calico

Home spun—looks like burlap

Roller print

Pillar Print

Calicos from early 1900's

Political Commemorative (Garfield and Arthur)

See #37 Quilt Collection Catalog

Best Wishes for a Joyous Holiday Season,

Mary[11]

Included in Mary's letter was a photocopy of two old quilt blocks accompanied by a note, which read "A pair of blocks from Betty Harriman's estate. The blocks are signed Angie Blodgette, 1883. Henry Bakeman, Cape Rosier Maine. Mary Schafer Collection."

Mary's letter is typical of her study and documentation method honed from years of exchanges with her pen pals. She is thorough with what she knows and careful about what she doesn't know. Despite her vast knowledge, she represents herself as a seeker rather than an authority. Unwilling to supply easy answers, she points to the complexity of the issues. She makes it plain that history is not necessarily linear and that writing history is a process, and a collective one at that.

Women like Mary and her friends dug the foundation for today's quilt scholars. They restlessly pursued leads and published findings. They proved themselves to be generous correspondents, intrepid explorers, and faithful documentarians. As Cuesta Benberry and Joyce Gross so poetically wrote, "Today's world of quiltmaking did not just 'spring from the head of Zeus' after 1970."[12]

Mary's Correspondence

MARY'S ADDRESS BOOK AROUND 1970 READS LIKE A "WHO'S WHO in Quilting." Since discovering quilt magazines, Mary had been participating in vigorous postal exchanges with quilters from all over the country. Some were round robin exercises in which quilters exposed each other to "new" designs by sending blocks and/or patterns back and forth. Other correspondents were also history buffs and quilt detectives. It was the work of this group that would come to occupy Mary's heart and mind as she continued to make and collect quilts.

This informal network of quilt investigators seemed to mirror her curiosity and match her spirit of adventure, diligence, and cooperation. Far-flung and operating individually as quilt makers, collectors, editors, writers, and publishers, they didn't give themselves a name or even refer to themselves as a group. Yet together they would build a bridge between a mostly oral tradition and modern quilt scholarship, observed, verified, and well documented.

After forty years of neglect by mainstream American culture, the come-again/go-again hunger for quilts surfaced during the years leading up to the bicentennial. Thanks to Mary and her quilting pen pals, the planners had twenty plus years of solid quilt data to consult for authenticity, and America had a sturdy frame on which to stretch the coming quilt revival.

Among Mary's correspondents were Lenice Bacon, Barbara Bannister, Cuesta Benberry, Joy Craddock, Sally Garoutte, Joyce Gross, Betty Harriman, Dolores Hinson, and Florence Peto. They corresponded with Mary, and they corresponded with each other. Ideas and information about quilts were shared with impunity as these women sought to better understand the intricacies of quilt history. Although most of their interchanges were conducted through the mail and less often by phone, there were also occasional visits. Oh what a tangled web of quilt enthusiasts was woven when Barbara Bannister introduced Mary to Betty Harriman, Cuesta Benberry introduced Mary to Dolores Hinson, and so on.

BARBARA BANNISTER

In a round robin letter dated October 29, 1964, Mary wrote, "Visited Barbara Bannister two weeks ago. She is a delightful person, bought the Carlie Sexton applique patts from her. She does many types of needlework-weaving. 'till the next time 'round. Mary."[1]

Barbara Bannister was a one-woman quilt industry in northern Michigan. From her home in Johannesburg and later in Alanson, she ran a mail order pattern business. She sold quilt books and reprints of old patterns by Nancy Cabot, the *Progressive Farmer*, Carlie Sexton, Grandmother Clark, the *Farmer's Wife*, the *Kansas City Star*, and others.

Barbara coauthored two books with her friend Edna Ford, with whom Mary also corresponded: *The United States Patchwork Pattern Book: 50 Quilt Blocks for 50 States from "Hearth & Home" Magazine* (1976) and *State Capitals Quilt Blocks: 50 Patchwork Patterns from "Hearth & Home" Magazine* (1977).

In the introduction to *The United States Patchwork Pattern Book*, the authors write: "The appearance of these fifty state quilt block patterns at the time of our country's Bicentennial celebration may seem to be a carefully planned event. Actually, the juxtaposition of these two occurrences is a happy coincidence, for the search for a complete set of these interesting, old quilt patterns has taken us many years.[2]

The cover notes on the back of *State Capitals Quilt Blocks* state the following.

In 1912 Hearth & Home, a popular farm magazine of the time, inaugurated its state capitals series of quilt blocks for which readers from around the country were asked to contribute. The best patterns, whether original designs or the senders' "favorites," then appeared in the magazine. After years of searching for these legendary and rare quilt blocks, the editors have collected all of them and prepared full-size patterns. They are reprinted here along with the blocks for the capitals of the then "outlying possessions" of Alaska and Hawaii.[3]

The timing for both of these books couldn't have been better. Barbara seemed to have a talent for guessing where the quilt world would likely go. In a letter dated November 8, 1964, Barbara wrote Mary that she could envision a future interest in doll quilts.

I have always felt there was a MARKET for doll quilts. So many women who collect the bisque dolls have doll beds or big cribs for them, and loads of the doll collectors can't sew, and BUY doll clothes for their dolls, so they'd be prospects for sheets, cases and QUILTS. This would be so easy to do, and the price could be low, as they don't take long.[4]

In 1976, she published a pattern book called *Doll Quilts*, effectively ushering in a trend that endures today as more and more quilts are made for the wall and not the bed.

Mary and Barbara met on several occasions. They wrote to each other until Barbara passed away in 1988. Mary had finished a quilt for Barbara in exchange for a kit quilt. "Barbara asked me to applique 2 panels (single bed size) of a Paragon kit in a Horn of Plenty design—she gave me the American Glory kit in exchange. Paragon No. 0117, 'American Glory' Quilt."[5]

In 1985 Cuesta Benberry visited Barbara in Alanson, Michigan:

Barbara kept her quilt materials in her studio which was a double sized large mobile home placed on a foundation, permanently placed on her property, several yards from her large white house on her extensive property. It was a virtual treasure trove of wonderful needlework items, including patchwork quilts, a collection of real and the later woven Marseilles spreads, Kashmir shawls from Persia, all kinds of stuff, her private book & periodical collection absolutely the finest I have ever seen.[6]

Cuesta wrote an article about Barbara for *Quilter's Newsletter Magazine* called "The Face behind the Familiar Name: Barbara Bannister" in which she says, "In the current resurgent period of heightened quilt interest, Barbara Bannister must be regarded as a pioneer."[7]

In a letter to Gwen Marston dated November 19, 1988, Cuesta Benberry wrote with the news that Barbara had died in her sleep a few days earlier, on November 16.

CUESTA BENBERRY

Cuesta Benberry's particular interest and expertise is in pattern collecting and researching African American quilt history. She began researching quilt history and collecting and cataloging patterns in the early 1960s. She holds a master's degree from the University of Missouri, St. Louis.

Since 1975, her research has centered primarily on African American quilt history. Her book *Always There: The African-American Presence in American Quilts* (1992) was a groundbreaking document. Recognized for her research, Cuesta is cited in the seventeenth edition of *Who's Who of American Women,* in the twenty-third edition of *Who's Who in the Midwest,* in the eleventh edition of *Who's Who in the World,* and in the *Directory of African-American Folklorists,* Smithsonian Institution Office of Folklife Programs. A restless researcher and prolific writer, her impact on the quilt world has been considerable.

Cuesta's interest in quilts inspired her to design a quilt using blocks found in quilts made by blacks from the days of slavery to the late twentieth century. She named the quilt Afro-American Women and Quilts.[8] Mary Schafer pieced the ninth block, a version of Robbing Peter to Pay Paul. Mary got the idea for her block from a picture she saw of a quilt attributed to a black woman in Florence Peto's *Historic Quilts.* Other participants were Annette Amann, Jinny Beyer, Carol Crabb, Shirley Conion, Alma Finney, Katherine Finney, Irene Goodrich, Jean Johnson, Lena Moses, Lois Muller, Frances Noack, George Amann, and William Mitchell.

Mary and Cuesta corresponded for years before finally meeting in the summer of 1985. In a letter to Gwen Marston, dated June 15, 1985, Cuesta wrote:

> *The Michigan trip was a memorable one! . . . the high point was to see Mary's fantastic quilts! Whew! I am still awe-struck. Everyone should know we have a Master Quiltmaker living among us today—Mary Schafer! I have seen photos of Mary's quilts for 20 years and always thought they were beautiful. But those quilts have to be seen to be believed—they are just that fabulous!*[9]

Their friendship went beyond correspondence. Over the years, Mary sent Cuesta more than one hundred quilt blocks, which Cuesta later donated to the Quilters Hall of Fame.[10]

In a letter to Gwen Marston dated February 11, 1985, Cuesta wrote of her friends:

> *Give my love to Barbara Bannister and Mary Schafer. Barbara almost killed me Christmas! She gave me a Quilt!! The shock was almost too much for the old lady! Talk about Pretty! It is a sensational quilt—embroidered—"Siesta." It's Feb. and I'm still walking around—smiling to myself about that Quilt! Whew!*[11]

FLORENCE PETO

Florence Peto (1884–1970) was a quilter, collector, author, lecturer, and a consultant and generous donor to museums. More than any other, she laid the foundation on which the quilt world we know today was built. She was known for her generosity and the encouragement she gave to other quilt enthusiasts.

Her interest in quilting began as a collector and researcher. Initially a hobby begun after she was married and a mother of two, she soon began to lecture and write about quilts. Her *Historic Quilts* (1939) and *American Quilts and Coverlets* (1949) set the standard for scholarly research.

She also wrote for leading magazines of the time, including *American Home, McCall's Needlework and Crafts, Woman's Day,* and the *Antiques Journal.*

From the beginning, Florence was interested in recording the history of old family quilts. She was intent on documenting information about the quilters themselves, who were so often ignored and forgotten. Boldly prowling the countryside, she earned a reputation for knocking on doors and asking people to share their quilts with her.

As a well-known authority on quilts and quilt history, Florence often worked as a consultant to museums in the selection and documentation of their collections. These included the Smithsonian, the Philadelphia Museum of Art, the Shelburne Museum, and the Newark Museum. Many of the quilts she discovered she eventually helped place in museum collections. Seventeen of her quilts became the nucleus of the Shelburne collection. Three of these are shown in *55 Famous Quilts from the Shelburne Museum* (Oliver 1990).[12] She donated two quilts to the Newark Museum collection.[13]

In 1997, two of her quilts were shown in the 20th Century Quilts, 1900–1970: Women Make Their Mark exhibit in Paducah, Kentucky. According to Joyce Gross and Cuesta Benberry, the curators, "Florence Peto was the most influential quilt authority of the mid–twentieth century."[14]

Florence had become good friends with Maxine Teele, another quilt enthusiast. These two women corresponded frequently. Florence sent Maxine enough antique fabric for at least three quilts. Maxine visited Florence at her home and was spellbound as Florence showed her her many quilts. Maxine said "she bubbled over with joy at our interest in her truly amazing collection of antique quilts."[15]

Shortly after Florence died, Maxine wrote a wonderful remembrance of her friend in an article called "In Partial Payment."

> *Even yet I marvel at her willingness to share time, ideas, and information with me. That Mrs. Peto was willing to take time for me (and many others) is an indication of her generous spirit and boundless enthusiasm. . . .*
>
> *Mrs. Peto was a lady of wide ranging interests and these letters sparkled with observations on many subjects. Often she wrote of her fondness for antique fabrics, toile, calico, oil calico, historicals, chintz and homespun. . . .*
>
> *Because she gave of herself so freely, we are inspired to do likewise. Because of her many of us have had our intellect challenged, our horizons widened, our knowledge deepened and our hearts warmed.*[16]

Maxine Teele was a Methodist minister's wife from Des Moines, Iowa. Maxine was an accomplished quilt maker, scholar, writer, lecturer, and teacher. For more than eight years, she taught the craft twice a week at her local YWCA. She organized quilt exhibits and lectured about quilts. One of her lectures was called "Quilts, a Textile Sandwich."[17]

Maxine came from a family of quilters: "I learned quilting at my mother's knee—literally. Of course I read and study and never stop learning."[18] When asked if she ever sold her quilts, she replied, "Almost never. A lot of the work in quilting is the kind of drudgery you can do for love but not for money."[19]

Maxine was a regular writer for *Nimble Needle Treasures.* At the conclusion of her articles, she had a little piece she called "Hit and Miss" in which she would write briefly about some interesting aspect of quilting.

> *Because quilts are such great fun it is strange that few quilt jokes come to our attention. Here is one: Mary Ann had attended church on the morning when the minister used as his text "Fear Not, for the Comforter has come." When she was asked what the minister had talked about, Mary Ann's version was as follows: "Don't be scared, you'll get the quilt."*[20]

In addition to writing a great deal of published material about quilts, Maxine was a loyal and contributing correspondent. In an article published in 1973, she expressed a sentiment that was widely held by quilters of her generation, who had personally witnessed the change in society from farm to factory: "Like anything else done with the hands, persons feel a sense of satisfaction after completing the job. In fact, in today's mechanized society, we need this satisfaction more than ever."[21]

Lenice Bacon

Lenice Bacon (1895–1978) from Rockwood, Tennessee, attended Belmont College in Nashville. In 1921, she married Frederick S. Bacon of Newton, Massachusetts, and moved to Boston. Lenice was a quilt collector, quilt maker, author, and lecturer. She was friends with Florence Peto and Ruth Finley, the author of *Old Patchwork Quilts and the Women Who Made Them.* Lenice's book, *American Patchwork Quilts,* was published in 1973. The book not only includes some very fine quilts but is well written and fun to read. Lenice not only knew about quilts, she knew how to turn a phrase. She begins the first chapter of her book with this sentence: "Indigenous as Vermont maple sugar, picturesque as a split-rail fence in Appalachia, dignified as a New England sea captain's mansion, romantic as the white-pillared plantation houses of the deep South, patchwork is uniquely interwoven with the story of America."[22]

The book jacket offers a glimpse of Bacon's background: "The Rockwood area remained a stronghold of quiltmaking even when the art seemed forgotten in many parts of the country, so that quilts are part of her family heritage. Mrs. Bacon made her first quilt top, a traditional family pattern, when she was a young married woman in New England. She extended her researches in earnest in the early '40s, traveling to interview the skilled quilters who still could be found in the mountains of North Carolina and other parts of the South."[23]

SALLY GAROUTTE

Sally Garoutte, a quilt historian from California, founded the American Quilt Study Group (AQSG). She served as the editor of *Uncoverings*, published annually since 1980 by the AQSG. Although Mary was not a member of group, she corresponded with Sally, exchanging information with her about historic patterns and quilts. Sally came to visit Mary in the late 1970s. They spent a busy day looking at quilts, and Sally spent the night at the Schafers' house in Flushing.

JOYCE GROSS

Joyce is a quilt collector and historian from California. During the 1970s and 1980s she published the *Quilters' Journal.* The apparent aim of *Quilters' Journal* was to further scholarship and research into quilt history. The publication featured articles about important historical quilters: Bertha Stenge, Florence Peto, Carrie Hall, Rose Kretsinger, Pine Hawkes Eisfeller, Mary Schafer, Betty Harriman, Cuesta Benberry, and others. Mary compiled the information for an article about her friend Betty Harriman in a *Journal* issue published in 1978. Over the years, Mary sent Joyce many quilt blocks to assist her in her efforts to explore quilt history. Joyce was another friend who paid Mary a visit in the mid-1980s and spent the night.

DOLORES HINSON

Dolores Hinson was a quilt maker, quilt collector, pattern collector, author, and lecturer. She lived in the Baltimore area for many years before retiring to Austin, Texas. She authored *Quilting Manual* (1970) and *A Quilter's Companion* (1973), which featured more than two hundred full-size pieced and appliqué patterns, border designs, and quilting designs. She also wrote for *Antiques Journal, Workbasket, Popular Needlework,* and *Antique Trader.* She helped her friend Pat Almy start her magazine *Nimble Needle Treasures.* She was writing for *Quilter's Newsletter Magazine* when it was in its infancy.

Dolores was an organizer of the National Quilting Association (NQA). She repeatedly urged Mary to send her CLAMSHELL quilt to the first NQA exhibit at the Greenbelt Library in Greenbelt, Maryland, in 1970. Mary's quilt won the Best Pieced Quilt and Viewers' Choice awards.

Dolores was the one who first encouraged Cuesta Benberry to write about quilts.[24] Dolores and Cuesta exchanged patterns and often wrote twelve- to sixteen-page letters to each other, written on both sides of the paper. She said she used to end her letters to Cuesta with "I'll stop now before you have to get it published."[25]

Dolores also corresponded with Maxine Teele and Barbara Bannister. In fact, when asked how she knew Barbara, Dolores said, "Oh, Honey . . . she was the first quilt person that I found." She referred to Cuesta as "the Godmother of American Quilters. . . . She got everyone together, and she knew what everyone in the country was doing in quilts. You could write to her and ask any question, and she would write back, yes, I have that information."[26]

In my personal experiences with Dolores, she, like Cuesta, was very generous with sharing information. During the writing of this book, I had numerous conversations with Dolores. Not only was she helpful, but she was also a highly entertaining conversationalist. Dolores passed away in October 2002. She will be fondly remembered by many as an interesting, vibrant, and generous woman as well as for her contributions to the quilt world.

Joy Craddock

In the early 1960s, Mary began her correspondence with Joy Craddock, who published the *4 J's* from her home in Denison, Texas. Mary and Joy were in a round robin together. Joy was also a pattern collector very much interested in researching and documenting quilt history. Her letter to Mary cited in "Quilt Study" makes it clear that Joy was a very enthusiastic and determined pattern collector.

Ruth Parr

Mary met Ruth Parr through Mr. Robert May, a mutual friend, who was an antique dealer in Detroit, Michigan. Knowing both women and their particular interests, Mr. May decided to introduce them to each other. He was correct in thinking that Mary and Ruth had a lot in common and would enjoy knowing each other. The two began a brisk correspondence, exchanging letters at least once a month during the early 1970s.

Ruth is an antique dealer, collector, and quilt maker from Meridian, Mississippi. She and Mary not only shared quilt information, patterns, and antique fabrics, but they actually mailed quilts, quilt books, and antique clothing back and forth for study purposes.

In one letter, Mary sent some antique fabrics she had acquired from Florence Peto as a gift to Ruth.

I'm enclosing some pieces of material I bought from Mrs. Florence Peto. When I asked whether she had old material she told me all she had left were small pieces. I wanted

*the material even though they are just small pieces—these are commemorative centennial
of U.S. Independence prints. They are especially interesting now that we will be celebrat-
ing our second centennial soon.*

*You were asking who is Nancy Cabot. She offered quilt patterns in the Chicago
Tribune (the newspaper) in the late 1920's and during 30's—much like Laura Wheeler
and Louise Brooks does [sic] today. There would be a drawing of the quilt block—quite
often a brief history of the pattern and the price of the pattern—about 15 cents."[27]*

In another letter, Mary thanked Ruth for sending her some antique clothing
for study as she returned the favor.

*Enclosed in the package is a piece of fabric from Mrs. Peto. It is like the English
roller print pictured in your book [Printed Textiles] fig. 397. Mrs. Peto used antique
fabrics in the quilts she made. It seems she was partial to the historical prints. I'm
enclosing 3 pictures of two quilts she made. The piece of fabric in the pkg is like the eagle
print in the quilt. I got three pieces of the fabric but the eagle was all ready cut out from
them. She wrote 'The Wild Goose Chase' was entered in the Eastern States Quilt
Exhibition one year and was awarded a blue ribbon in the Pieced Quilt category. It
also was made of antique fabrics.[28]*

Mary Schafer had to leave school when she was fifteen years old to work in
her father's dairy. She discovered quilts when she was forty-two years old in the
notions section of a department store in downtown Flint, Michigan. Yet within
a decade of discovering the craft she had begun a collegial correspondence with
a group of quilters, collectors, researchers, writers, editors, and publishers, five
of whom would later be inducted into the Quilters Hall of Fame: Lenice
Bacon in 1979, Florence Peto in 1980, Cuesta Benberry in 1984, Sally Garoutte
in 1995, and Joyce Gross in 1997.

Mary donated most of her letters, a veritable library of grassroots quilt
history, to the Michigan State University Museum in 1998. In this trove is
some of Mary's correspondence with Betty Harriman, an accomplished quilter,
historian, and collector from Bunceton, Missouri. Betty was Mary's de facto
mentor, her dearest pen pal, a frequent collaborator, and the person for whom
Mary had the most respect of all. It is telling that Mary kept some of Betty's
correspondence. In a conversation with Mary about Betty and their correspondence, Mary said she still had some of Betty's letters, explaining "I couldn't
part with it all."

Part Two

Mary Schafer and Her Quilts

Because she was my friend.
—*Mary Schafer*

 MARY CHOSE TO LIVE HER PERSONAL AND professional lives close to home. From the day I met Mary in 1977 until I moved to Beaver Island in 1983, we spent many hours together in quilt study and quilt talk. Because Mary didn't drive in those years, Fred would drive her to Flint to visit me in his beloved Chevrolet Monte Carlo. More often I would go to her house in the suburbs. If the timing happened to be right, Mary and Fred would ask me to stay for "dinner," which they took at noon.

Although Mary's neat little house has a formal dining room tastefully furnished with a Duncan Phyfe dining room

Mary at the Detroit Jewel and
Gwen in Mary's kitchen

set, we always ate in the kitchen. Past the mint-condition Detroit Jewel stove, there is a pine paneled breakfast nook with a maple drop leaf table surrounded with ladder-back chairs. Before dinner could be served, the two porcelain chickens that have served as a centerpiece for as long as I can remember had to be removed and the drop leaf engaged in an upright position. The table was then covered with a flannel pad to protect its surface. This, in turn, was covered with a print tablecloth.

One of the house specialties was Mary's cabbage rolls. She would serve these with mashed potatoes she had beaten with a hand masher. Fred, a gentleman from the old school, would punctuate almost every mouthful with a plea for me to "Eat! Eat!"

Once in a while, if I was lucky, Mary would serve her apple cake for dessert.

MARY'S APPLE CAKE

4 cups coarsely chopped apples and 2 cups sugar over the apples.
Let stand 15 to 20 minutes.
Add 2 cups flour, 2 tsp baking soda, dash of salt, 1 tsp cinnamon,
*   and stir.*
Add 2 large eggs, ³/₄ cup vegetable oil, ¹/₂ to 1 cup walnuts.
Pour into greased, floured 9 × 13 pan. Bake at 350 for 1 hour or
*   until done.*

The Schafer and
Harriman Collaboration

 In the annals of quilt history, the story of the friendship between Mary Schafer of Flushing, Michigan (1910–),
and Betty Harriman of Bunceton, Missouri (1890–1971),
may well stand alone. Mary Schafer, quilter, collector, and amateur quilt historian, was already engaged in a fruitful correspondence with the
nation's leading quilt researchers, writers, and publishers when a mutual pen pal,
Barbara Bannister, introduced them by post. While their lives, and to some
degree their professional reputations, would become forever intertwined, it is
an irony of dramatic size that Mary Schafer and Betty Harriman would never
actually meet.

Through their correspondence, and less frequently through telephone calls
over the years, their quilting friendship grew. In no other had they found the
same degree of interest in quilts. They discovered a mutual passion for historical quilts, especially patriotic ones, and rare old patterns. They proved to be
equals in craftsmanship, as both were able, indeed eager, to tackle technically
difficult quilts. Each was a polished needle woman actively engaged in quilt
making. Both chose to stay home, making quilts and investigating quilt patterns, blocks, and lore quietly rather than operating in the public eye. Both generously shared their knowledge with others. Together and sometimes
collaboratively they made hundreds of exquisite quilts.

Early photograph of Betty Harriman.
(Photo by Suellen Meyer.)

29

PRIDE OF IOWA block. Made by Betty Harriman. (Photo by Suellen Meyer.)

Mary and Betty discovered other bonds: a love of gardening and American history. Betty collected dolls and made authentic period clothing for them. She also designed and made cloth dolls, which she dressed in period costumes. She also became skilled in the art of china painting, taking her redware into town to be fired.[1]

Betty came from an aristocratic family that counted no less a personage than Gen. Robert E. Lee as a forebear. She married a man descended from President George Washington. Mary came from an immigrant, working class family, and married a man from the same. Betty graduated from Warrensburg State College. Mary was forced to quit school at age fifteen. When Betty was a young girl, her grandmother showed her how to make quilts. When Mary was a girl, motherless, a neighbor lady showed her how to darn. Yet, through sisterhood and a shared interest in history and textiles, these women came to understand each other in a unique way and speak each other's language.

When her husband died in 1925, Betty Harriman moved from Missouri to Newport News, Virginia, where she owned and operated a hotel. Upon retirement, she returned to the family farm in Bunceton. While in the East, Betty found that she had access to historical houses, museums, and antique shops full of quilts and textiles. She began collecting old quilts and fabrics. She kept the rarest textiles as she found them, but she also bought old fabric for the purpose of repairing old quilts and making reproduction quilts.

When Betty found quilts that she considered historically significant, especially those that were deteriorating, she resolved to duplicate them as closely as possible in order to preserve them. Mary said of her friend, "When she liked a particular quilt, she would buy it. If it were not for sale, she would ask permission to copy the pattern. If that was denied she would sketch it, and if circumstances prevented her from sketching it, she would sketch the pattern at her first opportunity from memory."[2] Like

Three dolls made by Betty Harriman. Each doll is stuffed with cotton, and each wears individually designed dresses and exquisite underclothes. Each has meticulous details, with the fingers individually marked. (Collection of Suellen Meyer. Photo by Suellen Meyer.)

Betty, Mary was compelled to reproduce old quilts. Unlike Betty, she was likely to endow her reproductions with her own distinctive characteristics, especially in the overall quilting and the border designs.

From years of correspondence with Betty, Mary knew her mind: "I think she bought quilts that took her fancy. She seemed to like any quilts of antique textiles—English prints, copperplate, roller prints, linsey-woolsey, homespun, resist prints, oil-boiled chintz, etc. She liked historical prints, quilts and quilt patterns from historical places. If the article had the above qualities, poor or worn condition was not an important consideration."[3]

Betty Harriman's modus operandi of quilt making is embodied in one of her favorite quilts, the Laurel. On visiting George Washington's home at Mount Vernon, she wanted to search the attic for quilts. It was off limits, but she persisted and was finally allowed as far as the doorway. A quilt was crumpled in the corner of the room. Betty snapped a picture and left satisfied. When she saw the photograph, she saw an image of a quilt that was only about an inch tall. Working from this tiny reference, she was able to draft the pattern.

Another reproduction Betty made from a quilt at Mount Vernon was her WASHINGTON PLUME. Mary tells me that the original quilt was a gift to the Mount Vernon Ladies Association of the Union in 1876 and was said to be very old even at that time. The minutes of the 1886 association report state that the quilt dated to the eighteenth century and was made of flax. Betty wrote to Mary about the pattern, and each woman set about making this quilt. Mary says that Betty used antique fabrics from her collection to make her quilt. Here was an ambitious, old-fashioned, historically significant quilt that could not have appealed more to these two women. Because the design was so large, it was difficult to copy. Betty decided that the easiest thing to do would be to send her partially completed top to Mary. Mary hurried to copy the pattern so she could return Betty's top as quickly as possible.

In 1967, Betty reproduced a Tree of Life quilt she had seen in Virginia at Wakefield, the birthplace of George Washington. Once a grand showpiece, the old quilt was in tatters, so worn that batting was showing through. Betty sketched the pattern. The finished quilt was presented to the Wakefield Historical Society, which then retired the original quilt. The February 1972 issue of *McCall's* contained an article entitled "Treasured Recipes from Washington's Day," which featured the Wakefield home. One of the photographs was of a four-poster bed on which lay Betty's Tree of Life.

A few months before Betty's death, the Wakefield Historical Society invited her to oversee the redecorating of the house. In appreciation of this honor, Betty's family after her death gave Betty's Laurel and WASHINGTON PLUME, both careful reproductions of eighteenth-century quilts, to Wakefield.

When Betty was given the opportunity to copy a quilt pattern from the Robert E. Lee home, she shared the pattern with Mary. Letters flew back and forth as both women set out to make a reproduction of the quilt. Betty chose to make the quilt as close to the original as possible. Mary chose to take the pattern and interpret it in her own personal style. Characteristically, she used fewer blocks, bolder color, and a four-sided border and drafted her own quilting designs.

While riding through Kentucky in 1969, Mary stopped in Bardstown to see the home where Stephen Foster wrote "My Old Kentucky Home." This lovely home is a Kentucky State Historical Shrine. On one of the beds was a rose appliqué quilt called WASHINGTON ROSE. She tried to take a photograph of the quilt, but her camera failed. She then resorted to drafting the pattern from a picture of the quilt shown on a postcard she had purchased at the home. She sent the pattern to Betty. The name alone was enough to set Betty into gear. When Betty got the pattern, she wrote to Mary about it.

> *Especially like the "Kentucky Home" quilt. My own Grandmother was born in Bardstown, Kentucky, living there until she married and came to Missouri. My Great Great Grandfather designed "My Old Kentucky Home," so there is a tender feeling for Bardstown and "My Old Kentucky Home" and I love having the quilt pattern.*
>
> *Thank you, Mary for the quilt pattern. . . . I do like it and will be impatient now to work on it.*[4]

Mary was thrilled. Little did she know when she sent the pattern to Betty that her friend had a family connection to the house. Betty's great-grandfather had built the house, known as Federal Hill, for Judge John Rowan. It remained in the Rowan family for several generations. Betty's grandmother, Marcie Pash Harned, was born in Bardstown and lived there until she married and moved to Missouri in 1855. This is the house in which visiting relative Stephen Foster wrote his famous song "My Old Kentucky Home."

Betty wrote to My Old Kentucky Home State Park asking for information about the quilt and her relatives. In February 1970, she received a reply from the superintendent.

> *In looking through our correspondence, I find you are speaking of the "Rose" quilt. Some call it "Washington Rose." It is very beautiful, and the work is nice.*
>
> *Mrs. Harriman, I have been here for a year, but our records are very incomplete, and I have no way of finding out who made the quilt. This quilt is on the largest bed in the "Home." Each square is 12 × 12 inches, and it is approximately 2 yards 24 inches square.*
>
> *There are some Pash's who still live in Bardstown and the Harned family lives in Boston, a small town west of Bardstown. Mr. Atkinson Hill, I believe, helped develop the Park when it was in its infancy. Some of his relatives live in Louisville.*

We are enclosing a brochure and other information for you to see. Please come to see us if you come to Kentucky.[5]

Betty was unsatisfied with this response or perhaps the brochure referred to in the first letter had a picture of another quilt. In any event, she wrote another query and received this response: "Princess Plume is the pattern of the quilt on the bed in the guest bedroom. It is sometimes called the 'Feather' pattern."[6]

Betty began work on WASHINGTON ROSE. She was so interested in this pattern that she began two tops according to her letters to Mary. She finished one, and when she died Mary received the unfinished top. Mary eventually finished Betty's "start" in 1984.

Betty was sought out by the *Kansas City Star* as an authority on quilts and was interviewed for the following article.

Skill of Long-Ago Eras in Quilts

Dateline: Bunceton, MO—Mrs. Betty Harriman didn't start out to be a collector of quilts. It was just a hobby that grew with the years. And now she has more than 100 quilts, all carefully stored in cedar chests on her 300-acre family farm in Cooper County, where she lives with her twin sisters, Marian and Marcia.

Driving through the stone gateway to their farm, visitors see a neat sign, "Windmere." The road leads across a blue-grass pasture and comes to a white fenced yard in a grove of elm trees. The large homey farmhouse, surrounded by porches, looks like a Currier and Ives print. The farm has been in the family since 1903 when Mr. and Mrs. Ben Harned, Mrs. Harriman's parents, bought the place and reared their eleven children there. Mrs. Harriman is a first cousin of Mrs. John Rhodes, Rockhill Manor, Kansas City.

Modern, but Unspoiled

Many changes have come to the farm with electricity, bringing all the conveniences and comforts of city living, but none of the clutter and confusion.

A large friendly collie dog greeted us. The hostess told us we must stay for lunch. The table was already set in a south window, with a green linen cloth and a bowl of fruit.

Mrs. Harriman's corner bedroom on the first floor was flooded with sunlight. The antique four-posted bed was covered with a rare all white padded quilt.

"That's one of my dated quilts," Mrs. Harriman remarked. "The name of the maker, Annabelle Smith 1853, is hand cross-stitched on the back."

She escorted me into her room and we settled down in two low rocking chairs. A sewing table, covered with spools of colored thread, scissors and a small stack of calico triangles, showed she was working on another quilt.

Keeps Every Project

"Don't ask me why I'm making another quilt," Mrs. Harriman laughingly said. "I would give you too many reasons. It has become an avid hobby. The quilts are like my children and what's more I never part with a quilt. I remember making my first quilt for my doll's bed: my grandmother gave me the scraps. Then years later in the early '20's a friend of mine asked me to help her finish some squares for her.

"Since then I estimate I've made about 75 to 80 quilts, besides collecting dozens of rare old ones, some of historic value. Often when they are worn I repair places and even dye the material to match and replace whole squares, circles, triangles. This takes patience and ingenuity.

"It seems to me American history is reflected in quilts. It is recorded that George Washington purchased from Belois estate at Fairfax 19 coverlet quilts to take to Martha Washington at Mt. Vernon."

A few years ago when Mrs. Harriman lived in the East, she visited Washington's home and was allowed to photograph and sketch an original design quilt which was in the attic of Mt. Vernon. The pattern was inspired by the laurel leaf. From her sketch she cut an exact copy of this quilt from Revolutionary times. She proudly lifted it out of her many cedar chests and spread it on the bed.

In her search for antique patterns she was permitted to take colored photographs of quilts at Rockefeller Museum in New York, at the Smithsonian in Washington, and in Williamsburg, Va. From these records she has been able to cut the patterns and recreate exact copies of the designs. The biggest problem was finding material of similar color and design.

Story with Quilts

From out of her treasure chests came quilt after quilt, all with a story to tell. She chatted as she showed them.

"The earliest quilt that I have is the one dated 1780. It is on copper plate print and Indian print. I found it at Marblehead, Mass., in an old house which had been owned by a clipper ship captain's wife. The house had been in the same family for generations. When the last member of the family died the house and entire furnishings were sold at auction. I also got some yard material from the attic, which I feel sure the captain brought back from England.

"Quilts of that period were made of piecings with calico, making a center design, which was then set together on a large spread of copper plate chintz. The chintz was very decorative and was used not only for the background of quilts but for bed hangings and window curtains.

"Here is one of my earliest American quilts, produced by material woven in our country and called linsey-woolsey. It was very warm and also scratchy. The two materials were sewed together and then quilted, but there was no applique.

"The earliest American reference to calico prints which I have found was made by Benjamin Franklin in a letter written from London to his wife in 1758. In it he tells her that he is sending home 56 yards of cotton material curiously printed from copper plate, many colored, for bed and window hangings in the great room.

"After the Revolution era, exquisite French materials were produced and imported. These earliest copper plate monochromes, using just one color, were pastoral, allegorical and historical in pattern. During the late 18th and early nineteenth century, Toile de Jouy was produced first at Jouy, a town in France. Hence comes the name of the material of Jouy still used today. The colors were blue on white background, red on white and later brown and mulberry. Many of these same pictorial story-telling materials are popular today with decorators."[7]

During the course of their friendship, Betty sent Mary gifts. One year she sent Mary a birthday gift: a quilt fragment, called Diamonds, made around 1835–40 and shown in *Mary Schafer and Her Quilts* (MSHQ).[8] Mary also purchased five outstanding antique quilts from Betty: SUNBURST (ca. 1825),[9] Four-Patch (ca. 1800–1825),[10] Mariner's Compass (ca. 1830–50),[11] and Framed Square (ca. 1800–1825).[12] She also bought an all white stuffed quilt (ca. 1800–1810), which is now a part of the Michigan State University Museum collection. The Mariner's Compass is the quilt Betty referred to in the newspaper article as the earliest quilt in her collection, found in Marblehead, Massachusetts.

The last quilt Betty completed was FREEDOM, which was finished in 1971. She worked on this quilt for several years. In her Christmas letter to Mary in 1968, she sent snapshots of twelve of the blocks, which were pinned to a sheet hanging on a clothesline. Suellen Meyer was fortunate enough to see the FREEDOM quilt and took some slides of it, which she generously shared with me. Suellen wrote about this last quilt Betty finished.

She held her standards to the last. Her final quilt, in 1971, was the Freedom Quilt, a reproduction of one originally made to commemorate a man's twenty-first birthday. Its blocks are complex applique scenes: two red birds holding a cherry in their mouths hover over a tree branch; an eagle perches on the U.S. flag; a basket of lattice-work holds heart-shaped flowers and stuffed cherries; and in the center blocks stands Major Ringold's monument framed by flags, guns and a dove. Every day Betty spread this quilt out on her bed. Turning on her tensor lamp, she pulled it close to the quilt, picked up her large magnifying glass and worked through it to get her stitches right. Her eyes might threaten to betray her, but her standards held firm. When she took the last stitch, she patted the quilt and said, "This is my $1500 quilt.[13]

Betty died with a quilt top on her lap. Her twin sisters wrote to Mary and said that Betty had been gardening that morning and had come in and begun working on a quilt, which Mary remembers was Lee's Rose and Buds. Over her lifetime, Betty had made

FREEDOM quilt. 1971. Made by Betty Harriman. (Photo by Suellen Meyer.)

FREEDOM quilt, detail. 1971. Made by Betty Harriman. (Photo by Suellen Meyer.)

between eighty and one hundred quilts and had collected about one hundred antique quilts. The exact number of quilts Betty made and collected isn't known. Just as the cobbler's kids want shoes, Betty's body of work went without documentation.

Upon her death, family members were given their choice of quilts. The Rhea Goodman Gallery bought the remainder of her finished quilts and took them to New York City to sell. Betty's sisters remember that a moving van came to the farm and picked up all the finished quilts. Much later, Gwen Marston tried to track down Betty's quilts through Rhea Goodman. Rhea also had not kept records of the quilts. Occasionally, a picture of a quilt appears in a publication that Mary recognizes as one of Betty's.

Mary remembers Betty saying the Smithsonian had approached her regarding her quilt collection. Betty didn't want them to go to the Smithsonian because, as she said, "they would put them in storage for fifty years and then maybe let them out." Betty didn't want her quilts to languish in storage units.[14] Mary completely understood Betty's position. This fear colored Mary's thinking when she accepted the Michigan State University Museum's offer for her first collection, and it continues to influence her in reaching a decision on the remaining collection.

Mary wanted to buy Betty's unfinished work sight unseen. The sisters set a price of six hundred dollars, which Mary accepted. She was shocked at the amount of material she received. In the many boxes were completed tops, partially finished tops, patterns, quilt patterns. Some were not even begun, just the pattern and fabric folded neatly together. Mary even received her own letters, the ones she had written to Betty over the years.

Among the patterns were original Marie Webster and *McCall's* patterns from the 1920s. In one box was a *McCall's* transfer pattern for an appliqué basket quilt, which Betty had begun. Betty's pattern and one completed block are shown in *Twentieth Century Quilts, 1900–1950.*[15]

Betty's sisters told Mary that they had two more quilt tops, an ENGLISH PLUME and an Oriental Poppy. Mary offered to finish the Oriental Poppy in exchange for the ENGLISH PLUME. The Oriental Poppy was a copy of a quilt made by Rose Kretsinger that was shown in a number of books.[16] The Kretsinger quilt is now housed at the Spencer Museum of Art in Lawrence, Kansas.

In one of the boxes, Mary found Betty's Lee's Rose and Buds quilt. Mary received Betty's quilt as a completed top partially marked for quilting. Betty's notes were attached to the top: "History 'Rose and Buds' . . . made in 1852 by mother and Grandmother of cousin Mamie Lee—Mamie Lee was born 1860 the night Abraham Lincoln was elected president . . . Quilt now owned by Robert E. Lee, son of Mamie Lee— This quilt is large. This old quilt is in perfect condition and very beautiful."

Mary didn't hesitate. She and Betty had each been working on a Lee's Rose and Buds quilt, and Mary characteristically decided to finish Betty's first. She finished her own version later, in 1972.

Sometime in the 1920s, Betty bought the Marie Webster pattern GRAPES AND VINES. The pattern came with all of the fabric for the quilt. Betty had never gotten around to making it. Mary got the pattern and all the fabric needed from Betty's estate. She went to work and made the quilt, finishing it in 1972. Mary made the quilt to exact specifications with the exception of the outer border. The original pattern showed a scalloped border. Mary chose a straight border

Marie Webster's Grapes and Vines pattern, dated April 15, 1916, complete with swatches for fabric suggestions, blueprint, and tissue paper pattern.

GRAPES AND VINES
83½" × 97", 1972. Mary received the original Marie Webster pattern for this quilt from Betty's estate, completing the quilt in 1972. More than once, Mary commented on how she never thought she'd finish sewing on the grapes. (Collection of the Michigan State University Museum, Mary Schafer Collection. Photo by Alan Zinn.)

but tipped her hat to the original by quilting in the scallop.

Like a sentimental inscription on a nineteenth-century friendship quilt, Betty and Mary's friendship transcended death. Mary set about immediately to finish Betty's "starts," as she calls them. She worked on them in no particular order. She decided which project to finish based solely on whatever caught her interest. Mary often signed these special quilts with both Betty's name and her own. When Betty had done much of the work, Mary embroidered Betty's name first, with her own directly beneath it.

Eventually, she would finish twenty of the quilts Betty had started and three antique quilt tops from the Harriman estate (see "Complete Inventory of Mary Schafer Quilts"). Seventeen of these quilts went to the Michigan State University Museum as a part of the First Collection. Subsequently, three of the Harriman/Schafer quilts were sold by the museum. After 1980, Mary finished five more tops begun by Betty. She also finished an antique top from the Harriman estate. These six quilts are part of her Second Collection, shown elsewhere in this book.

Realizing the importance of Betty's correspondence to the history of quilting between the quilting revivals of the twentieth century, Mary donated most of them to the Michigan State University Museum when they acquired Betty's quilts.

When asked by Gwen Marston why she wanted to finish, and did finish, so many of Betty's starts, Mary answered, "Because she was my friend."

Coming to America

IT WAS A CLOSE CALL. MARY TOLD ME THE STEAMER THAT brought her to America was the last peacetime ship to cross the International Date Line before the Great War began in 1914. Mary, her mother, and her brother were on the last passenger ship allowed to exit Austria-Hungary until the war ended in 1918. A year later the Treaty of Versailles would redraw the map of Europe and Mary's homeland would cease to exist.

In other ways, Mary's coming to America story is the quintessential immigrant story of her day. She was born in Tarany, Somogy County, in 1910. Her mother, Julianna Zelko, and father, Josef Vida, a widower with a four-year-old son, had been married there the previous year. In 1911, Josef Vida realized he couldn't support his family on the little farm he had inherited. He made the hard decision many Europeans made in those days. He decided to seek a better life elsewhere.

Josef Vida struck out alone for Brazil, where he labored on a plantation. When this first adventure turned out to be disappointing, he moved to Mississippi and tried growing peanuts. When his peanut crop failed, he moved to West Virginia and worked in a coal mine. Later he moved to Ohio and found work in a rubber

Mary with her brother Josef and her mother, Julianna Zelko Vida, before leaving Austria-Hungary

Mary's father, Josef Vida

Mary with her brother and "Aunt Nellie." Aunt Nellie wasn't a relative; rather she was a neighbor who took care of Mary and Josef for a few years after their mother died.

Mary's First Communion picture

factory. None of these first attempts earned enough money to reunite his family. Undaunted, he moved to Kansas City, Kansas, and began working as a boilermaker for the Union Pacific Railroad. There his fortunes took a turn for the better. Four years after emigrating to the New World, he bought and furnished a small house and sent for his wife and children.

Tragedy struck not long after they arrived in Kansas City. Julianna fell ill with tuberculosis and died on January 11, 1916. Mary was just five years old. Her father, not yet thirty, found himself widowed for the second time.

Unfortunately, the bad times didn't stop there. A few years later Mary contracted a serious eye infection, and Josef took her to a nearby Catholic hospital for treatment. While they were there, he learned that the nuns at St. Margaret's Hospital ran an orphanage for girls in a wing of the hospital. He decided that Mary would receive better care at the orphanage than he could provide. He made arrangements for Mary to stay with the nuns until his situation improved.

Mary stayed at the orphanage for over a year. It was so crowded, she recalls, that the girls slept two to a bed, one at the head and the other at the foot. With World War I in full swing, food, clothing, and even medical supplies were hard to come by everywhere, and St. Margaret's was no exception. As if things weren't bad enough, 1918 was the year of the terrible influenza pandemic that raced around the globe killing between 20 and 40 million people. Mary remembers that many of the little girls in the orphanage died while she was there.

Late in 1919, Mary's father visited her in the orphanage and asked if she wanted to stay there or go home. Mary wanted to go home. Listening to her talk about these times, I've found it hard to imagine just how alone and terrifying a time this must have been for little Mary Vida, a girl without a home, a homeland, or a mother.

In 1920, Josef packed up the children and moved to Flint, Michigan, where he found work at General Motors. They rented two rooms on the second floor of a house that Mary remembers as being identical; no kitchen to speak of and no running water. Mary carried pails of water for drinking, cooking, and bathing up the stairs from the pump in the backyard. She did the laundry in a wash bucket for the whole family. Mary, at age ten, was considered old enough to take on all the other housekeeping chores, too. She tells me there were only two chairs at the kitchen table so she served her father and brother their meals first and she ate later.

In spite of how much time Mary had to spend on housekeeping, she did very well in her studies. Mary liked everything about going to school except for the second- and thirdhand clothes she wore. Her father brought home clothing for the children that he had "rescued" from the ragbag at work. Although she was embarrassed at the time, later in her life rescuing textiles would become a major factor in her artistic development.

Mary's Confirmation picture. Julianna Gyorkosz was a Hungarian woman who was a friend of Mary's father. She was chosen as Mary's godmother. Mary told me she found it interesting that her mother and godmother shared the same first name. Mary is wearing her first pair of high heels. She said they were called "cuban heels" and were quite popular at that time.

Mary vividly remembers an act of kindness from this period. One of her teachers recut and remade one of the hand-me-down dresses to fit Mary correctly. She tells me she was thankful to this teacher for altering her dress, especially because she did it in a quiet way.

Inevitably Mary, like many women of her generation, would learn to sew. Josef intended to bring his daughter up with skills she needed to be marriageable. Knowing how to cook and clean was only part of it. Sewing and other types of needlework were considered crucial to her education.

With no mother to teach her these essentials, Josef arranged for Mary to take lessons from neighbor women. Her needlework lessons included crocheting, tatting, embroidering, and knitting. Josef expected perfection from Mary.

He inspected all of her work. If he detected the slightest flaw, he would rip it out and make her redo it. This early experience of striving for perfection would later manifest itself in Mary's quilt making.

Ambitious and frugal, Josef saved enough money by 1925 to buy the Flint Creamery. The dairy processed pasteurized milk, cream, buttermilk, cottage cheese, and a little butter. Customer deliveries were made in a horse-drawn wagon. When Josef had to fill big orders on the other side of town, he hired Fred Schafer, a young man in the neighborhood who had access to a car.

Mary was now fifteen, old enough to work full time in the business, or so Josef thought. He told Mary that what she needed to know wasn't taught in school. And so it was that Mary's high school education, like those of many women of her generation, came to a premature and abrupt end. Mary did continue sewing for pleasure in her spare time. She told me that as a teenager she loved to embroider and did a great number of pillowcases, dresser scarves, buffet pieces, and tablecloths.

Although Mary's childhood may sound short and harsh to us today, it is important to put it in its historical context. Hers is the classic immigrant story. Her family experiences were no different from those of many others who came to America seeking a better life. Josef followed Old World ways in raising Mary, and it was common in those days for everyone to do their part to support the family unit.

Mary kept long hours at the creamery. Because she was family, however, she wasn't paid for her work. Her father did give Mary a check, but it was only for tax purposes. Mary was expected to cash the check and give the money back. Her father thought that Mary didn't need money because he provided for her.

Mary was good at math, and she took over the bookkeeping for the new business. When she wasn't occupied with bookkeeping, she washed bottles and did other chores. While this arrangement seemed perfectly normal to Josef, it wasn't satisfactory to Mary. When she was sixteen, she rebelled. She left her father's employ and joined other young women operators at Michigan Bell.

In Josef's eyes, Mary was fast approaching marriageable age. He considered it his responsibility to select a husband for her. He told Mary who he had in mind. Mary had to tell her father that the boy he had chosen wasn't the one for her. She was beginning to exercise her independence. She wanted to make her own decisions.

The Schafers, a family of German immigrants, lived down the street from the creamery. Mary went to school with Ann, one of the older daughters. Ann's younger brother Fred was one of the rowdy boys she had seen around the neighborhood and at the creamery. She didn't like him much.

Mr. Schafer, a man whom Mary remembers fondly, encouraged his son to court Mary. Fred took his father's advice and began paying attention to her. At first, Mary wasn't interested, but he persisted, giving her little gifts and being attentive. Once he gave Mary a watch, which she still has. She began to change her mind about Fred, and they began to see each other. They found out that they liked the same things. They went to see silent films; they took in vaudeville shows at the Palace Theater in downtown Flint. They danced. In the summer, they went to dances at Potters Lake, east of Davison, Michigan. On Saturday nights in the winter, they went to the Dance Box in downtown Flint.

As a Catholic, Josef wasn't at all happy about his daughter dating a Lutheran. Fred told me that when he was courting Mary he would catch glimpses of Mr. Vida spying on them from behind buildings.

Fred was a hard worker. He was a welder at "The Buick," as the largest factory in the world was known in its hometown of Flint. Even before the Great Sit-Down Strike of 1936–37 in Flint, which resulted in major improvements for workers, a job in a General Motors factory was coveted. After about a year's courtship, and despite her father's objections, Mary and Fred married on June 22, 1929. Mary was nineteen when she took Fred's hand at St. Paul's Lutheran Church on North Saginaw Street in Flint. On this formal occasion, Mary wore a white wedding gown with a long train. She had six bridesmaids. Six friends in black tie stood up with Fred.

Fred Schafer, 1936. This picture was taken shortly after Mary and Fred moved into their first home. Mary told me that "Fred was quite like his mother. He believed in dressing up."

Fred and Mary moved into their own apartment and set up housekeeping. With both of them working at paying jobs, they enjoyed relative prosperity. They loved being together and making their own decisions. The honeymoon period was short-lived, however. Only three months into their new life together, the stock market crashed. Fred lost his job at Buick in the first wave of layoffs.

Shortly afterward, Mary lost her job, too. In those days, married women were the first to be laid off, as they presumably had husbands to support them. In 1929, there was no such thing as unemployment benefits. When you were laid off, you were out of work and that was that. Mary says she and Fred were so poor that they couldn't afford to buy a newspaper. Instead they relied on friends to tell them what was happening downtown and what was going on in the country.

Fred and Mary found enough work at the Flint Creamery to remain independent during the first four years of the Depression. I remember Fred telling me that when he was on his usual route, delivering milk with the horse and wagon, one of his stops was the Balkan Bakery. Fred used to get a loaf of bread there and feed it to his horse. Despite all the things that have changed in Mary's lifetime, the Balkan Bakery is still in business in Flint and still making wonderful Old World bread.

In October of 1934, Mary and Fred were blessed with the birth of their son Ronald, born at Hurley Hospital in Flint. When Mary left the hospital, she went directly to Fred's mother's house where they lived for the next two years. It had become financially impossible to keep their apartment. For the next two years, Fred was called back to work and laid off repeatedly. Finally, in the fall of 1936, Fred was called back to work permanently. He worked as a welder for "The Buick" until his retirement in 1972.

In 1936, Fred and Mary bought their first home. It was a little two-bedroom white frame bungalow on Gracelawn Avenue in Flint, next to the Gracelawn Cemetery, which is still there. This first home cost $1,600. Mary reminded me that $1,600 was "amazingly low but not for the time. The Great Depression was in full swing. We had to borrow $200 from my father for the down payment."[1]

Now Mary was finally in charge of her own home. She knew how to do it, and she was good at it. She used her needlework skills to make her home more beautiful. She embroidered tea towels and pillowslips, tatted edgings for linens, and crocheted doilies for the tabletops and the arms and backs of chairs. Needlework of all kinds was popular, and many homemakers practiced a variety of needle arts.

Women's magazines during that period were full of patterns and sewing projects. Mary made most of her own clothes. She knitted ties for Fred. As many women did in those days, she also mended clothes and darned socks. Fred's job as a welder meant that his shirts often had little burn holes in them, so Mary was constantly mending his work shirts. Eventually, she designed and made special protective sleeves for him to wear at work, which helped cut down on her mending.

Mary gained her citizenship in 1943 and Fred in 1944. During World War II, Fred's job as a welder was important to the war effort and kept him safely at home. Life had become easier for Mary. She was happy being a housewife and a mother. Despite the loss of homeland and mother, her time in the orphanage, and all the many hardships she had encountered in America, Mary had not only survived, she had prospered. She had managed to glean goodness from the harsh lessons of life. And, very importantly, as she moved toward what would become her life's work she learned that sewing can be an act of redemption and kindness from one woman to another.

Mary's Early Quilts

Pioneers john and "aunt" polly todd built a tavern at the "grand traverse" of the Flint River Trading Post in 1830. One hundred and twenty years later, Mary shopped in a grand department store there in the city of Flint. Everything was up to date at Smith Bridgeman's, including the quilts on display in the Notions Department. These were sold as kits. Mary, who had never actually seen a quilt, had seen references to quilt patterns in needlework magazines. Intrigued, she bought a kit. In the privacy of her living room, she opened the kit and read the instructions. She was shocked. An experienced needleworker, she calculated the amount of time and work that would be required to make this quilt. Intimidated by the instructions, she did not think she had what it took. She carefully boxed up the kit, returned it to the store, and got her money back. The year was 1949. Mary had seen her first quilt and decided that making a quilt was not for her. She forgot about it, or so she thought.

In 1952, Mary and Fred moved into a brand new house in Flushing, a sweet little bedroom community adjacent to Flint. They bought a brick two-bedroom ranch house with a large back yard. Later that year her son Ronnie would join the navy. Mary told me she was devastated when her only child left home. She found herself with more time on her hands than she liked, time spent worrying about her son. She decided she would be better off if she stayed busy.

Mary's home, 1991. This is the house she and Fred bought in 1952. Mary has lived there ever since.

Mary loved to garden and she intensified her efforts. She kept the hedges well trimmed, did the mowing, raked the leaves in the fall, and planned and executed all the landscaping. But even this did not fill the spaces left by her son's departure. She went back to Smith Bridgeman's and bought a quilt kit. It was a Progress Company pattern called Rhododendron.[1] Typical of quilts from this era, Rhododendron was a medallion-style quilt in soft pastel pinks and greens with a scalloped binding. She took it home, read the instructions and felt that this time she was up to the challenge. Mary soon found that the work posed no particular problem for her. The kit included numbered, precut appliqué pieces. The quilt ground was marked with corresponding numbers showing the exact placement of all the patches. Mary positioned the patches where they belonged and needle turned the edges under. She found the work easy and enjoyable. She realized that quilting had become a comfort to her as well.

The quilting lines were marked with little blue dots. Mary hadn't quilted before, and she didn't have a quilting frame. She solved this problem by basting the three layers together and quilting them in her lap. Having taught herself this way, she still uses this method of quilting. Rhododendron was finished in six months. Mary never considered this quilt part of either collection. The last time I saw the Rhododendron, it was still in Mary's bedroom.

Mary enjoyed making Rhododendron and decided to make another quilt. She bought a Progress Company kit called POPPY WREATH, another medallion-style quilt with a center oval wreath of flowers and four floral sprays in the corners. Like Rhododendron, POPPY WREATH had a scalloped binding. She finished POPPY WREATH in 1953. She felt satisfied with these two quilts and didn't have plans to make any more.

A few years went by before Mary thought about quilting again. In 1956, her son Ron completed his military duty. His friends threw a beach party to celebrate his homecoming. The next day Mary decided to clean out the car. When she opened the trunk, she found an old beach blanket, which upon closer inspection turned out to be an old quilt. It was wet and sandy. Mary gave it a good shaking. Then she examined it more carefully. It was different from the two appliqué quilts she had made. This was a pieced quilt, worked in solid red and white.

Mary, having made two quilts, albeit of the kit kind, now had a good understanding of the time and talent it had taken to make this quilt. She thought about the unknown quilter who had put so much of herself into its construction. She thought about how this quilt had most likely been the pride and joy of its maker. It seemed such a shame that the old quilt had fallen so low that no one cared for it any longer.

Mary decided that the least she could do was to wash the old quilt, which she carefully did. Then, still thinking about the unknown quilter, she decided to do everything she could to restore its dignity. She set about repairing the quilt. While she was mending it, her curiosity got the best of her and she decided to at least find out what the pattern was called.

Then Mary took another step, which marked her quilt making from that moment on. She decided that the best way to honor the unknown quilt maker

POPPY WREATH
78″ × 93″, 1953. Mary's second quilt. (Collection of the Michigan State University Museum, Mary Schafer Collection. Photo by Alan Zinn.)

and preserve the old quilt itself was to make a copy of it. Little did she know that she was hooked. The old red and white quilt had won Mary's heart, and it opened her mind to a new world of exploration.

Making a reproduction quilt began as a labor of love. It turned into a romance with quilts that never ended for Mary. It forged her interest in the history of quilting. It shaped the very way she made quilts from then on.

Mary's first two quilts had been appliqué kit quilts complete with instructions. Reproducing the old red and white quilt posed a different set of challenges for Mary. First she drafted the pieced block pattern on paper. Then she made cardboard templates the exact size of the finished shapes. She drew around each template and cut

it out a quarter inch beyond the pencil line for the seam allowance. Once she had constructed the blocks she set them together on point with alternate plain blocks, just like the original. The old quilt had thirty blocks. Mary made twenty. She altered the finished size of the old quilt, enlarging hers so that it would fit a full-size bed. Mary continued this practice throughout her quilt-making years, making quilts that covered the bed with an adequate drop on the sides and long enough to cover the pillows.

The old quilt did not have a border, and Mary decided to add one to her quilt. In creating this first border, she began a tradition of designing original borders that would develop into a signature characteristic of her quilts. She used a portion of the block design to create a harmonious border. Because the quilt was rectangular, Mary designed a center resolution on the long sides and worked out a corner arrangement that was identical in all four corners. Symmetrical borders would also become characteristic of Mary's quilts.

Another notable feature of this first pieced quilt was Mary's use of fabric. She began piecing the blocks with a red print cut from used clothing. When she ran out of the print, she switched to a solid red and then arranged the blocks, print and plain, in a clever, symmetrical pattern.

Once the top was completed, Mary turned her attention to the quilting. True to the original quilt, she chose feathers for the alternate plain blocks. She decided to draw her own quilting motifs for the side triangles and inner borders. To transfer the quilting designs to the top, she turned to the only method

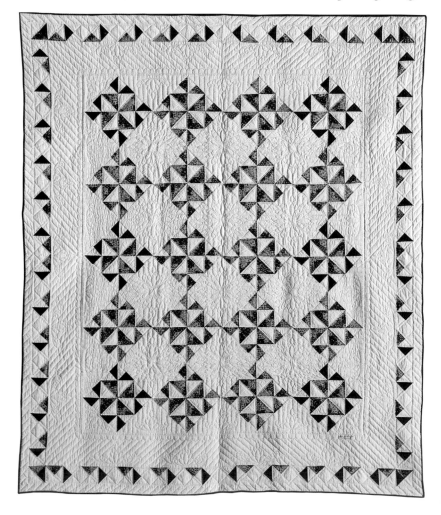

LINDEN MILL
81" × 96", 1980. Made by Mary Schafer.

she knew. The quilting designs in the kits were premarked with a series of little blue dots. Mary drew her designs on brown grocery sacks and poked little holes every quarter inch with a darning needle, creating a perforated pattern. She then positioned the pattern on the quilt top and marked a dot through each hole with a lead pencil. That was her system of marking, and she never gave it up. She used a ruler to mark the straight lines. She completed the quilt in 1956. When it was done, she signed and dated it in embroidery, something else she would continue to do throughout her quilting life.

While she was making the quilt, she continued looking for the name of the block. She looked through all of her needlework magazines and started buying every magazine that pictured quilts, but the name of the block eluded her. Finally she named it herself. As with everything Mary did, she was thoughtful and resourceful as she pondered an appropriate name. The beach party that had resulted in Mary finding the quilt had been at a lake near Linden, a nearby town. She knew that an old mill in Linden had recently been declared a historic site. It was the first such site in Genesee County to be registered with the state of Michigan. Mary thought the pattern resembled a mill wheel, so she named the quilt Linden Mill. Both the old Linden Mill and Mary's reproduction are shown in *Mary Schafer and Her Quilts* (Marston and Cunningham 1990, 5, 7).

The die was cast. Mary's defining characteristics as a quilt maker stemmed from this first pieced quilt: a passion for pattern collecting and history, a commitment to honoring unknown quilt makers, the idea of preserving old quilts by reproducing them and often incorporating original borders and quilting designs, and the belief that a quilt should fit a bed. In essence, these were her fundamental concepts of how a quilt should be imagined, pieced, marked, and quilted.

In 1980, Mary made another LINDEN MILL for herself in blue and white. In 1991, she turned to the original red and white in making a gift for her son Ron. LINDEN MILL had captured Mary's heart and mind and demonstrated that quilting can be a transforming act. From a damp and sandy throw drooping toward obscurity, it had become the launching pad that hurtled Mary into a life of new purpose.

Pattern Collecting

With the completion of LINDEN MILL in 1956, MARY HAD A quilt for each of the three beds in her house. For the next few years, she kept herself busy with embroidery, crochet work, tailoring, and the usual mending. But every time she looked at her bed quilts, Mary wondered about the names of quilt patterns and their origins.

She continued to buy needlework magazines, and early in 1963 she noticed an advertisement in one of them for "thousands of quilt patterns." Thinking that she might discover something about her Linden Mill, Mary was quick to subscribe. *Aunt Kate's Quilting Bee* arrived in the mail. It not only provided interesting reading, but it listed other quilt publications. Mary eagerly subscribed to every one of them. Soon she was receiving *4 J's, Jay Bees,* and *Little 'n Big* in the mail, too.

Through *Aunt Kate's Quilting Bee,* Mary also discovered a system for exchanging patterns called round robins. This was an ingenious method similar to the chain letter, by which a group of women shared patterns in their personal collections. The way it worked was that one woman would make up a list of seven or eight other women. She would then send a pattern to the second woman on the list who would copy it, add her contribution, and send the two patterns to the third woman on the list. It would continue in this way until the patterns came back to the first woman, who would copy them, take her pattern out, replace it with another, and send them all to the second woman on the list. Sometimes the women in the round robins would contribute several patterns. They were often drawn on onionskin paper to make the envelopes lighter. Mary says there were sometimes as many as thirty patterns or more in one envelope. She was sometimes involved in as many as five round robins simultaneously.

Some of the patterns Mary collected from the round robins were taken from old quilts in private collections; some were undocumented. Some were from the *Farmer's Wife,* which was published in Saint Paul, Minnesota, from the nineteenth century through the late 1930s. Some were from Aunt Martha's Quilts, a mail order pattern business begun in the 1930s. The majority of patterns, however, were *Progressive Farmer* and Nancy Cabot patterns. *Progressive Farmer* was founded in 1895, and during the 1930s and 1940s it sold mail order patterns from the Spinning Wheel Company.[1] The Nancy Cabot patterns were carried by the *Chicago Tribune* beginning in the early 1930s. Many of the *Progressive Farmer* and Nancy Cabot patterns were the same.

The round robins were usually limited to one particular type of pattern. Mary primarily collected *Progressive Farmer* and Nancy Cabot patterns. I made copies of Mary's round robin patterns early in our friendship and carefully cataloged them in notebooks. In reviewing these some twenty years later, I can't be sure I copied every single pattern Mary had, but I do have 195 *Progressive Farmer* and 99 Nancy Cabot patterns.

One of the many hand-colored patterns Mary drew on onionskin paper

Mary used onionskin paper to copy the patterns, and often she hand colored them with colored pencils. Other women sent Mary hand colored patterns, too. It is an indication of how important the patterns were to these collectors. Mary's patterns always included all the pertinent information regarding them. Each gave the source of the pattern, instructions, finished block size, number of blocks needed, size of border, and material requirements. These patterns reveal Mary's meticulous attention to detail and her love of precision. She was also keenly aware of the need for correct documentation of patterns. In a letter to round robin participants, for instance, she questioned the sources of several *Progressive Farmer* patterns.

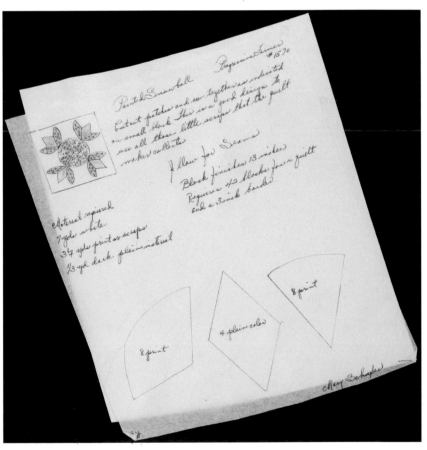

*#1575 and #1177—California Sunflower—is being circulated as being the same.
I am sending #1177, with just one # on it for your consideration. I can't say for cer-
tainty it is the true copy for #1177—perhaps one of you have an original or some way
of checking. At first glance they appear to be the same, but pattern parts are a different
size—block size is also different. If this is a true copy of PF#1177 I should not like it
to lose its individuality as is the case of "Forget-me-not." Speaking of the "Forget-me-not"
patterns—I have three different (somewhat different) sets for this pattern—you will notice on your list of PF patterns #1055 is Forget-me-not. . . .*

*Today is a red letter day for me—for months it's been my project to check, study and
search for a true copy and block set of "Constellation",#1702. With the information I've
gathered I'm reasonably sure the enclosed patt is The One. I want to thank all the ladies
who sent patts and info., each has been a help and I'm sending a copy to share with you.*[2]

Cuesta Benberry, noted quilt historian, also wrote of her early round robins.

*After a time I joined a number of RRs and that is the way I got to correspond with
a lot of different people from all over the country. I don't know how many RRs I belonged to. . . .*

*Sometimes I would extract 20 patterns from one RR. With the number of RRs I
belonged to and the personal exchanges, it got to be a real chore. You had to copy by hand
(that was in the days of pre-photocopying) as many patterns as you wanted within the
5–7 day deadline. I prided myself on being accurate so sometimes I would stay up until
2 or 3 o'clock tracing and copying and then get up with George Jr in the morning.*

*Some of the women in the RR were real sticklers. They wanted every bit of the in-
formation text. They wanted to know "name of the pattern," "what was its original
source,""when was this pattern published," and "was it a syndicated pattern." They
wanted as much information about it as they could possibly get and if you sent in patterns more than once without the complete information, they would strike your name
from the list, take your patterns out and send them back to you. I was glad to have the
association of different kinds. My first RR was an experienced group of women and a
good training ground. They were a no-nonsense type of pattern collector and extremely
strict about the rules.*[3]

Joy Craddock, publisher of *4 J's,* a favorite magazine of Mary's, belonged to
one of her round robins. I include a letter from Joy to Mary here because it is
typical of the many letters Mary received from her quilt detective colleagues,
terse with pattern jargon. In this undated letter, Joy wrote:

*Mary, I'm giving you a few days to get out from under the R Robins before I send
this batch along. Most are ones I've redrawn from Round Robins. (Progressive Farmer)
patterns only—part are some block diagrams—I'd like you to check over, such as
#1659. I got my Carnation Bowl from Gladys Phillips—1st one. Second one that sent*

*in R.R. was used original pattern which I traded 5 copies of others for. (Gladys Phillips)
has the following original patterns: #1728 Violet Wreath; #1718 Bed Time; #1705 The
Bride's Bouquet; #1685 Forget-Me-Not. I got #1734 Yellow Cosmos from her. She has
#1914 Rockets; #1900 Wreath; #1790 October Foliage; #1762 Sapphire Net;
#1822 Crazy Loons—I also have it now; #1455 Bell of St. Mary's. I sent her in
R.R. or an exchange Church Bells, #16 . . . Mexican Vista, #1686 and it is in R.R.
which should reach you sometime. #1593 Rail Fences; #1649 Wheel of Fortune;
#1755 Rope Block; To be sure just which ones went out in R.R. I just checked. . . .*[4]

Mary sometimes included little personal notes to the round robin participants, as this 1964 letter shows.

> *LeJean—my husband is an arc-welder also—at Buick. Maintenance—sheet metal
> shop. Has been for 35 years. Will retire in 4½ years.*
> *Bonnie—yes I heard about the covered bridges you have in that one county—as a
> matter of fact I sent for a brochure on the big celebration you're having in Indiana all
> this 150th year.*
> *Vesta, I'm sending all info on Forget-me-not patts I have. The info written by a
> friend may be from a Martha Madison pattern—but they are usually the same as PF, I
> understand. I really get involved with these patts at times and have to put the brakes on.*
> *May, sorry about your illness—hope it was of short duration.*
> *Phyllis aren't you glad you decided to join these wonderful robins? Till next time
> around. Mary.*[5]

Mary could also personalize an introduction to the round robins: "Welcome
aboard, Mrs. Folmer. Happy to have you join us. Thank you girls for the fine
patterns. . . ."[6]
Some of the round robin participants also corresponded individually, and
in these letters personal struggles and experiences were more likely to be
included, as this letter from Carol Lynch of Lyons, Kansas, indicates.

> *February 26, 1965*
> *Dear Mary:*
>
> *Enclosed find 14 patterns. I hope you are satisfied with them. I find I have only
> Nasturtiums of Nancy Cabot that you ask for. Do you have the Progressive Farmer
> list? If so how far back does it go? I also have a list of Nancy Cabot if you would care
> for them. There are some of the patterns I do not have of the P.F. I am returning your
> list so that you will be able to send for others.*
> *I am so glad Milt is home from hospital, was there for 19 days. His temperature
> came up and Dr. could not find the trouble. Finally located the congestion in his lungs.
> Even cut windows in his cast to see if the infection was there. Thank goodness, no. I
> have enough of that for this family. Barbara is back perking on all four again. In fact*

*things have leveled off for us around here. And we have found our sense of humor
again. So now things will be better.*

*Yes you understood. I will have need to stop quite a several of the R.R.'s. Milt put
his foot down and said I was not to continue with the patterns. But don't think he
realized just how many Robins I was in. I am keeping the P.F., N.C. Rainbow and a
few special to me. So you can see I have cut away down. The P.F. is my pet. And I
really love to receive them. Of course Nancy Cabot patterns are strewed throughout the
P.F. Also some of the other patterns too. Wm Clark for one, has patterns in the P.F.
Also I find Ladies Art and some K.C.S. [Kansas City Star] with script added to
them. I could really cry when I think how many R.R.'s I have stopped. But like you, the
ladies have been so kind and have sent word of encouragement. Just when I needed it
most. Not all the ladies will know how much I appreciated the lovely cards, birthday,
and letters. Things had been a little rough for awhile. And the letters came just at the
right moment to help me find my balance and sense of humor again. One lady said that
quilt pattern collectors are a breed apart. Willing to share and offer encouragement, not
only on patterns, but on the daily happenings of life. You know she is so right. Guess I
had not really realized that, until I was the recipient. Oh how I do appreciate and hug
the words and thoughts to myself and take them out and examine them often. Did not
know how the ladies felt about me. But I really know now. The wonderful, darling
ladies. God bless them, everyone.*

*I really appreciate your sending for patterns. Now I can put out a few letters, that
have been waiting for postage. Thank you so much and do hope you visit my house again
with another order. B Cing U.*

Carol Lynch.[7]

Never mind the coffee klatch prose; the round robin women were serious
pattern collectors. Mary told me that for some pattern collecting was an end in
itself. She knew that some women collected patterns and didn't make quilts. On
February 8, 1966, she sent a note to a group of women in a round robin in
which she asked about this trend.

*Hi Gals, Hope every one is well, and aren't you glad we're no longer in the deep
freeze.*

*Your notes about your handwork is interesting. Do any of you make quilts. I do and
would like to know if you do too, also collect sampler blocks and old and antique quilts:
books and articles on quilts, and of course quilt patterns. 'Till next time Round,
Mary Schafer*[8]

Barbara Bannister wrote to Mary about her observation of this phenomenon.

*makes me think of all these women who are collecting PATTERNS so frantically.
One lady, in response to my question was amazed to think I thought she made quilts.*

(She has HUNDREDS of patterns) . . . she had never even made a single BLOCK, just collects them. Another friend of mine, Maryella Walling (in Des Moines) has a curious hobby. She REALLY collects—has thousands of patterns, and she puts them on MICRO-FILM!! She doesn't do much in the way of quiltmaking. I think she said once, it was a lack of room or some reason like that. . . . So, I have done a LOT of thinking about this hobby of collecting quilts, patterns, etc. How to use it in a decorative manner, so one can SEE the pretty designs and get some daily pleasure from them.[9]

With good organizational skills, Mary worked out a system for cataloging data that stood many years as a model of efficiency. Before many of her collected items went to the Michigan State University Museum, I could ask Mary for information from her vast archive and she could find it in a matter of minutes. Sometimes she would get letters from quilters asking if she had a specific pattern. In response, she would diligently go through all of her pattern collections and cross-check her books and other sources. I have a copy of a letter Mary wrote to Joan Kaim in response to such a query. The letter includes six drawings of blocks, which Mary describes in detail. Here is what she says about three of the patterns.

October 1, 1965
Dear Joan,

Perhaps I'd best send you drawings of some of the Cabot patterns you wonder about to avoid unnecessary duplication. Holly Hock Wreath: This looks like the Holly Hock Wreath in the McKim book. Haven't checked whether there is a difference. Will send if you want it.

Shooting Star: Have this pattern. Have another Shooting Star, but can't find it now. no source on it. Done in orange, red yellow and burnt orange. (Drawn from memory). This is a Workbasket pattern.

I have the Cabot Sunbonnet baby with no pocket, but I have a pattern (don't know source) of a Sunbonnet Baby with hand in pocket—pattern given to me by an acquaintance here in Flushing—it is very pretty I think. Pattern parts almost like Cabots Print dress—pocket is defined by outline stitch in black embroidery—an arm boot and bonnet in harmonizing solid color. Buttonhole or blanket stitch all around. Black lazy daisy flowers on bonnet, yellow centers. Crown of bonnet has running stitch, two lazy daisy stitches for bow and running stitch streamers (all embroidered in black except French knots in yellow).[10]

Dolores Hinson wrote me a long letter about round robins, speculating about how and why they eventually disappeared.

The robins started dying out when quilt pattern books became available and magazines started showing up on Supermarket shelves. (oops! I just realized, I'm

*probably the chief murderer, as my pattern books were the first since the McKim book.)
Mt. Mist put out patterns on the backs of their wrappers—but about one or two
patterns a year and to get others you had to send—Money—. It was still near enough
to the depression for that to be a large consideration. Remember for the round robins the
postage was still below 10 cents for a letter and the P.O. didn't weigh each letter to make
sure you didn't try to send 1/50 of an ounce more than your stamp paid for.*[11]

In the years between the end of one quilt revival (ca. 1940) and the beginning of another (ca. 1970), round robins were an essential ingredient in the
survival of quilt making in America. Membership in round robins allowed a
continuous flow of information on patterns and spurred independent field
study. They also offered a means by which far-flung, socially diverse, and very
often isolated women could share intimate struggles and triumphs in a safe
forum. Thus, many quilters between the revivals continued another important
tradition: women coming together to support themselves and others.

Mary Makes Quilt Blocks

NOT ALL ROUND ROBINS IN THE QUILTING WORLD ARE PAPER based. Mary participated in some that exchanged fully realized quilt blocks. But these exchanges turned out to be less satisfying in her efforts to educate herself about quilt making. Often, in exchange for her precisely pieced or appliquéd blocks, Mary would receive blocks that were poorly made. While she found interest in these primitive blocks because she valued effort, she also realized that her own energies could be more productively employed elsewhere.

Cuesta Benberry gives an eyewitness account of one such block exchange.

> *There were other kinds of RRs. Mary Schafer of Flushing Michigan joined several block RRs. Mrs. Schafer always put her name neatly in the seams as she became disenchanted that many of the blocks she received had the name written across the front in large black letters. I received many lovely blocks for my collection from her which she had originally planned to exchange.*[1]

In earlier times, quilters made and kept blocks as a way to remember different quilt patterns. In a time when paper, patterns, and books were scarce, ingenious quilters made their own quilt block catalogs. Dolores Hinson wrote a letter to me about what she calls "quilters' catalogs." She came across the term while doing research in 1954. When Dolores was giving a lecture, she often asked members of the audience to share their own quilts. "I asked the groups to bring in their quilts, and at a meeting in Fairfax, Virginia, I met the first 'Great-grandma's quilter's catalog.' It was made in 1842 for a bride who was to leave for the west, only the couple changed their minds about leaving."[2] Dolores said that there was a note attached to the batch of blocks, which read "My Quilter's Catalog, 1842." Dolores had "run into it in other places also, from 1810 to 1850s on the east coast."[3]

For more information about this interesting subject, refer to Dolores Hinson's "Quilters' Catalogs," an article written for *Antiques Journal* in 1970.[4] Wilene Smith researched quilters' catalogs for an article entitled "Quilt Blocks? Or Quilt Patterns?" originally published in *Uncoverings* 1986.[5] This article was reprinted in 1994 in Laurel Horton's *Quiltmaking in America: Beyond the Myths.*[6]

One of the most famous block collections was made by Carrie Hall. She talks about her collection in *The Romance of the Patchwork Quilt in America* (Hall and Kretsinger 1935), which features her blocks:

> *After completing my "baker's dozen," I realized that I couldn't continue making quilts indefinitely, and yet I was so fascinated by all the numerous and beautiful patterns that I conceived the idea of making a collection of patches, one like every known pattern, little realizing the magnitude of the undertaking. The collection now contains over one thousand patches and is to be placed in the Thayer Museum of Art of the University of Kansas.*[7]

Knowing the names of blocks, of course, is very important in a discussion of traditional quilt making. I can remember, as a beginning quilter, many a night going to bed with the Hall and Kretsinger book, fascinated by the quilt block section. Oh what a tangled web our foremothers inadvertently wove into quilt posterity. Shoo Fly, for instance, is also called Duck and Ducklings, Double Monkey Wrench, Love-Knot, Hole in the Barn Door, Puss in the Corner, Lincoln's Platform, and Sherman's March. Duck and Ducklings is also called Corn and Beans, Handy Andy, and Hen and Chickens. This makes good, if somewhat confusing, reading for the rookie quilter—and necessary reading. In my own experience in the 1970s, there was a convention among quilters of mentioning a pattern, Crown of Thorns, for example, and then lowering the voice, as if speaking in parentheses, and saying, "also known as Single Wedding Ring or Georgetown Circle."

Within a short time of meeting Mary in 1977, I realized how important it was to have a good working knowledge of quilt pattern names. How can you talk quilts, especially across geographical regions, if you don't know all the names? By then, Mary had twenty-five years of intense research, study, and classification under her belt, not to mention a remarkably quick memory. This mix of knowledge and wit made her *really* good at identifying patterns. I can still remember her telling me that Jacob's Ladder was also called Road to California, Wagon Tracks, Trail of the Covered Wagon, Stepping Stones, Underground Railroad, Tail of Benjamin's Kite, and other names that I have since forgotten. Mary noted that all of the names used to describe a diagonal row of little squares placed like stepping stones on a pathway referred to movement or travel.

It was clear that pattern identification and documentation were important to Mary and her generation of quilt scholars. As these women devoted themselves to collecting and documenting quilt history, much of the attention was focused on gathering the patterns, identifying them, and researching the sources. As a witness of this phenomenon, I would say that today there is far less attention paid to being well versed in quilt block identification. Perhaps this is because the excitement of discovery has passed.

One of the ways in which Mary had studied quilt making was by making and collecting quilt blocks, which over the years added up to a substantial record. Mary always signed each block of her own manufacture in the quarter-inch seam allowance along the outer edge. The name of the pattern and the date she made it were also written on the outer edge of each block.

Part of my quilting education was sitting at Mary's knee, literally, leafing through her blocks. There was a reason for making or collecting every block. Usually it was a historical reason. Sometimes it was natural curiosity about how the blocks would fit together or an exploration of color possibilities. Sometimes she made one block to check the pattern for accuracy. At other times, she made a new block just for the transparent joy of making it.

When she decided to make a Feather-Edged Star quilt, she drafted patterns of the nine versions she liked best and made the blocks. It was her way of choosing the pattern and color combinations she preferred. I remember looking through that group of blocks and noting the amount of piecework Mary had done even before she sewed the first stitch on the new quilt. Each sample was meticulously hand sewn from scraps and each in itself was an item of considerable beauty.

Always interested in American history, Mary was intrigued by blocks with historical references. She made blocks with patriotic themes to illustrate her lecture about quilts with historical names. In 1992, she gave me four red, white, and blue blocks with historical names: Nelson's Victory, Union Square, 54–40 or Fight, and Tippecanoe & Tyler Too. In the quarter-inch seam allowance of this last block, Mary wrote: "U.S. Pres. Campaign 1840, 'Tippecanoe & Tyler Too', pg. 69 Finley, Mary Schafer, June 5, 1992." Mary, true to form, even documented this sample block. Later she donated the majority of her blocks to the Michigan State University Museum. She kept the part of the collection she couldn't part with, including the Feather-Edged

Star blocks, the patriotic blocks, and some twenty-five blocks she'd made specifically to illustrate her lectures.

Mary sent blocks to people she thought would use them to promote quilting, a cause near and dear to her heart. She knew the importance of blocks in quilt research and sent them to friends such as Cuesta Benberry and Joyce Gross, who, among others in her quilt circle, were gaining reputations as historians and writers of note. Although Mary had chosen to stay home and work quietly in the background, she admired what her quilting friends were doing and was always there to support them in any way she could.

By 1984, Cuesta Benberry herself had a collection of around six hundred blocks. She wrote about her block collection in an article published in the *Quilters' Journal:*

> *I have not seen the Carrie Hall block collection but I think my collection would pretty well match it. Many of mine are different from the ones she has, because through the years my friends have just sent me made up blocks. Mary Schafer has been the largest contributor and they are probably the finest as far as being well made but I appreciate each one block because they were all sent with love.*[8]

By 1996, Cuesta's block collection had grown to more than eight hundred blocks. In a Christmas letter dated December 16, 1996, she mentions her block collection and says: "I now have 800+ of those sample blocks, of which 100+ were the very elegant blocks that over the years Mary has given to me."[9]

In 1977, Cuesta announced she would donate her block collection to the Quilters Hall of Fame in Marion, Indiana, which included the blocks Mary had sent her over the years. The Hall of Fame hosted an exhibit of Cuesta's blocks on July 15–18, 1999. It was held at the Marion Public Library and Museum and was curated by Hazel Carter, president and founder of the

MICHIGAN ROSE
12″ block, 1987. Original design, made by Mary Schafer. (Collection of Gwen Marston.)

Quilters Hall of Fame. The exhibit included sixty blocks made by Mary Schafer.

Dolores Hinson sent me a list of the twenty-one blocks that Mary had sent her from 1967 to 1979. Reviewing the list, I noticed that five of the blocks were of the same patterns Mary had sent to me. There were also duplicates in the blocks Mary made for Cuesta. When Mary's enthusiasm for a particular pattern took over, she couldn't resist making more to share with quilting friends.

Over the years, Mary has given me fifty blocks, including MICHIGAN ROSE, a Schafer original. Often I would receive the block accompanied by the pattern, the templates (made from cereal boxes), the quilting design, and historical information about the pattern. Because Mary was a stickler for documentation, she usually included everything she knew about the block. When Mary sent anything too large to fit in a standard envelope, she made her own ingenious one. She used a brown paper grocery sack and cleverly constructed a study envelope, just the right size to hold the contents.

I don't know the total number of blocks Mary made and gave away. Nor do I know the number of blocks she made for herself. In 1998, she donated 208 blocks to the Michigan State University Museum. During a visit in late 2000, she and I went through the remaining lot, as we had done together many times before. Her current block collection includes about seventy blocks: the beloved patriotic blocks, some twenty-five blocks made to illustrate her lectures, and the nine Feather-Edged Star blocks she made as a way to determine the variation she liked best.

The Challenge Period

BY 1966, MARY HAD MADE SEVEN QUILTS: RHODODENDRON in 1952, POPPY WREATH in 1953, Linden Mill in 1956, Fox and Geese and Star and Cross in 1964, and RADICAL ROSE and Yankee Puzzle in 1965. She had become an accomplished quilt maker and was deep in pursuit of pattern collecting and quilt history. Her library contained all the important books that had been written about quilts. One of her favorites was Marie Webster's *Quilts: Their Story and How to Make Them* (1915). Some of Marie's words touched Mary deeply and inspired her to begin a new phase of her quilting, which she calls her "challenge period." Marie Webster wrote in the introduction to her book:

> The work of the old-time quilters possesses artistic merit to a very high degree. While much of it was designed strictly for utilitarian purposes . . . Every now and then there comes to light one of these old quilts of the most exquisite loveliness, in which the needlework is almost painful in its exactness. Such treasures are worthy of study and imitation, and are deserving of careful preservation for the inspiration of future generations of quilters.
>
> To raise in popular esteem these most worthy products of home industry, to add to the appreciation of their history and traditions, to give added interest to the hours of labor which their construction involves, to present a few of the old masterpieces to the quilters of to-day, such is the purpose of this book of quilts.[1]

The phrase "to raise in popular esteem" roused Mary to a new purpose. She decided to challenge herself. She would make a series of quilts as tributes to women who had been most inspirational in her quilt making. Mary thought that a series of this nature might make a meaningful contribution to quilt history and tradition.

Mary's first challenge quilt honored Ruth E. Finley, author of *Old Patchwork Quilts* (1929). Ruth gave thorough descriptions of old quilts and wrote about the times in which they were made. In one of her discussions of patterns, Finley described a quilt in her collection called the CLAMSHELL.

> *A quilt wholly constructed of convex-concave patches, and hence exceedingly difficult to make, is the "Clam Shell." This typically Cape Cod design appeared more frequently in quilting than in actual patchwork. "Clamshell" quilting is not especially rare as quilting goes, but the quilt photographed is the only perfectly preserved specimen of "Clam Shell" patchwork I have ever seen. A glance at the exacting requirements of its needlework explains why the pattern went out of fashion, soon after 1800.*[2]

The CLAMSHELL pattern was exceedingly difficult, rare in patchwork quilts, and out of fashion—three good reasons for Mary to make this her first challenge. Finley showed a photograph of a quarter section of her CLAMSHELL on page 70, which was all Mary needed to get started. She found a pattern in one of her *Aunt Kate's Quilting Bee* magazines. Even though the piecing was complicated and tedious, Mary was so familiar with fabric that she knew exactly how to use the grain to make the curved edges comply. She began piecing the clamshells, carefully arranging the fabrics so that they mirrored each other both vertically and horizontally.

As the piecing continued, she noticed that she had pieced together a diamond shape. She liked the shape and decided to emphasize it by making a medallion-style CLAMSHELL. She filled the corners of the triangle with white clamshells to form a rectangle and added still more white clamshells to emphasize the medallion. Around this center, she added five more rows of printed clamshells, again mirroring the fabrics right and left and top and

CLAMSHELL
79" × 97 1/2", 1966. Made by Mary Schafer. (Collection of the Michigan State University Museum, Mary Schafer Collection. Photo by Alan Zinn.)

bottom, to make an inner border. Then more white clamshells followed by colored ones were grouped in a unique way to create another border. She finished the quilt with white clamshells.

Encouraged by her friend Dolores Hinson, she entered it in the first National Quilting Association show in 1970 and won two blue ribbons. This first NQA show was an important event in the quilt world, predating the nationally touted quilt shows at the Whitney Museum in 1971 and the Smithsonian in 1972.

Nimble Needle Treasures cited Mary and her winning quilt in an article in the spring of 1971.

> *[Mary Schafer,] quilt maker par excellence, also has an extensive collection of antique and modern quilts. Her deep interest in quilts has been the inspiration for making quilts and collecting quilt patterns. Mrs. Schafer has consistently been a sweepstakes and blue ribbon prizewinner for quilts of her own making at Fairs in Michigan. At the first Quilt Show of the National Quilting Association, Washington, D.C., Mrs. Schafer's "Clamshell" won two blue ribbons for "Most Popular Quilt in the Show" and for "Best Pieced Quilt."*[3]

The CLAMSHELL took Mary a year to make.

Her next challenge was an appliqué quilt called Coxcomb. Mary had made friends with Glenna Boyd, publisher of Mary's favorite quilt publication, *Aunt Kate's Quilting Bee.* Glenna published some of her own original designs, and one of them, Coxcomb, caught Mary's eye. She decided to appliqué only five of the nine blocks, carrying out the design of the other four blocks with quilting rather than appliqué. Mary designed her own border and drafted her own original quilting designs for the quilt.

In 1968, she began to make a HONEY BEE quilt to honor Ruby McKim. She took the pattern from McKim's 101 *Patchwork Patterns* (1962). Ruby operated McKim Studios, a mail order house for patterns located in Independence, Missouri. She was well known in quilt scholarship circles as she had written a syndicated newspaper column on quilting in the 1920s and 1930s. Dover Publications reprinted one of her early pamphlets, "101 Patchwork

WASHINGTON PLUME
93″ × 93″, 1968. Made by Mary Schafer. (Collection of the Michigan State University Museum, Mary Schafer Collection. Photo by Alan Zinn.)

Patterns," in 1962, and the book became a standard resource for many years afterward.

As had happened before, Mary began with a simple pattern that grew into a more complicated project. She made the two center blocks out of a printed fabric so that they would stand out from the other blocks, which were made in solid-colored fabrics. This was intended to represent the queen and drone bees. All the other blocks were made in solids to represent the worker bees. Bees need flowers, from which they gather food, so Mary designed a lovely floral border. As a final touch, she appliquéd little honeybees caught in flight at each corner.

In 1968, Mary began working on a WASHINGTON PLUME to honor her dear friend Betty Harriman. It was a reproduction of a historic quilt Betty had seen at Mount Vernon. Both women made quilts of this design. In fact, the pattern was so large that instead of drawing it Betty sent her completed top so that Mary could draft it directly.

One of the books Mary studied was Florence Peto's *Historic Quilts* (1939). Mary corresponded with Florence and held her in high regard. Peto had worked endlessly to bring quilts to the attention of museums and to the public as well. Mary appreciated the fact that Peto's own quilts were masterpieces of design and execution. In 1968, Mary began working on a LOBSTER quilt, inspired by the Peto book. According to the book, LOBSTER dated from the American Revolution and the name of the design referred to the red uniforms of the British soldiers, which earned them the nickname "Lobsterbacks." The threatening display of pincers and tails was one of the most unusual patterns Mary had seen. As with the WASHINGTON PLUME, it was just the kind of rare, historic pattern that interested her most.

Florence Peto wrote to Mary about her LOBSTER quilt: "Do you know I have never seen another 'Lobster' quilt since the one pictured in *Historic Quilts.* I am happy to know you are keeping the design alive."[4]

With Mary's theme of honoring people in the quilting world who inspired her, it was only natural for her to commemorate Rose Wilder Lane, the only child of Laura Ingalls Wilder

LOBSTER
77" × 93", 1969. Made by Mary Schafer. (Collection of the Michigan State University Museum, Mary Schafer Collection. Photo by Alan Zinn.)

(author of *Little House on the Prairie*). Rose Wilder Lane wrote the *Woman's Day Book of American Needlework* (1963), a beautiful book with an accompanying box of full-size patterns. Mary chose to make one of the rarest patterns in the book, Oak Leaf and Cherries. The cherries in this exquisitely crafted quilt are padded, and Mary created original quilting and border designs. Oak Leaf and Cherries demonstrates Mary's ability to master difficult patterns with seemingly effortless grace. Rose Wilder Lane's homage quilt is shown in *Sets and Borders* and *Mary Schafer and Her Quilts*.[5]

From 1967 through 1969, Mary's work was characterized mostly by the truly difficult CLAMSHELL, Coxcomb, WASHINGTON PLUME, HONEY BEE, LOBSTER, and Oak Leaf and Cherries. Each was made as a testament of Mary's admiration for important figures in the quilt world. However, when she discovered and purchased an old SAVANNAH STAR quilt in 1969 she returned to her original purpose—to elevate the work of ordinary quilters.

With the idea to pay homage to the unknown quilt maker, Mary went to work on her own version. The old SAVANNAH STAR was a scrap quilt made in the 1920s. Mary used the block pattern and color scheme from the old quilt, but she changed virtually everything else and added a complementary original border. Her refined treatment of the old quilt highlights the inherent elegance of simple patterns. *Sets and Borders* shows both quilts. Mary's version of the old quilt is shown in *Mary Schafer and Her Quilts*.[6]

While Mary was making the challenge quilts, she looked for easy projects to give her a rest from the more demanding work. While making her Coxcomb homage quilt for Glenna Boyd, Mary began an uncomplicated Nine Patch intended for her grandson. From a simple beginning, this quilt, like many of Mary's ideas, grew wings and began to fly on its own. While making the blocks, Mary was thinking about former president Dwight D. Eisenhower. She told me that something in the Nine Patch construction suggested his humble, rural background. The quilt evolved over time. To replace the center block, Mary inserted an eagle surrounded by five stars, representing the Eisenhower presidency and his status as a five-star general. She designed a border of laurel leaves and stars to stand for all the honors Eisenhower had received. The continuous vine border was Mary's way of suggesting Ike's unity with the people and the nation. Mary also incorporated forty-eight stars in the design, some appliquéd, some quilted, to represent the number of states during his presidency. Mary purposely made the quilt narrow as a reminder that Ike had slept many a night on a narrow army cot.

EISENHOWER[7] is a prime example of quilts Mary would begin making with specific historical themes. It was shown in the exhibit 20th Century Quilts, 1900–1970: Women Make Their Mark, held at the American Quilter's Society, Paducah, Kentucky, in 1997 and pictured in the exhibit catalog.

The EISENHOWER quilt had another meaning for Mary. It was the first time she attempted to express her patriotism by exploiting the symbolic possibilities of quilt design, something she would investigate more fully during the 1970s.

Mary considers the years 1966 through 1970 her challenge period. It was a time when she focused on making quilts to honor women who she felt had furthered the art of quilt making. During the challenge period, Mary also began to introduce patriotic themes in her quilts, which later culminated in six quilts made for the U.S. bicentennial. I think of Mary's challenge period as her glorious period because of the number of outstanding quilts she made during this time. But it was by no means the end of exquisite work by Mary. She immediately began two more unusual appliqué quilts, OCTOBER FOLIAGE and NORTH CAROLINA LILY.[8]

OCTOBER FOLIAGE
84½" × 94", 1971. Made by Mary Schafer. (Collection of the Michigan State University Museum, Mary Schafer Collection. Photo by Alan Zinn.)

The challenge period ended when Betty Harriman, Mary's mentor, friend, and longtime collaborator, passed away. She left a cache of unfinished quilts, which Mary purchased from Betty's estate. Mary, in loving memory, would finish Betty's work because she saw them as "treasures . . . worthy of study and imitation . . . deserving of careful preservation for the inspiration of future generations of quilters."

The Bicentennial Quilt Revival

THE QUILT WORLD WAS PERCOLATING WITH EXCITEMENT, as Mary worked to complete her own Lee's Rose and Buds and Betty's unfinished one. The blockbuster quilt shows of 1971 and 1972 at the Whitney Museum and the Smithsonian, respectively, heralded the beginning of a new, dynamic era in quilt making in America. Mary, continuing to work quietly in the heartland, was nevertheless aware of trends, especially in quilting. In a letter to Ruth Parr, she set forth her impressions of the Whitney show:

> I have read in several places about the quilt show under the direction of Gail van der Hoof and Jonathan Holstein, the collectors of the quilts. Their collection has created quite a stir not only among quilters but has caused art-minded people to see them as op art. I guess I'm old fashioned. I still see them as bed covers, their original intended purpose—strictly speaking, I use them as bed spreads.[1]

Locally, Mary noticed an increase in public awareness of quilting. She was thrilled to see this growing popularity and felt that it placed a new responsibility on experienced quilt makers like herself. She wanted to do everything she could to encourage this new, positive development.

At the same time, every village, township, and city in the United States was gearing up for the bicentennial celebration. As had been fashionable preceding the centennial, anything thought to be early American enjoyed a revival in the 1970s. Quilting, an art form innovated by American women, was back in the forefront of the national consciousness.

In April of 1971, Mary was asked to present a quilt workshop at the YWCA in Flint, Michigan. She was also asked to speak at church group gatherings, craft clubs, and antique study groups. Unlike today, when quilt professionals travel on a circuit of coast to coast engagements, Mary and her colleagues rarely traveled any great distance.

Mary never really enjoyed public speaking. She did it because she felt obligated to fulfill Marie Webster's maxim "to raise in popular esteem these most worthy products of home industry."[2] Mary prepared lectures on various historical and technical topics. She wrote her lectures in longhand and read them to the audience. Mary wanted to have concrete examples of everything she discussed. This became yet another reason to make new blocks and quilts or to collect them.

Mary was content with a ten-dollar lecture fee. While this fee seems surprisingly low by today's standards, it was an acceptable fee in the early 1970s. And even though she never enjoyed lecturing she was loyal to Marie Webster's mission, which she had taken as her own. Mary didn't drive, so her husband Fred chauffeured her. Later, as I began to plan exhibitions of her quilts and to lecture about them, Mary was only too happy to relinquish public speaking. She always said "my quilts speak for me."

In 1973, Jonathan Holstein published *The Pieced Quilt: An American Design Tradition*, and Patsy and Myron Orlofsky came out with their *Quilts in America* in 1974. Robert Bishop and Carleton L. Safford published *America's Quilts and Coverlets* in 1974, and Bishop published *New Discoveries in American Quilts* in 1975. Mary and her quilting friends, who had spent so much time beating the bushes, publishing their findings in little magazines and round robin letters, could see that quilt information was now being broadcast on a grand scale.

Quilting magazines began focusing attention on the approaching bicentennial. Announcements for contests and exhibits proliferated, and writers began to focus on articles with patriotic themes. In 1970, Dolores Hinson wrote an article for *Nimble Needle Treasures* called "The Spirit of '76." It began, "Have you started designing your Bi-Centennial Quilt yet?"[3] That same year Cuesta Benberry wrote a number of articles reminding quilters of historical patterns. She wrote an article about quilts from World War II called "Victory Quilts"[4] and another called "More Patriotic Quilts of the World War II Era."[5]

As an immigrant herself, and as a person with a keen interest in American history, Mary enjoyed the bicentennial as much as anyone I know. As 1976 approached, she was in her element. To contribute to the celebration, Mary made a series of quilts with patriotic themes. Mary already had the Mount Vernon reproduction WASHINGTON PLUME she had made to honor Betty Harriman.

Mary decided she would make more symbolic historical quilts to celebrate the coming bicentennial. Knowing full well the amount of time needed to finish a quilt, Mary began work on the series in 1972. By the time fife and drum corps piped the floats down American main streets on July 4, 1976, Mary had researched, designed, and completed five more major quilts: QUEEN CHARLOTTE'S CROWN, Burgoyne Surrounded, Lafayette Orange Peel, Molly Pitcher, and Spirit of '76.

Mary's bicentennial series is outstanding in several unique ways. First of all, I don't know of anyone else who offered six full-size, "museum quality" quilts for the occasion. Second, the amount of research that went into these quilts is no less impressive than the stitching designs that hold them together. They are scrolls of symbolism. They exemplify Mary's deliberate, meticulous approach to process. Third, they explicitly honor the role of women in the Revolutionary War. Finally, in a national celebration defined by clichéd patriotic symbols, there isn't a tired idea in the lot.

Her idea was to commemorate some of the less celebrated figures of the American Revolution, just as she had championed the less celebrated artist, the "anonymous" quilter. In a surprising departure from standard bicentennial themes, Mary made a quilt honoring Queen Charlotte, King George's wife and America's last queen.

As she explained to me, "Charlotte was our last queen and, as wife of the reigning monarch, she played an important role in her time. One of the most difficult aspects of the revolution for the colonists was severing their lifelong allegiance to their queen." I did a little research of my own. What Mary said was correct. The British campaign, which successfully captured Georgia at the end of 1778 and South Carolina in 1779, for instance, was won in part with the aid of local loyalists.

Ruth Finley refers to Charlotte as a "seemingly gentle, self-effacing woman." Finley goes on to remind us that "In Virginia there is a county

QUEEN CHARLOTTE'S CROWN
76″ × 98″, 1973. Made by Mary Schafer.
(Collection of the Michigan State
University Museum, Mary Schafer
Collection. Photo by Alan Zinn.)

named in her honor—Queen Charlotte County originally, but just Charlotte now. Undoubtedly Virginia also is responsible for another honor paid her—an old old quilt pattern called Queen Charlotte's Crown."[6]

Mary wanted this quilt to be fit for a queen. As with her other bicentennial quilts, this one is a steeple of simplicity, symbolism, and elegance.

Mary's Burgoyne Surrounded, completed in 1974, commemorates the Battle of Saratoga, where British general John Burgoyne met defeat at the hands of General Horatio Gates in Saratoga, New York, on October 17, 1777.[7]

Mary's third quilt, Lafayette Orange Peel, proved to be another uncommon choice for the bicentennial celebration. Mary got the idea for this quilt from Dolores Hinson's *A Quilter's Companion.*[8]

Spirit of '76, a red, white, and blue quilt replete with stars and stripes, was Mary's salute to the American flag. Mary says it was "dedicated to the patriots of 1776 and those who followed in service to our country." She explains that she chose the pinwheel design to suggest "the Spirit of '76 is dynamic and still in motion today."

After honoring Queen Charlotte, she turned her attention to the efforts of American women in the Revolution. She first considered Betsy Ross but decided that was too obvious a choice. After searching her history books for an appropriate heroine, she settled on Molly Pitcher (1754–1832), so named because she carried pitchers of water to thirsty soldiers at the battle of Monmouth. According to legend, she took her husband's position at the cannons when he was overcome by heat and fought in his place for the duration of the battle.

Mary had her heroine, but there was no quilt pattern named for Molly Pitcher. Mary found an old, unnamed pattern from Connecticut in her collection. Perfect! An unknown quilt design by an unknown maker would create a link to the innumerable anonymous heroines of American history. She designed an original center appliquéd block and set the other blocks on point. Molly Pitcher was finished early in 1975.

Mary raced to complete her bicentennial quilts by the deadline and appreciated Fred's help. Now retired, he stepped in and gladly helped Mary with the housework, cooking, and gardening chores. Fred was always proud of Mary's accomplishments and supportive of her quilt making.

Fred never made suggestions about what quilt Mary should make or what fabrics would work best. Sometimes Mary did ask him for ideas about a quilt on which she was working. When asked, he would tell her what he thought, but generally he stayed out of it. Fred and Mary had a mutual respect for each other. He knew quite a bit about quilts; you couldn't live in the same house with Mary and not know about them. When I would visit, the topic of conversation centered around quilts and there was always a pleasant and comfortable exchange between the three of us.

Mary had an opportunity to exhibit her bicentennial quilts in Flint, Michigan. In 1976, Goodwill Industries sponsored a bicentennial music production at Whiting Auditorium. The sponsors of the show invited Mary to display all six bicentennial quilts. Mary accompanied the quilts, dressed as Betsy Ross.

Mary used the bicentennial quilts in her lectures and used her extensive written descriptions of them as the text of her presentations. All of Mary's bicentennial quilts went to the Michigan State University Museum in 1998. They appear in *Mary Schafer and Her Quilts* (Marston and Cunningham 1990).

For Mary, the year 1976 was like none before in her quilt-making experience. Celebrations called for colonial costumes, decorations, muskets, and of course needlework. At the same time, quilting literature was beginning to proliferate. Old texts were being reprinted, and more quilting magazines and books were being published.

Quilt shows and contests abounded in 1976, and Mary entered as many as she could. She entered six quilts in the National Bicentennial Quilt Exposition and Contest in Warren, Michigan, which Robert Bishop and Bonnie Leman judged. Her Molly Pitcher won third prize in the Bicentennial Pieced Division. She entered competitions at the Michigan State Fair in Detroit and won three divisions: Pieced Quilts for her Attic Window, Bicentennial Theme for Molly Pitcher, and Pieced and Appliquéd for her Single Chain and Knot. At the Saginaw County Fair that year, she entered four quilts and won a first-place and three second-place ribbons.

As Mary worked on her bicentennial quilt series, she hoped it would lead to something. It was her wish to donate the entire series to a historical society, where they could be placed among revolutionary era artifacts. She was unsuccessful in this and disappointed. Yet she accepted that while her quilts had historical themes historical museums were primarily interested in housing antique artifacts.

Mary's interest in historical themes did not cease with the end of the country's birthday celebration. In 1977, she made Georgetown Circle and TOBACCO LEAF, the latter a quilt full of symbolism commemorating Native Americans and Europeans in the Jamestown settlement.

TOBACCO LEAF
79½" × 96½", 1977. Made by Mary Schafer. (Photo by Alan Zinn.)

As usual, Mary researched the subject before beginning TOBACCO LEAF. She found that before tobacco-growing developed Jamestown was a virtual prison camp riddled with disease and want and constantly on the edge of failure. When the local Indians introduced tobacco to the Jamestown settlers, it became the settlement's first commercial crop. Tobacco was the salvation of the new settlement.

Mary chose a green and brown color theme to suggest the tobacco leaf. She designed a pieced border using a traditional pattern called Tree of Life. She saw this design as reminiscent of American Indian design and used it to symbolize Indians surrounding the tobacco fields as they surrounded the Jamestown settlement. American history was a subject of which Mary never tired.

Gwen and Mary talking quilts over Mary's fence

Mary's Quilts for Others

 MARY WAS NEVER INTERESTED IN SELLING QUILTS. SHE WASN'T looking for commission work, but she did make and sell three quilts and one top upon request. Robert May commissioned Mary to make two quilts for him. Mr. May worked at the Irwin Galleries, an antique shop on Grand River in Detroit. He had seen Mary's WASHINGTON PLUME when it was on exhibit in Detroit in 1976. He called her to see if she would sell it to him. She told him it wasn't for sale as it was part of her bicentennial series. Mr. May knew a good thing when he saw it. Since he couldn't buy the WASHINGTON PLUME, he asked her if she would consider making a quilt for him. She agreed, sent him several ideas, conferred about color choices, and made Tea Leaves for Mr. May.

Later he asked for another quilt. I can remember Mary showing me Pumpkin Vine when she was making it. Obviously, Mr. May appreciated Mary's work as art, and he had a frame built to house the Pumpkin Vine quilt and proudly displayed it in his home. The two never met, but they formed a friendship through letters and phone calls. Mary treasures the antique sewing bird Mr. May sent her as a gift (the sewing bird is discussed and depicted in "The Second Collection").

In the mid 1980s, Mary honored a request from her dentist, Dr. Raymond Hagan, and made a PINEAPPLES for him. In a conversation with Mary in April

2000, she told me that she had been to see her dentist recently, where the subject of the Pineapples quilt came up. She said that he was quick to report that he was taking good care of his quilt. He told Mary that the Pineapples was on the bed in the spare bedroom and he kept the shades pulled to protect it from the sun.

More than most gifts, the gift of a quilt is a gift of love. Giving a quilt to someone special is very much a part of the history of quilt making. The literature is full of examples of quilts made for ministers, friends who were moving away, and children. There is even a quilt block that was used specifically to make a group quilt as a gift: Album.

Most quilters make sure that their loved ones all have quilts. For myself, making quilts for my family is thrilling. I think all of us who fall into the category of "mom/quilter" are enthusiastic about making quilts for our children and grandchildren. I have seen and heard about many quilts made for parents' twenty-fifth or fiftieth wedding anniversaries. In fact, years ago I participated in the making of a quilt to celebrate my own grandparents' fiftieth anniversary. Everyone in the extended family made blocks with the shape of their hands and their names and birth dates embroidered in white on a blue ground.

Mary has given more quilts away than anyone I know; sixty-five by my count. She gave them to her extended family, friends, worthy causes such as benefits, people she barely knew, and people she had never met.

A favorite pattern of Mary's seems to have been Tea Leaves. She made six Tea Leaves quilts for other people: one for Sophie Ignotov, one for Robert May, three for family members, and one for a Whaley Historical House benefit. Another of Mary's favorite appliqué patterns was RADICAL ROSE. She made one for her own bed and two more for her quilter, Ida Pullman. Ida quilted two quilts for Mary in exchange for the two RADICAL ROSE quilts, which she wanted to give to her sons.

Quilts for Her Family

Mary always made sure that her husband Fred had his favorite quilts on his bed. Fred's very favorite quilt was a Shoo Fly, made with a black print on unbleached muslin. Mary made quilts for everyone in her immediate family: her son Ronnie and his wife Esther; her grandchildren, Deborah, Carey, and Jennifer; and her brother Joe. In 1991, Mary made yet another LINDEN MILL and gave it to her son. When her granddaughter Jennifer had a baby, a quilt was not far behind. Mary made little Samuel J. Schmondiuk Little Skipper. And when Jennifer gave birth to her daughter Natalie, Mary gave her SAVANNAH STAR.

Then she began making quilts for Fred's family. Fred's brother Alex and his wife Mary received a quilt called COUNTRY HOME. Fred's sisters, Ann and Molly, both have Tea Leaves quilts. All three of Molly's sons, Robert, Charles, and Edward Hilgendorf, received full-size bed quilts. Mary then began making crib quilts for all of their children.

QUILTS FOR HER FRIENDS

When Mary moved to Flint in 1920, she was ten years old. One of the first friends she made was Sophie Ignotov. They are still friends. Mary says that Sophie asked her if she would make her a quilt, and so she did. She made Sophie a Tea Leaves quilt in a medium blue print and a plain blue fabric. Mary remembers finishing this around October 1969.

Hazel and Bill Gillanders lived across the street from Mary for many years. The Schafers and Gillanders were always good neighbors. When Hazel and Bill celebrated the arrival of new grandchildren, Mary made quilts: a Hearts appliqué crib quilt for Heather Gillanders and an Attic Window for little Steven Joseph Kamorny.

After years of friendship, Mary also wanted her neighbor Hazel to have something of hers. Surprised and delighted with her quilt, Hazel explained how she received it.

FEATHER-EDGED STAR
75" × 96", 1993. Made by Mary Schafer.
(Collection of Hazel and Bill Gillanders.)

We lived across the street for 17 years. Mary brought over some material, and templates one day, and showed me how to piece a doll quilt for my granddaughter who is now 14. From that time on I was hooked. She was such a kind and patient teacher and I count Mary as one of my dearest friends.

I had observed Mary piecing the feathered star quilt and admired it, never dreaming one day it would be mine. One day Mary came across the street with six quilt tops and told me to choose one, as I had indicated I would be honored to have one of hers. How thrilled I was to see the star quilt top and did not even consider one of the rest. She helped me select the quilting pattern and Bill helped me mark it and Shirley Neff in Shipshewana quilted it for me.[1]

Hazel's FEATHER-EDGED STAR is a reproduction of an old top in my collection. Mary admired it, borrowed it, and used it as inspiration.

I know about Mary's generosity firsthand. In 1979, Mary gave me a

ROSE OF SHARON quilt. Since then, six of Mary's crib quilts and seven doll quilts, not to mention fifty quilt blocks, have come my way. Sometimes Mary would not only send a quilt but also the pattern (hand colored, of course) with complete instructions.

When Mary "discovered" Amish quilts, we talked about them a lot. She made a series of Amish crib quilts and gave me Streak o'Lightning, because she knew I particularly liked that pattern. It was based on an antique quilt shown in *Crib Quilts and Other Small Wonders* (Woodward and Greenstein 1981, pl. 104, p. 61).

On three other occasions, Mary made me copies of quilts she'd made for herself. The original HONEYCOMB, BOW TIE, and HIT AND MISS are depicted in "The Second Collection."

Mary is always interested in knowing what the theme of my annual Beaver Island Quilt Retreat is going to be. Not only do we have lengthy discussions about the specific theme, but she often sends blocks, patterns, and sometimes quilts in support. HOLE IN THE BARN DOOR VARIATION is one such quilt. I can remember talking to Mary about a Midwest Amish quilt in one of the Quilt Engagement Calendars.[2] Mary and I talked about how this old quilt was a perfect example of how color placement can radically change the look of a block, which was the theme of the retreat in 1990. She offered to make a small version of the quilt, and after much conversation we decided which blocks in the old quilt were the most exciting and would make the best examples. It wasn't too long before the quilt arrived in the mail. When Mary got excited about a quilt, she went right to work.

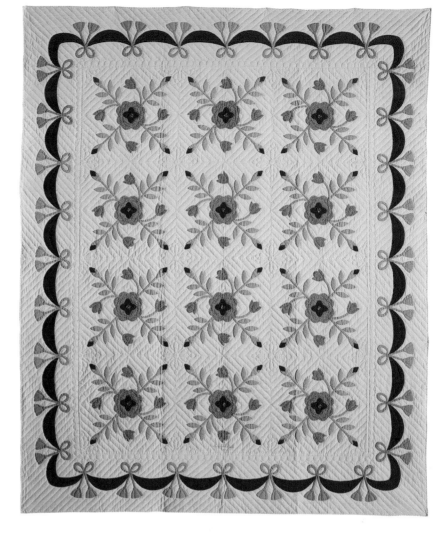

ROSE OF SHARON
77" × 93", 1979. Made by Mary Schafer.
(Collection of Gwen Marston.)

Quilts Given in Appreciation

Mary had a wonderful way of saying thanks. Her gratitude often took the form of a quilt. Hazel and Bill Gillanders weren't the only neighbors to be given a quilt. Charles and Joyce Johnson lived across the street, and Mary gave them a Nine-Patch Variation. Charlie, as Mary calls him, kept her driveway

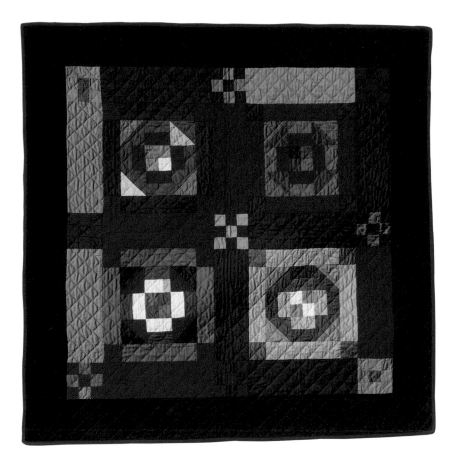

HOLE IN THE BARN DOOR
VARIATION
44^1/$_2$″ × 44^1/$_2$″, 1991. Made by Mary
Schafer. (Collection of Gwen Marston.)

and sidewalks clear of snow for years. Mary said, "Charlie would never take a penny. To show my appreciation, I gave them the quilt. Charlie always tells everyone 'it's my quilt' because he was the one who shoveled the snow."[3]

When Charlie had to give up shoveling, Mary's younger neighbors stepped in. It appears that John and Barbara Zintsmaster wouldn't take any "compensation" (as Mary says) either. In appreciation for their help, she made a quilt for their five-year-old daughter Kathleen.

Virginia Anderson received a ONE PATCH doll quilt from Mary in appreciation for her friendship and help. Virginia lives in Flushing, not far from Mary's house. She is an active member of the Genesee Star Quilters Guild in Flint. She helped Mary select the archival materials that Mary donated to Michigan State University Museum. Virginia was the one who painstakingly recorded all of the materials that were given to the museum. She has been a good friend to Mary, always quick to lend a helping hand.

Over the years, I've become great friends with many of the women who are regular attendees at my Beaver Island Quilt Retreat. Informally, they form the Mary Schafer Fan Club. In 1989, I took one of my retreat friends to meet Mary. Deb Ballard is a quilt maker, teacher, and lecturer from Midland, Michigan, who had long admired Mary and wanted to meet her. Deb, her seven-year-old daughter Megan, and I drove out for a visit. Little Megan had brought along a few of the quilts she had made to show Mary. Well, guess what happened. Megan went home with a new Mary Schafer One-Patch doll quilt. Mary has always had a soft spot in her heart for children, in part because her own childhood was bleak.

Benefit Quilts for Worthy Causes

When Mary was a schoolgirl, she rode the streetcar to school every day. And every day, the streetcar took her past the Buzzell home. Constructed in a Greek classical style, the home had been built by John Buzzell around 1854–1856. Buzzell had moved to Flint from Vermont and made his living as a carpenter and joiner. After his death in 1900, the house was passed on to a son, then grandchildren, staying in the family until almost 1949.

The Buzzell home barely escaped the wrecking ball. Slated for demolition, Flint citizens finally realized the value of the home, which was still in almost original condition. It was eventually moved to Crossroads Village, an open air museum north of Flint. Updates about the house appeared in the local newspaper, and Mary was thrilled that it had been saved. She was inspired to make a Fox and Geese quilt, which she presented to the Buzzell house in 1976. Mary loved that house. More than ten years later, I asked her to refresh my memory about the quilt and the Buzzell house. She sent me a long letter about the house with a newspaper clipping, photographs of the house, and a snapshot of the Fox and Geese quilt. The letter concluded with "The Buzzell House will always have a special meaning for me."[4]

Between 1979 and 1983, Mary made six raffle quilts for the Whaley Historical House in conjunction with the annual exhibits of her quilts. The money was used for the restoration of the house. She donated a quilt top to the Flushing Area Historical Society, too, in support of its preservation efforts. The Railroad Crossing top was quilted by the Genesee Star Quilters Guild. Mary even helped the Michigan State University Museum raise the money to buy her collection. She donated a Maltese Cross quilt top to raffle off as a fund-raiser. In the mid-1990s, she donated a SUNSHINE AND SHADOW crib quilt to the local branch of Planned Parenthood for a benefit auction.

QUILTS FOR PEOPLE SHE HAD NEVER MET

In 1995, Mary saw an article in the *Flint Journal* about a little girl who had not won a handmade quilt in a raffle at her school. The photograph showed weepy little six-year-old Jessi McConnell, saddened because she hadn't won the quilt. Mary never missed anything in the news that had something to do with quilts. She said she "wanted to do something to comfort Jessi, as she once was comforted by a teacher when she was a little girl around Jessi's age." Mary spent about four days making a doll quilt for Jesse called Dear Hearts. It was a twelve-block appliqué heart quilt. Before mailing it to little Jessi, Mary personalized the quilt by stitching in a message: "For Jessi."

Mary sent me a clipping from her local newspaper, which covered the story. The article quoted Mary, saying, "Every quilt has a story. Even Dear Hearts. It includes my seeing Jessi's picture but I also think it tells something about myself." It went on to say, "Schafer said her decision to create the quilt may have been a motherly act springing from her yearning for a mother when she was growing up."[5]

Mary also made a quilt for her quilting friend Cuesta Benberry before she actually met her in person. In a Christmas letter, Cuesta had announced: "Also from the 'old days', my close friend Mary Schafer, made a beautiful little heart *Charm* Quilt for me."[6]

Giving as many quilts away as she did to both family and acquaintances, Mary was obviously a generous person at heart. Also, it seems to me that she was so thrilled when *anyone* expressed an interest in quilts that she probably would have made one for anyone who asked. That may be a slight exaggeration but not by much.

The fact is that Mary simply loved making quilts. As she has said many times, "I make quilts for enjoyment. I get a certain high out of the accomplishment." I am sure that everyone who has a Mary Schafer quilt cherishes it. I know I do.

Recognition Comes to Mary

 By the mid-1970s, Mary had gained both local and national recognition as a quilt maker. She had entered many quilt contests in her home state of Michigan, which yielded shoe boxes full of ribbons.[1] Winning two blue ribbons at the first National Quilting Association quilt show in 1971 was the beginning of broader recognition. She won two blue ribbons for her CLAMSHELL.

Nimble Needle Treasures cited Mary for her accomplishments in a 1972 issue, describing her as a

> quilt maker par excellence, [who] also has an extensive collection of antique and modern quilts. Her deep interest in quilts has been the inspiration for making quilts and collecting quilt patterns. Mrs. Schafer has consistently been a sweepstakes and blue ribbon prizewinner for quilts of her own making at Fairs in Michigan. At the first Quilt Show of the National Quilting Association, Washington, D.C., Mrs. Schafer's "Clamshell" won two blue ribbons for "Most Popular Quilt in the Show" and for "Best Pieced Quilt."[2]

She had won ribbons in every category in state and national competitions. She had encouraged her friends to enter quilts in competition. But, knowing well what her own track record was, she didn't want to encourage her friends to enter and then take the chance of winning the blue herself. She eventually began to inquire as to what category her friends were entering. Then she made it a point to enter some other category. Mary wanted to encourage her friends in quilt making, so she made sure she avoided competing with them. When Mary told me about this, I was moved. What a wonderful attitude, and how gracious she was. For Mary, it was always about quilts, not about personal acclaim.

When Mary and I met in 1977, it was the beginning of a new phase for both of us. My first meeting with Mary convinced me that the best thing I could contribute to the world of quilts was finding ways to make Mary Schafer visible to the larger public. Although she certainly was a player in the quilt world, she had been a quiet player.

I was a novice, new to quilts and unfamiliar with promotional efforts. Still, it occurred to me that a good start would be to arrange exhibits of Mary's work. In 1978, I approached the Whaley Historical House in Flint with the idea of mounting an exhibit of Mary's quilts. The Whaley House had only recently been granted historical status and was in the early stages of restoration. I suggested arranging the exhibit as a fund-raiser, and the board of trustees agreed to give it a try.

I wanted the exhibit to make an impression, so I selected thirty-six sensational quilts. I showed Mary's six bicentennial quilts, her CLAMSHELL, Dutchman's Puzzle, all three NORTH CAROLINA LILYs, Oak Leaf and Cherries, and five showy Harriman/Schafer quilts. It worked! The show was so successful that it became an annual event. The Whaley Historical House exhibits ran from 1978 to

HONEY BEE
79" × 95", 1968. Made by Mary Schafer and pictured at the Whaley Historical House. (Collection of the Michigan State University Museum, Mary Schafer Collection. Photo by Alan Zinn.)

1983. Over the course of six years, I eventually showed all of Mary's quilts. The quilts were arranged throughout the house draped over beautiful Victorian sofas and chairs and on beds, as was Mary's HONEY BEE quilt.

Remembering the first Whaley Historical House exhibit many years later, I can still remember how exciting it was for both of us. Mary and I were thrilled. I don't know how to say it any other way than this: it was a really big deal. And to top it off we got a glowing review in *Quilter's Newsletter Magazine.* "Dr. G. Stuart Hodge, director of the Flint Institute of Art, expressed his opinion that the collection is a contribution to the world of art."[3]

As the curator of the show each year, I arranged the quilts and was there to meet the public and walk them through the exhibit.

Mary found new inspiration in these shows. If she lacked enough samples for the current theme, she made more quilts. After that first year, she decided it would be nice to make raffle quilts to raise money for the ongoing restoration of the Whaley House. She said she remembered seeing the house from the streetcar on her way to school as a young girl. Every year thereafter, Mary made a full-size quilt to donate for a raffle in conjunction with the annual exhibitions. It was her way of saying thank-you and supporting the grand old historical landmark. In 1979, she made Hands All Around, which raised almost a thousand dollars. In 1980, she made Broken Dishes. In 1981, she made a Nine-Patch Variation and then Tea Leaves in 1982. Preparing for these annual exhibits was time consuming for both Mary and me. By the time the sixth show rolled around, Mary and I shared the making of the 1983 raffle quilt. We decided to make a Roman Stripe, which I pieced and Mary marked and had quilted.

From the beginning, I felt it was important to document Mary's collection. After being turned down by the National Endowment for the Arts in 1977, I applied to the Charles Stewart Mott Foundation for financial support in 1978 and, after almost a year of waiting for its decision, was turned down. Determined, I turned to the Ruth Mott Fund. I remember my discussion with fund officials as they questioned whether my proposed budget of five thousand dollars would be adequate to perform the work of documenting Mary's collection. They thought it would most likely cost more. I was so happy to be taken seriously and given any support that I assured them I could manage on the proposed amount. With a budget secured, I hired Alan Zinn to photograph all of Mary's quilts, measured all of the quilts, and recorded Mary's information regarding them. In 1980, I published a small catalog entitled *The Mary Schafer Quilt Collection.*

When I look at this publication more than twenty years later, I see its limitations. At the time, however, it was the best I knew how to do. And to this day I refer to it and find it useful when looking for basic information. Mary used this catalog to define what she calls her "First Collection" or the "A Collection." She referred to this catalog to determine the cutoff date for the quilts that were sold to the Michigan State University Museum. The catalog lists 121 quilts, and of these Michigan State University (MSU) acquired 118. Mary retained three quilts listed in the catalog for personal reasons. I continued to promote Mary through lectures, exhibits, articles, and books.

On September 9, 1986, the Michigan State Senate adopted Senate Resolution 605, honoring Mary for her "many contributions to the art of quiltmaking."

WHEREAS, When the rest of the nation was re-discovering quiltmaking, Mary Schafer was nearing her fourth decade of involvement in this art. . . . Mary Schafer has devoted countless hours to researching the history of quilting as well as creating new patterns and duplicating old. . . . Her contributions to the history and culture of our state and nation will have a lasting influence far into the future.[4]

Senator Jack Faxon presented Mary with a proclamation as evidence of the State of Michigan's highest esteem. It was quite a thrill for me to see Mary fairly beaming as she graciously accepted the proclamation.

In 1987, the American Museum of Quilts in San Jose, California, mounted an exhibit entitled Reflections on American History: Quilts from the Mary Schafer Collection. Another event in 1987 was the publication of my little alphabet book *Q Is for Quilt.* I wrote the book, and Mary made all twenty-six blocks. It was a project that we both enjoyed. I donated both the book and the quilt to Michigan State University Museum to be used to raise funds for the purchase of the Schafer quilt collection.

On May 25, 1988, Mary was one of eleven Michigan women honored by the Michigan Women's Foundation for outstanding contributions to the arts. She was presented with a Hearts and Hands Award for her lifetime contributions to the tradition of quilt making. The program said of Mary, "Her work has been recognized by many authorities as beautiful, extraordinarily crafted, and conceptually rich." It went on to say, "She is a member of yard and garden clubs and tends the landscaping as artistically as she does her quilting." I can remember how proud and happy Fred was that night. Fred had always supported Mary's involvement with quilts. He was fighting cancer at the time and passed away in December of that year. I've always been glad he lived to see Mary receive public acclaim for her accomplishments.

Mary Schafer and Her Quilts: A Retrospective was the name of an exhibit presented by the New England Quilt Museum in Lowell, Massachusetts, in 1989. It included seventeen full-size quilts made by Mary, eight of Mary's finest antique quilts, and three crib and two doll quilts made by Mary.

Always hoping to publish a book about Mary, I had settled for showing as many Schafer quilts as possible in *Sets and Borders* (Marston and Cunningham 1987) and *American Beauties: Rose and Tulip Quilts* (Marston and Cunningham 1988). The year 1990 saw the publication of *Mary Schafer and Her Quilts* (Marston and Cunningham 1990). Another milestone along the path had been realized.

By this time, all the quilters who came to my annual Beaver Island Quilt Retreats were big Mary Schafer fans. We had a party to celebrate. Mary came with some of her quilts to share with everyone. We had a cake decorated with an album block and a dozen red roses for Mary. Best of all, thirty quilters made album blocks. My late friend Sally Goodin—to whom this book is dedicated—put them together and appliquéd the words "Thanks Mary." What a day it was!

The American Lung Association used four appliqué blocks on their stickers for the summer 1990 regional fund-raiser mailing. Three blocks were Mary's, and one was made by Mary's dear friend Hildegard Hoag. Two of the blocks on the stickers are Mary's original MICHIGAN ROSE and her Rose Wreath.

In 1991, the American Quilter's Society opened the doors to its new museum in Paducah, Kentucky. Forty-four Mary Schafer quilts comprised that prestigious first exhibit. Simply called Mary Schafer Quilts, the exhibit included antique quilts and quilts made by Mary. It opened April 25 and ran through June 1, 1991.

Christopher R. Young curated an exhibit called Michigan Directions: Flint Area Artists at the Flint Institute of Arts. The exhibit opened November 27, 1994, and ran through January 15, 1995. Young's purpose was to select the best artists from the greater Flint area and to include all media. He wanted to show avant-garde and traditional work on an equal footing. Mary's INDIA, CLAMSHELL was included in the exhibit.

In 1995, the Greater Flint Arts Council organized an exhibit of Mary's quilts at Crossroads Village. One hundred quilts were chosen for the exhibit, entitled Mary Schafer Retrospective. No antique quilts were shown, only quilts made by Mary. Three more quilts somehow found their way into the exhibit, making the grand total 103: 40 full size, 29 crib quilts and 34 doll quilts. It was an impressive showing by anyone's standard.

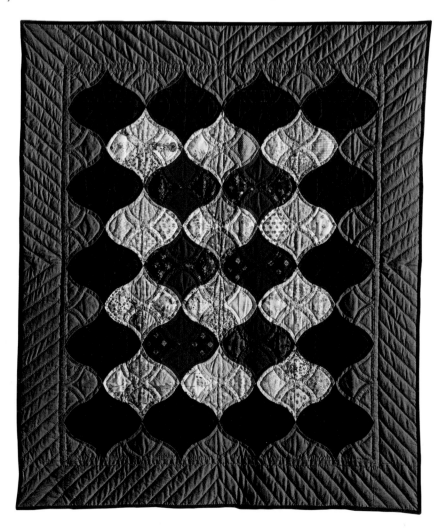

INDIA, CLAMSHELL
36″ × 43½″, 1984 or 1985. Made by Mary Schafer.

I worked closely with organizers Valerie Clarke and Mary Whaley as the quilts were measured, dated, carded, cataloged, and hung. As anyone knows who has ever hung a quilt show, sleeves have to be sewn to the back of the quilts so that they can be displayed. This is no small feat. Sewing sleeves on one hundred quilts takes a lot of muslin and a lot of stitching. As always, Mary was willing to get right after it, but the job was overwhelming. It was necessary to call in reinforcements. The call went out. My quilting friends from Southeast Michigan rose to the occasion, and, as you know, many hands make light work.

The opening reception for Mary's exhibit was highlighted by the appearance of Dan Kildee, chairman of the Genesee County Board of Commissioners, who bestowed an official government proclamation on Mary. A warm letter of congratulations to Mary from First Lady Hillary Rodham Clinton was read. Mary graciously accepted the acclaim but noted that the quilts were made because they were "fun" to make and useful in teaching others about the art of quilt making. Mary's show set a record for attendance at a Greater Flint Arts Council exhibit.

In 1997, Mary was chosen to participate in an exhibit called 20th Century Quilts, 1900–1970: Women Make Their Mark. This exhibit was curated by Joyce Gross and Cuesta Benberry and held at the Museum of the American Quilter's Society in Paducah, Kentucky, March 22 through June 29, 1997. In the introduction to the catalog, the curators say:

> *Here for the first time ever, some of the most exciting and famous quilts and quiltmakers from 1900 to 1970 can be seen together. . . . some of the quiltmaker's names may not be familiar, but it is our hope that those who have the opportunity to see these quilts with the archival material in the exhibit will realize that fine quilts and today's quilt scene come from a strong background. Today's quilt world did not "just happen." It moved forward step by step as women left their mark.[5]*

Mary certainly made her mark, and it was a thrill to see her so recognized. In my estimation, this was a landmark exhibit containing many of the quilts made by quilters I'd known about since my introduction to the quilt world. I was able to arrive early, as the exhibit just opened and before it became crowded. I was touched to see Betty Harriman's LINCOLN quilt and Mary Schafer's EISENHOWER hanging in the same exhibit. The EISENHOWER quilt is discussed in more detail in "The Challenge Period." They were in good company with quilts by Charlotte Jane Whitehill, Pine Eisfeller, Marie Webster, Bertha Stenge, Florence Peto, Rose Kretsinger, Carrie Hall, and others.

CHERRY BASKET was inspired by an antique quilt in my collection and was interpreted on a slightly smaller scale by Mary in 1985. The original was made in the early 1900s by Lucy Ann Brown, an African American activist in Flint. Mary's CHERRY BASKET was part of the Red Beret Exhibit, organized by Valerie Clarke to honor the Women's Emergency Brigade of the Great Sit-Down Strike at Flint, 1936–37. Mary is the only quilter among nine in this exhibit, including me, who personally witnessed the forty-four-day strike, which is known as "the strike heard 'round the world." The Red Beret Exhibit traveled from 1999 through 2001.

A special showing of Mary's quilts was hung at the Michigan State University Museum July 29 through December 31, 2001. The Mary Schafer Collection: A Legacy of Quilt History was a beautiful exhibit and left no doubt of Mary's contributions to the world of quilts and art. I was invited to present the feature lecture accompanying the exhibit. November 17 was a memorable day. I gave the

LINCOLN
85″ × 85″, ca. 1930. Made by Betty Harriman. (Collection of Suellen Meyer. Photo by Charles R. Lynch, courtesy of the American Quilter's Society.)

EISENHOWER
56″ × 102″, 1968. Made by Mary Schafer. (Collection of the Michigan State University Museum, Mary Schafer Collection. Photo by Alan Zinn.)

CHERRY BASKET
39³/₄″ × 47″, 1985. Made by Mary Schafer.

Mary Schafer lecture with Mary sitting in the front row. When I was uncertain of any small detail, I asked Mary, and she rose to her feet and deftly provided the information. She was the star of the evening and received a standing ovation at the end of the lecture. I am sure this was a night that will be remembered by all who were there.

In 2002, Mary was honored with the Michigan Heritage Award, an award given by the Michigan State University Museum. The award is given to those who are seen as supporters of traditional arts in their communities.

In September 2002, Mary's hometown of Flushing honored her for her "outstanding contributions in the field of quiltmaking, and in extending our sincere congratulations for her many achievements."[6] Mayor Gensel presented Mary with a proclamation designating September 27–29 as Mary Schafer Days. Mayor Gensel thanked Mary for her contributions. "Mary has been a staunch supporter of local history organizations, loaning her quilts for exhibitions, and regularly donating quilts to raise funds for numerous charitable causes and benefits."[7]

In January 2003, an exhibit of sixty important American quilts opened in Tokyo. Of the sixty quilts chosen by the Japanese, eight were Schafer quilts from the Michigan State University Museum collection. The exhibit included Pineapple, OCTOBER FOLIAGE, and Oak Leaf and Cherries, all made by Mary; and Alice Blue Wreath and DEMOCRATIC ROSE, two Schafer and Harriman collaborations; and three early-nineteenth-century quilts: Boxes, Four Patch, and Whig Rose.

Mary chose to stay home and make quilts. Although it was never her aspiration, she has made a name for herself in the quilt world. This alone is interesting to me and validation of something I have long thought: if you work hard enough and long enough at something, you may eventually get good enough at it that others will notice. I really believe that your chances for doing something noteworthy are enhanced if you follow your heart rather than succumbing to popular trends. The proof is in the pudding.

Mary, 1990 to the Present

 IN 1990, MARY MADE TWO EXQUISITE APPLIQUÉ QUILTS. POMEGRANATE was made from a Pennsylvania German pattern Mary had collected. The original quilt was made around 1820 by Mrs. Henry Zeller. Having detailed documentation about this old quilt delighted her. Mary was so excited about this pattern that she sent me all the information about the quilt. She drew and hand colored the pattern, which included complete instructions. She also sent me a template and a finished appliquéd block. As was her custom, Mary also gave me the other names by which this pattern is known: Tulip and Star, Star and Tulip, and Pomegranate and Star.

The second full-size quilt Mary finished in 1990 was ROSE WREATH. For the first time, she agreed to allow me to mark a quilt for her, asking me to reproduce the feather designs on the original quilt's borders. The First Collection included a ROSE WREATH from Pennsylvania made around 1850. While the old ROSE WREATH was indeed worn, it was a prime example of the kind of quilts from that period. The old quilt was quilted within an inch of its life. What can I say, worn yes, beautiful yes. It was impressive. So appreciative of it, Mary decided to reproduce it. It is good that she did. As part of the First Collection, which was purchased by the Michigan State University Museum, the old quilt was promptly sold at auction.

POMEGRANATE
82″ × 94″, 1990. Made by Mary Schafer.

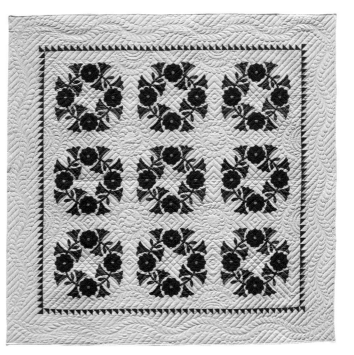

ROSE WREATH
82″ × 82″, 1990. Made by Mary Schafer. This quilt is a reproduction of an antique quilt in the First Collection, which has since been sold.

ROSE WREATH
76″ × 76″, ca. 1850, Fayetteville, Pennsylvania. (Photo by Alan Zinn.)

This proclivity for reproducing old quilts is not common in today's quilt world, and therefore it is interesting to consider. Both Mary and her friend Betty Harriman were known to reproduce old quilts that were worn and fragile. Both women saw this as a way to preserve the artistic ideas of an earlier era and to pay homage to the unknown quilters of the past. These were the very concerns that had brought Mary into quilting in the first place, as she first repaired and then reproduced the old red and white quilt she would christen Linden Mill. Throughout Mary's quilt-making years, central was the notion to document and honor. Mary never forgot Marie Webster's poignant words: "to raise in popular esteem, those most worthy products of home industry."[1] Knowing Mary as I do, I think it is conservative to say that Marie's words became Mary's battle cry.

In 1991, Mary made FRIENDSHIP STAR. The next year she made MONTEREY NINE PATCH, a return to a simple block pattern. Mary's MONTEREY NINE PATCH shows her ability to make quilts that look very much like quilts made in the nineteenth century.

Mary began to have problems with the circulation in her fingers sometime in the early 1990s. Her doctor felt she had ruined the nerves in her fingers in eighty years of hand sewing. With the loss of feeling in her fingers, she began to slow down in her quilt making. Mary didn't feel like she needed more quilts anyhow. As far as her quilting was concerned, her attention became focused on trying to take care of the quilts she had.

It was around this time that she quit cleaning out her own gutters. I was relieved to hear that she had finally decided she shouldn't be climbing the ladder anymore. I plan to give that up, too, when I'm eighty-five. Mary also began to accept a little help with the yard work. When winter comes to Michigan now, Mary's neighbors on both sides borrow her snowblower. They clear their own driveways and make sure Mary's is clear, too. Mary thanks them with gifts of quilts, which I discuss in "Mary's Quilts for Others."

Otherwise, Mary continues, as ever, to maintain her house neat as a pin. And, as always, she keeps up with the news. In December of 1996, Mary sent me an article from the arts section of a Detroit newspaper. She attached a note: "Gwen, this article by Ann Mullen of Ferndale MI is about quilters we both know. (The stains are spilled coffee). Thought you'd be interested. Mary. 12/16/96)."[2] The article featured two

FRIENDSHIP STAR
78" × 91", 1991. Made by Mary Schafer.

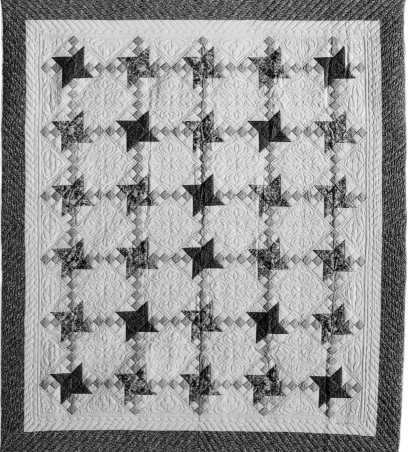

MONTEREY NINE PATCH
76" × 90", 1992. Made by Mary Schafer.

quilters, Carol Harris, a Detroit art quilter, and Mary Schafer.

While her quilt making had slowed down, occasionally she couldn't resist making a quilt, as in 1995 when she saw the story about Jessi, a little girl who had so wanted to win a quilt in a contest (see "Mary's Quilts for Others").

During the 1990s, Mary was also very involved in arranging four exhibits of her work. These exhibits are discussed in detail in "Recognition Comes to Mary." In particular, the large-scale exhibit of 103 Schafer quilts at Crossroads Village in 1995 required a lot of her time and effort.

In the spring of 1998, the Michigan State University Museum finalized the acquisition of Mary's First Collection and took possession of those quilts. This had been a long time in coming, and it still demanded much of Mary's time, attention, and energy.

After Fred died in 1988, Mary bought a Buick and took driving lessons from Sears. She was almost eighty years old at the time. Typical for Mary, this didn't deter her. I remember having lots of conversations with her during this period. She was a very cautious driver. She planned her trips during low traffic times and figured out routes to avoid heavy traffic. She also figured out how to get everywhere she needed to go without making a left-hand turn!

Mary had a narrow garage that didn't allow much room on either side of her car. Her solution to this problem was to hang a tennis ball from a string in the center of the garage to help her navigate safely. When she first began driving, she told me that "backing up is hard because you can never tell which way the car is going to go." That worried me a bit, but she managed to get herself around safely for a long time.

On August 17, 1999, Mary's friend Hazel Gillanders called to tell me Mary had had an accident. She had broken her "never make a left-hand turn" rule and had totaled her car. Besides breaking the rule, she had also broken her leg and a few ribs. Badly bruised, she ended up in the hospital. I talked to her a day after the accident. Although she faced a lengthy recovery, she had not lost her spirit. She was quick to tell me that it was the other person's fault and that she was definitely going to drive again. She came home from the hospital with a full leg cast, a wheelchair, and a pair of crutches.

Hazel told me that the day of the accident Mary had been out picking blueberries and was on her way home. Hazel said that after the accident the only thing on Mary's mind was her quilts. Hazel and her husband Bill showed up at the hospital within an hour of the accident. Mary asked them if they would please go to her house and make sure the humidifier in the basement was working. She was afraid it might quit and the quilts would be harmed.

Hearing this reminded me of Betty Harriman being caught in Hurricane Hazel in 1954. Betty was managing her hotel in Newport News, Virginia, when the hurricane struck. She worked her way down eight flights of stairs in the dark to rescue her quilts, which were stored in the basement. Of the guests at the hotel, she said that guests had legs and could take care of themselves but her quilts were helpless.[3]

On September 20, 1999, I got a letter from Mary. She said "I'm waiting for the day when I can stand on my own two feet and do things with my own two hands."[4] I called her early in November, and her first comment was "I'm on my own two feet." Within a few months, she was shopping for another car. She bought a pale gold Saturn, and by December she was driving, remembering her rule to never make a left-hand turn.

About the time Mary turned ninety, she decided she needed a hearing aid, and in her usual way of dealing with things she declared "and I'm going to get one, too." She also told me that some local quilters had asked if they could visit her regularly to learn more about quilts and she had agreed to be available to them. Anything she could do to promote quilting Mary always did.

In 1999, Mary became interested in Baltimore Brides' quilts. Perhaps it was the only area left that she hadn't explored. She began designing and making a few blocks, just for the enjoyment of it. Mary keeps the album blocks that she's made along with others given to her in a beautiful fabric-covered portfolio case.

In 2000, Mary gave a Tea Leaves quilt to Fred's sister Ann, her first friend in the Schafer family. Mary made an arrangement with the Genesee Star Quilters Guild to quilt Ann's quilt in exchange for a Churn Dash top that the guild planned to auction as a fund-raiser.

With her ninetieth birthday having passed, Mary takes her time. She isn't in a rush. She works a bit on her blocks when she feels like it and when her fingers are working properly. Yet to this day she is still full of surprises. In a phone conversation with her on April 30, 2000, she amazed me by saying, "Yesterday, believe it or not, I mowed the lawn!" To my response that I thought she must have enjoyed it, she said "Oh, I can't get enough of it, I love being outdoors. I'd rather be outdoors than inside." Later in the day, I called Mary again, and she answered the phone breathlessly. She said she'd been out picking dandelions.

Since Mary began making quilts, many parts of the quilt world have changed, even the terminology. When I learned to quilt from the Mennonites, they talked about "putting in," "rolling," and "taking out." These were common terms understood by all quilters. They described installing a quilt in the frame, rolling the finished section under in the quilt frame, and taking a finished quilt out of the frame. Everyone knew what you meant when you said, "I put in this morning," or "I rolled twice today," or "I finally got it done and took out this afternoon." No one "sandwiched" anything except her husband's lunches.

Mary saw these changes and many more. She never missed anything that was going on in the quilt world. She and I had many detailed conversations about current trends in quilting. The thing I always thought was wonderful about Mary was that she looked into everything, tried to understand it, and even when failing to understand maintained a completely tolerant attitude. While she definitely had her own way of doing things and stuck to them, she was not judgmental and never imposed her ideas on others. As long as people were making quilts, she was thrilled. How they did it was up to them. The important thing to Mary was that people were making quilts.

The years add up, and things change. But for Mary some things never seem to change. She's still involved with quilting and quilters. She still washes in a Maytag square-tub wringer washing machine. She still cooks on her Detroit Jewel stove, which looks like new. And she always ends our phone conversations the same way: "Bye-bye Dear."

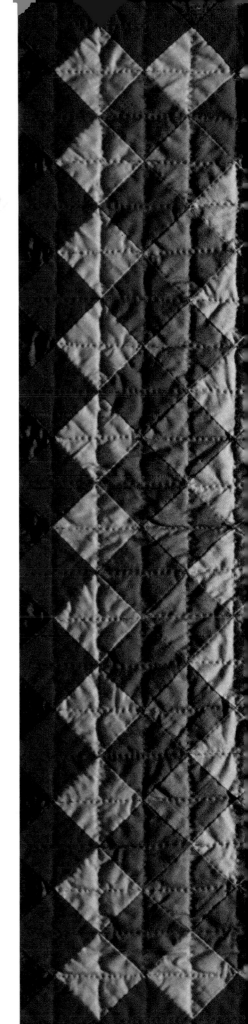

Part Three

The Schafer Quilts

*Pieced quilts make a special appeal to women who delight in
the precise and accurate work necessary in their construction.*
—Marie Webster

 COLLECTING QUILTS IS EASY. TAKING CARE OF
them and deciding what to do with them is hard.
There are 118 quilts in the First Collection, which
Mary also called the "A Collection." It contains some incredibly beautiful antique quilts and 38 quilts made by Mary,
including the bicentennial quilts. It also includes 17 of the
significant Harriman/Schafer quilts. These are quilts begun
by Betty Harriman and finished by Mary after her friend's
death, a unique story in the annals of quilting.

With the First Collection housed at the Michigan State
University Museum, Mary was left with the Second

Collection, which she also called the "B Collection." To date, it consists of 106 quilts plus quite a number of works in progress. The Second Collection contains 33 full-size quilts made by Mary. The Second Collection differs from the first in some major ways. While the First Collection is distinguished by Mary's challenge and bicentennial quilts, the Second Collection boasts Mary's series of medallion quilts and her 62 crib and doll quilts. Unlike the First Collection, which includes 56 antique quilts, the Second Collection has only 2. Mary got back to work on the Harriman quilts and finished 5 more of Betty's "starts" as well as finishing an antique top from the Harriman estate.

The question of what is to become of the Second Collection is now a subject that concerns Mary. To date, no solution has been found.

Mary's Technique

Most noticeable in a Mary Schafer quilt is a polish, an elegance, a rare beauty owed to her adept hand-sewing.
—*Cuesta Benberry*

 MARY'S TECHNIQUE DIFFERS LITTLE FROM THAT COMMON IN the eighteenth and nineteenth centuries. Her quilts are made *completely* by hand, and they are made with basic sewing tools. It always amazed me that Mary would piece the backing together by hand and then put the binding on completely by hand. But she was comfortable with a needle, and she enjoyed handwork. If you do something a lot, you get good at it and you get fast at it.

Mary made her first dresses, skirts, and blouses from purchased patterns, and she sewed them by hand. In the 1940s, she upgraded and bought a portable sewing machine to use for dressmaking. She made a lot of her own clothes. Years ago, when Mary and I got interested in Amish quilts, she gave me some of her old wool homemade clothing to turn into a Center Diamond quilt, which I did.

Mary's 1940s sewing machine was relegated to making clothes. When it came to her quilts, she simply preferred to make them by hand. Her experience with various kinds of hand needlework made her comfortable working this way.

Mary kept the project, or projects, on which she was working in the living room. There was always one neat little pile, and it was always in the same place, next to the couch. Everything she needed was right there. This is remarkable compared to the quilt studios most of us think we need. When I work, I'm all over the place, and, plainly speaking, it's messy. As do many of my contemporaries, I have a large room dedicated to quilt making and I've seen many quilters' studios that are far more extensive than mine.

When Mary was done with her sewing, the work was again folded and stacked neatly in a little pile by the couch. This style of working can be attributed to several factors. One is that Fred and Mary liked to keep things perfectly neat at all times. I visited them many, many times over the years, and the whole house always looked *exactly* the same. It was spotless, and everything was in its place. I do know that if Mary's pile got too big Fred complained and asked her to clean it up. Mary could make quilts in a limited work space because she hand stitched her quilts and used few tools. All she needed was a little pair of scissors, a pincushion, and a spool or two of thread.

Most often when she sewed, she sat on the floor next to her stack of materials, threads, and pincushion. When I visited Mary, we spent half the time on the floor. It always amazed me that she could jump up to go retrieve something, scurry right back, and make herself comfortable again on the floor.

Mary always sewed with a thimble. I think most proficient seamstresses of Mary's generation learned to sew with one. I don't know exactly when this changed, but almost everyone I know who learned to sew prior to 1940 sews with a thimble.

FEATHER-EDGED STAR
77″ × 97″, 1984. Made by Mary Schafer.

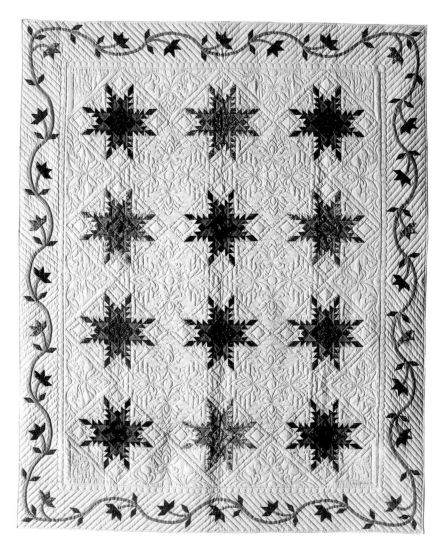

DRAFTING

Mary could draft patterns. She had always been a whiz at math and knew how to use a protractor, a compass, and a ruler. She delighted in drafting quilt patterns. She could draft very complicated ones such as the Feather-Edged Star in all its glorious variations. When Mary decided to make a Feather-Edged Star, she found it hard to choose among the many variations. To help her decide, she drafted nine of her favorites and made a block of each. Once she made up her mind, she set to work. Flawless in technique and artistry, Mary produced an astoundingly beautiful FEATHER-EDGED STAR with its scrappy stars and elegant border. She drafted the pattern, meticulously hand pieced the stars, and designed the border. It's hard to believe that there could be another FEATHER-EDGED STAR more artfully composed or executed.

One of my favorite Mary Schafer crib quilts is PAINTED CIRCLE. Working from a photograph, Mary drafted this complex curved pattern. She chose high-contrast solids to accentuate the circles. SAVANNAH STAR has one of Mary's perfectly drafted sawtooth borders. The side triangles around the pieced stars are quilted with one of Mary's original quilting designs. PERIWINKLE is another difficult pattern to draft, which Mary can make look deceptively easy.

Often she made quilts that were inspired by antiques shown in books and magazines. On numerous occasions she and I would work out a pattern from a picture of a quilt. Mary was incredibly accurate in her calculations. If a photo included the dimensions of the quilt, we were in business. It is a matter of counting the number of blocks across, comparing the size of the blocks to the width of the borders, and playing around with the numbers until it comes out right.

Mary aptly demonstrated her ability to take a pattern from a quilt when she and I visited the Detroit Institute of Arts for a special exhibit of Amish quilts during the 1980s. We both got excited about one particular quilt, and Mary whipped out her cloth tape measure to check a few measurements. The Museum guard was right on us and told us nicely that we weren't allowed to measure anything or take notes. Mary whispered to me that I shouldn't worry. We looked at the quilt and made mental notes, then slipped out of the gallery and recorded them. Then back in again to check our notes and complete our study. Between the two of us, we had enough notes to recall the quilt in its entirety.

FABRIC SELECTION

Early quilt makers made quilts from their scrap bag. Most did not go to "the quilt shop" and buy new fabric for pieced quilts. Mary continued this tradition by making scrap quilts from recycled clothing. She used her own old dresses and old clothing gathered from the Salvation Army and other thrift stores. One memorable Mary Schafer moment came when I showed her a Shoo Fly quilt top I'd found that had been made in the 1950s. Mary spotted a fabric in the quilt and excitedly asked me to wait just a minute. She jumped up and scampered down to the basement and back up again with a gathered skirt she'd made sometime in the 1950s. Mary's skirt was made with the same fabric she had spotted in my quilt top. She gave me the skirt and suggested I use it to make a border, which I did.

Mary preferred 100 percent cotton fabrics. She told me that she would occasionally use a blend if she just "had to have a particular print." She also said she used blends only for piecing and never for appliqué. When polyester

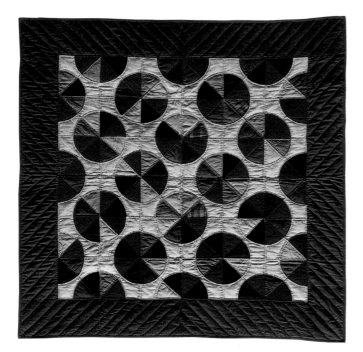

PAINTED CIRCLE
40¹/₄″ × 40³/₄″, 1982. Made by Mary Schafer.

SAVANNAH STAR
40¹/₂″ × 50¹/₂″, 1983 or 1984. Made by Mary Schafer.

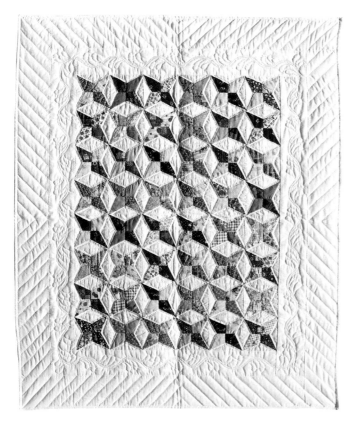

PERIWINKLE
36³/₄″ × 44³/₄″, 1983 or 1984. Made by Mary Schafer.

fabrics made their debut and cottons became harder to find, Mary began to rely more than ever on shopping at local thrift stores. It was there that she could still find the cotton scraps she liked.

Thread

When I asked Mary if she ever used cotton-covered polyester thread, she was emphatic. She does all of her sewing with cotton thread. She prefers it because it is easy to handle and doesn't fray, twist, or knot. Mary's antique quilts give loud testimony to the performance of cotton thread, and she listened. In the mid-1980s, Mary and I took a road trip together and we discovered an Amish store called Gohn's in Indiana. From then on, Mary ordered her thread from Gohn's.

Piecing

Mary hand pieced all of her quilts. She was good at it, and she enjoyed it. I was always amazed at how fast she could work. For example, she hand pieced the ambitious THE HARVESTERS in ten days. Techniques that are considered diffi cult by machine piecers, such as setting in patches and working with curves, pose no difficulty for the hand piecer. Her unusual SCALLOPS quilt is a good example of a difficult pattern made easy when worked by an experienced hand.

Mary drafted the pattern from an old quilt top she saw at an antique shop. SCALLOPS is similar to Mary's CLAMSHELL, except for the fact that it has one more seam. Mary says it was a lot of work to make, but she wanted to do it because she'd never seen the pattern before and hasn't again to this day.

For Mary, pieced quilts begin with a traditional pattern. She draws around her cardboard templates on the wrong side of the fabric and cuts them out (by eye) a quarter inch beyond the pencil lines. With right sides together, she lines up the pencil lines, placing a pin at both ends. As she sews, she keeps checking to make sure the pencil lines are lining up exactly. "You don't make mistakes that way. You don't have to do it over," she explains.

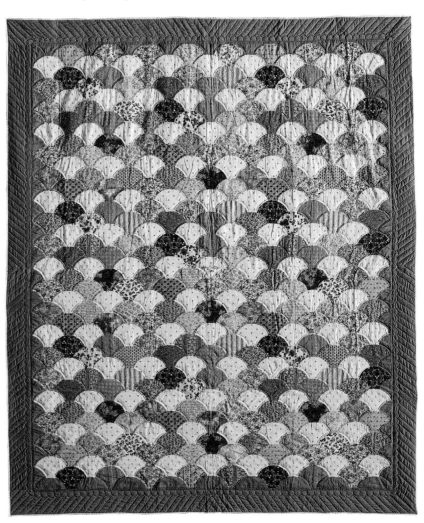

SCALLOPS
77″ × 95″, 1982. Made by Mary Schafer.

When Mary makes any pieced quilt, she makes a template from a cereal box, cuts each fabric piece out individually, and hand sews the pieces together. The rotary cutter is not a part of her quilt making. As we know, today the instructions for making a block are often given for rotary cutting. Mary told me she can't follow the instructions anymore because she doesn't understand rotary cutting. "And," she added, "I just don't want to do it."

Appliqué

Mary taught me how to appliqué, and I am forever in her debt. Her method is direct and uncomplicated. She showed me how to make the templates (actual size) and cut the patches by drawing around the template and cutting a quarter inch beyond the pencil line. As with pieced quilts, Mary cuts the seam allowance by eye. She reminded me that the cutting line doesn't have to be exact. She showed me how to needleturn, rolling the seam allowance under with the needle as I sewed. Then she sent me home to finish my block. When I completed the block, I took it back for her to critique. She looked at the front, turned it over, and looked at the back, then handed it to me, saying, "Make the stitches a little smaller." And that was that.

Mary favors precise work. Precision had been drilled into her as a child. She has an excellent system for positioning the appliqué patches accurately. She positions a completed drawing of the pattern under the background square and places tiny pencils dots to indicate the position of flowers, leaves, stems, etc. This system seems superior to the commonly taught method of tracing the entire design on the background because there are minimal pencil marks on the block. If you have tried the method of tracing the entire design on the ground, you know that it is hard to cover all the pencil lines with the appliqué. She also taught me to create placement guidelines by folding the background in quarters and diagonally and finger pressing the creases.

Templates

Mary preferred cardboard templates. Most of her templates were made from cereal boxes, and usually from Kellogg's Bran Flakes cereal boxes. For both piecing and appliqué, she cut the templates actual size. Mary sent me the pattern and the template for the POMEGRANATE quilt she made in 1990. The template shown here is typical of her work in every regard.

For Mary, making the template is always one of the required steps whether she is making a complicated design or a simple nine patch. In February 1989, she sent me a pattern for a nine-patch quilt. As always, she included *complete* instructions. There was a carefully hand colored drawing of the block and the whole quilt. The instructions included number of blocks, block size, size of the

Cardboard template for POMEGRANATE. Made by Mary for Gwen.

borders, and size of the quilt. Included in the packet was a cardboard template of a simple square labeled "Nine Patch." Some might find this level of detail excessive, but that is the way Mary consistently works.

BORDERS

Mary contends that cutting borders from the width of the fabric is best because the width has some stretch to it (unlike the length, which doesn't stretch) and therefore allows any easing or stretching that might be needed.

I wrote to Mary and asked her some questions about handling borders. Here is her response:

Sat. Feb 23, 1985

Dear Gwen,

About adding border strips to the body of a quilt, there is no one way that works easily all the time. Hand sewing tension can vary from one hour to the next, the difference in pull between cross and vertical grain of material—this last can vary between different materials used in the same quilt. In spite of all precautions taken, the body of the top can vary on sides and ends.

I've not had to write instructions of my method before, usually I show my way, however I must say I have to stretch or ease-in material at times. As you know I hand sew.

1. *First I fold the sides of the quilt-body together. Use the longest measurement (if there is an inch or less difference).*
2. *If there is more than an inch difference use a longer strip measurement,—remember this excess will have to be eased into the shorter side.*
3. *These instructions apply to the top and bottom also.*

4. To sew together—As you hand sew have the body of the quilt on top; the strip underneath. Fold the strip in half, pin to half measurement of quilt body—as you sew stretch or ease in to fit.

Note—Instruction given in many magazines say tear the strips from the length of material to a size as given. I don't do that any longer as there is no give in length-wise weaves. I tear the strips on the cross-wise weave of material—there is some give in the cross wise weaves.

Caution—this applies to cotton material—high content polyester blends don't stretch either length-wise or cross-wise.

You and/or your students may gain some comfort in knowing the quilting forgives moderate puckering and unevenness, but sometimes creates unevenness if the top is not put into a frame properly—in most quilts there is a variance in side and end measurements—some slight but others very visibly so. As with most handmade things we strive toward perfection, but seldom attain it. However, that fact should not keep us from trying.

We are quite well and getting back in the groove as much as weather and snow allows.

Fondly, Mary[1]

Taking her cue from antique quilts, Mary rarely miters her corners. Rather, she almost always butt joints them. If she wants to miter the corners, however, she knows how to do it. She used a directional print on the border of a quilt she made for me. Thinking the print should line up so it would flow continually around the quilt, she mitered the corners.

QUILTING DESIGNS

As her quilting designs are such an important part of her work, she always marks the tops completely before sending them out to be quilted. The quilting designs are one more way for her to express her creativity and put her distinctive mark on her quilts. She truly enjoys designing original quilting patterns. I have a large box full of Mary's quilting patterns as well as designs taken from her antique quilts. Thirty-three of Mary's original designs and nine Betty Harriman designs are included in *70 Classic Quilting Patterns* (Marston and Cunningham 1987).

MARKING

With no one around to tell her how to mark quilts, Mary got her ideas from looking at her first kit quilts. Kit quilts indicate the quilting designs with a line of dots and, as mentioned earlier, Mary devised a way to imitate the dot sys-

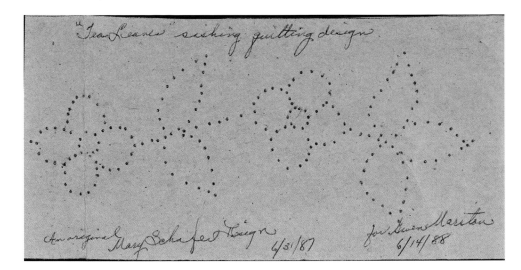

"Tear Leaves" sashing quilting design

An original Mary Schafer design 4/31/87   for Gwen Marston 6/14/88

Mary's quilting design template

tem. She drew the design on a brown paper grocery sack, and with a darning needle poked holes about every quarter inch. She laid the pattern on top of the quilt and made a pencil mark through every hole.

Mary's husband Fred made her a little board out of hard maple, about 9″ × 12″, upon which Mary marked her quilts. She sits on the floor with the quilt top and her quilting pattern and marks her quilts section by section.

With one exception, Mary always marks her tops before sending them out to be quilted. Although I'd offered many times before, Mary finally accepted my offer to mark a quilt for her. She decided she had too many projects to finish and accepted my help with her ROSE WREATH quilt in 1996. While she trusted the marking to me, she told me what to mark.

QUILTING

Mary quilted her first quilt in her lap. Later Fred had one of his friends at work make a quilting frame for her. Fred traded his welding skills for his friend's carpentry skills. Mary used the frame a few times but was never comfortable with it. Having quilted the first quilt in her lap, she prefers that method.

Her particular love is designing quilts, hand piecing, and hand appliqué. Early on, she realized that she wanted to spend her energies designing and making the tops and began to send her quilts out to be quilted. Professional quilters, and even professional quilt markers, have always been a part of quilt history. Many experienced quilters held the view that sending the tops to a professional was a wise choice. Mary's friend Betty Harriman sent her work out to be quilted, as did other notable quilters such as Rose Kretsinger.[2] In *The Romance of the Patchwork Quilt in America,* Hall and Kretsinger address this issue. On the common practice of one person making the top and a second doing the quilting, Rose writes that "the quilt top is made by one person, then passed on to some other worker to be quilted."[3] In the chapter "How to Make a Quilt," Carrie Hall advises that "When you have finished your 'top' turn it over to an experienced quilter, for a beautiful quilt may be made or marred by the quilting."[4]

Hannah Haynes Headlee and Charlotte Jane Whitehill, both from Kansas, are two more well-known twentieth-century quilters who sent their tops to professional quilters.[5] The Charlotte Jane Whitehill quilts are now housed at the Denver Art Museum.

Bertha Stenge is another great quilt maker who initially did her own quilting but later had it done, "following the traditional wisdom of the day."[6] In an article entitled "The Superb Mrs. Stenge," Cuesta Benberry writes:

> *In 1942, Mrs. Stenge was awarded the Grand Prize in the National Needlework Contest of Woman's Day Magazine. . . .*
>
> *The Art Institute of Chicago, in the summer of that same year—1943 honored Mrs. Bertha Stenge with a One Woman Show. Seventeen of her beautiful quilts were hung in the Art Institute's galleries—displayed as the art objects they were.*[7]

The fact that "The Superb Mrs. Stenge" had a one-woman show at the Art Institute of Chicago reminds us of her importance in the quilt world. In having her quilting done, Mary is following a long tradition of quilters who sent their tops out to be quilted.

Mary's custom is to mark her own designs before sending them to quilters. In the late 1960s and early 1970s, Ida Pullum, who lived in both Flint and Flushing, did most of Mary's quilting. Mary used other quilters as well: Mrs. Erb of Charm, Ohio, and Mrs. Runge of Reading, Pennsylvania. Later in the 1970s, Mary's quilters included Mrs. Miller of Dundee, Ohio, Mrs. Milton Unruh of Freeman, South Dakota, Alva Schlabach of Ohio, and Theda Yoder of Bemidji, Minnesota. In the 1980s, Mary's quilters included Mary Anna Bontrager of Centreville, Michigan, and Shirley Neff of Shipshewana, Indiana.

When Mary began making doll quilts, she returned to quilting them herself, quilting in her lap as she prefers.

Binding

Mary prefers a single-thickness binding cut on the bias. I remember talking to Mary about this shortly after we met. The Mennonite quilters who taught me to quilt instructed me to use a double binding. Their idea was that it was more durable. If it wore through the first thickness, there would be another layer. It

Mary sewing on a binding by hand

made sense to me, but Mary had another point of view. She told me that if the binding wore through she would want to replace it. She also showed me her antique quilts, all of which have single bindings. Single bindings are finer and lie flatter than double bindings, resulting in a more refined edge, which Mary likes. Her argument convinced me.

She uses a standard yardstick to mark the cutting lines, resulting in a bias strip measuring between $1\frac{1}{8}''$ and $1\frac{1}{4}''$. Right sides together, she hand sews the binding to the top side of the quilt, then turns the quilt over and slip stitches it down, turning the seam allowance under as she works.

SIGNING HER QUILTS

From the beginning, Mary has embroidered her name and date on her quilts. Her handwriting is very pretty, and she signs her name, including her maiden name, "Mary Vida Schafer." The majority of quilts in the First Collection are signed and dated. She faltered somewhat when she began to make crib and doll quilts, however, and many of these are not dated. With other records to rely on, we have been able to make plausible guesses as to dates when these were made.

Being a quilt maker myself, I have always been amazed at Mary's rate of production. A clue to how she has managed to make so many quilts is found in a letter written to her friend Ruth Parr dated February 23, 1973.

Dear Ruth,

Glad to know you are sticking with your Sunburst quilt—quite often that is the hardest part of quiltmaking, that is, staying with it 'till finished. That's one of the reasons I sew just about every day. If I get weary of applique I pick up pieced work or perhaps read thru (or look at pictures) of one of my books.[8]

And so it is that Mary made an astounding number of beautiful quilts, by hand, often from scraps, using basic sewing tools. Dolores Hinson said of Mary's quilts:

I have not seen any old quilts with better workmanship than Mary Schafer's in all the thousands of quilts I have seen, studied and photographed. . . . Her needlework in itself is flawless.[9]

$\mathcal{A}$rtistic Characteristics

 WHILE MARY HAS AMPLY PROVEN HER ABILITY TO MAKE COMplicated quilts, she showed an early and abiding love of simple layouts. Her first two quilts, the kit appliqués RHODODENDRON and POPPY WREATH, are models of design basics with a capital B. Each is a floral medallion framed by a small version of the central motif in all four corners. The first quilt Mary made from scratch, her pieced LINDEN MILL, is also a model of simplicity, although it differs from her first two quilts in just about every way a quilt can: pieced versus appliqué, primary colors versus pastels, abstract forms versus realism; and straight binding versus scalloped edges.

Throughout her many years of quilt making, Mary has moved easily between complicated and simple patterns. Two medallions, the BIRD OF PARADISE and THE HARVESTERS, are pieced quilts that require an experienced hand, as is her SCALLOPS. Her PINWHEEL and MONTEREY NINE PATCH are made with simple pieced patterns.

Mary has always been intrigued with rare and unusual patterns. ENGLISH PLUME, LOBSTER, TOBACCO LEAF, and OCTOBER FOLIAGE are examples of truly unusual appliqués. SCALLOPS and CLAMSHELL are examples of Mary's unusual pieced quilts. The scrappy EVENING STAR twinkles with its old-fashioned bar setting and border treatment. The stars are set into nine-patch blocks with an extra row at the bottom. These design choices emulate design elements common on eighteenth- and nineteenth-century quilts. What a great quilt this is.

She continued in her quest to seek out the unusual. Browsing through an antique store in her area, Mary ran across a small section of pieced work. She was very interested in it because she had never seen the pattern before. While it caught her eye, she thought the asking price was too high. She got permission to copy the pattern. Always vigilant to collect any information available, the only data she could get from the shop owner was that this remnant had come from a family named Taylor. Mary took her pattern, went home with her treasure, and started in on the SCALLOPS. SCALLOPS is discussed further in "Mary's Technique."

Always looking for the unusual, a quilt in *Country Living* magazine became the source and inspiration for VARIABLE STAR. What intrigued Mary about the antique quilt was that the stars were white and the background blue. In most cases, the star would be blue and the background white. She liked the idea of reversing the more common color arrangement.

While not old, GRANDMOTHER'S PRIDE is another unusual pattern. Mary found this pattern in a magazine article about classic fan designs. As it reminded her of Art Deco, she used the pastels popular in the 1930s to make this wonderful scrap quilt. She designed yet another one of her flawless borders, cleverly working out the corners.

EVENING STAR
78″ × 93″, 1982. Made by Mary Schafer.

Often she'd become so intrigued with a particular style of quilt that she'd work in a series as a way to explore the subject thoroughly. She did this with her medallion quilts, discussed in "The Second Collection." When she became interested in Amish-style crib quilts, she made fourteen of them. She saw that SUNSHINE AND SHADOW quilts offered room to experiment with color. First, she made two doll quilts to see how many ways she could manipulate the palette. The possibilities seemed unlimited, so she made four larger, crib-size quilts, continuing the color play.

Drawing on ideas taken from old quilts, Mary practiced a time-honored tradition in both word and deed. Before Mary's time, two well-known quilters,

VARIABLE STAR
77" × 87", 1983. Made by Mary Schafer.

GRANDMOTHER'S PRIDE
79" × 99", 1980. Made by Mary Schafer.

SUNSHINE AND SHADOW
47½" × 47½", 1982. Made by Mary Schafer.

SUNSHINE AND SHADOW
39″ × 39″, 1983. Made by Mary Schafer.

SUNSHINE AND SHADOW
46″ × 47″, 1984. Made by Mary Schafer.

SUNSHINE AND SHADOW
49″ × 49″, 1984. Made by Mary Schafer.

Rose Kretsinger and Charlotte Jane Whitehill, took designs from antique quilts, redrafting the patterns for their own use. Like them, Mary often drew inspiration from antique quilts, as did her longtime friend Betty Harriman. Both of these women reproduced antique quilts, among other reasons as a way to preserve them. Motivated by a desire to foster respect for early quilts and quilt makers, Mary also found that reproducing antique quilts helped her. Having grown up without quilts in her life, copying old quilts became a way to discover what she liked and did not like in quilts. Mary's study of old quilts helped her develop her preferences. Her ideas about how her quilts should look came from her intense, hands-on study of antique quilts.

Mary's and Betty's approaches to reproducing old quilts differed. Betty was more likely to copy an antique as closely as possible, using antique fabrics whenever she could. She followed the design layout of the quilt scrupulously. Mary, on the other hand . . . well, I don't know that Mary ever copied a quilt exactly. From the first LINDEN MILL on, she caught the essence of the old quilt, used it as inspiration, and always gave it her personal touch.

She excelled at designing original borders that harmonized with the interior of her quilts. Whether pieced or appliquéd, Mary's borders always "fit" exactly. She was especially clever in devising symmetrical border resolutions. Look at the pieced borders on GRANDMOTHER'S PRIDE, VARIABLE STAR, FLOWER POT, and CUPS AND SAUCERS, for example. Look at her appliqué border resolutions on ROSE OF SHARON and COUNTRYSIDE for more examples. Reviewing Mary's quilts, it is clear she has a preference for symmetrical borders.

When she saw an old Spools quilt I'd found at the Salvation Army store in Flint, Mary borrowed it and made her own version. Although in the arts it is commonplace for students to copy the acknowledged masters, I think watching Mary "copy" has made me appreciate this practice even more. I followed her lead early on in my own quilting. Sometimes I copied quilts in the Betty Harriman style as closely as I could. Most often I adopted the Mary Schafer style of drawing ideas from old quilts and reworking them in my own way. I encourage you to copy an old quilt and see what you discover. This practical exercise can make you appreciate the design elements that go into quilts as no other method of learning can. In the copying, you will gain a deeper understanding of what is exceptional and what is ordinary in any given quilt. I know it has helped me to get a handle on balance, color, scale, and texture in my own work.

Mary formed her own idea about what size her quilts should be. Quilts, in her mind, after all is said and done, are made to fit on beds, and she wants a certain drop on the sides, with enough volume to go over the pillows and tuck in at the foot of the bed. Often, in copying, this means that she has to add borders, which provides another opportunity for self-expression.

Mary studies old quilts as a way to understand scale and balance, but these are only part of what goes into a successful quilt. Mary is also interested in

FLOWER POT
79″ × 99″, 1980. Made by Mary Schafer.

CUPS AND SAUCERS
80½″ × 95½″, 1989. Made by Mary Schafer.

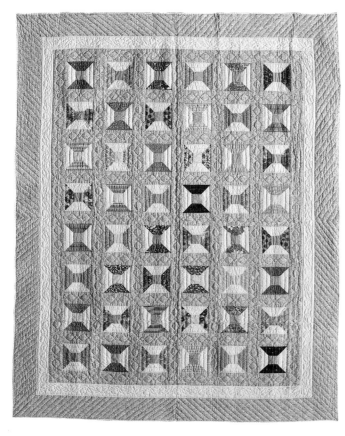

SPOOLS
76½″ × 95″, 1985. Made by Mary Schafer.

investigating and decoding the colors. She tries to capture the color ideas from the antiques, but she usually uses fabrics she has on hand rather than buying new fabric. A child of the Depression, Mary graduated from the "waste not, want not" school of economics.

Color and print choices have always been one of the things I like most about Mary's quilts. Most of her early quilts were made before the explosion of reproduction fabrics hit the market. Mary tried to get "the look" of the old quilt, using fabrics from the 1950s through the 1980s. Over and over again she cleverly used contemporary fabrics to create the look of quilts from an earlier era.

Mary did buy new fabric on occasion, but she didn't buy very much. I've been with her at big quilt shows with lots of tempting vendors displaying great selections of new fabrics. Mary would thoughtfully buy a quarter yard of one or maybe two fabrics. She purchased only what was intended for a specific quilt. She did buy a lot of muslin because she almost always chose muslin for the back of her quilts.

In the early 1970s, it was hard to find 100 percent cotton fabrics. Mary could find cottons at local thrift shops and began using recycled clothing for her quilts. In 1973, she wrote to her friend Ruth Parr about this.

It is unfortunate that now that there is a resurgence of quilt making, suitable cotton material is difficult to find. This past summer I have gone to garage and yard sales trying to find cotton prints (dresses and blouses) in good condition to cut up for quilts. I've found a few, but even at these sales there were less of cotton prints this fall than last spring. I heard though, cotton goods are coming back. I hope so.[1]

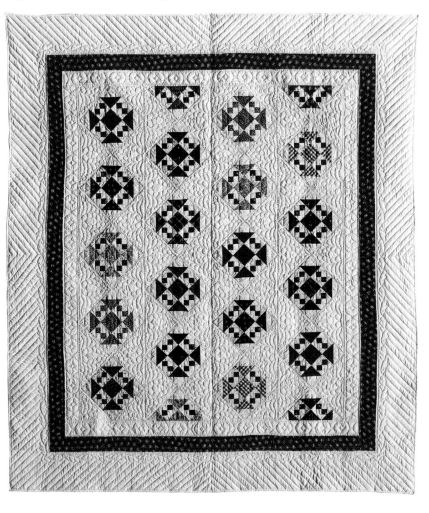

PRAIRIE QUEEN
82″ × 97″, 1984. Made by Mary Schafer.

Like many quilters before her, she continued to enjoy the challenge of making quilts from recycled clothing. This choice produced a distinctive quality in her quilts: They do not contain the contemporary fabrics seen in other quilts of the time.

Working from her scrap bag, Mary's PRAIRIE QUEEN and FLOWER POT are typical of her clever use of fabrics. In PRAIRIE QUEEN, she captured the look of scrap quilts made in the last quarter of the nineteenth century. She used stripes, checks, and plaid shirtings with browns, reds, and blues from her scrap bag. The Streak o'Lightning set contributes to the old-fashioned look of the quilt. Less common today, this set begins and ends every other row of blocks with a half block.

In Mary's FLOWER POT, she used a brown plaid for the baskets, thinking it gave the appearance of a woven basket. She repeated the red diamond-shaped flowers in her border design, using two diamonds in the corners.

She also liked using historical colors such as blue and white, which were popular in the mid–nineteenth century. Both VARIABLE STAR and CUPS AND SAUCERS are classic blue and white quilts.

Sometimes Mary had to imagine the colors because she was working from a black and white reproduction of a quilt or from a bare bones pattern. Less often she would use the fabric as a place to jump into a new quilt.

In a letter to me, Cuesta Benberry commented on Mary's skill and artistry as a quilt maker, saying:

> I knew years ago Mary was more than an excellent quiltmaker. Those quilts of hers attest to her technical skill, and more, to the wide knowledge of history, the symbolism with which she imbues each work, and finally to her own creativity which distinguishes her work. There's a slang phrase—"Some folks got it and some folks ain't." Well, Mary has 'IT!!'[2]

The final design element that goes into a quilt is the quilting itself. Quilting not only gives the quilter another way to express herself and continue ideas she began in the piecing and/or appliqué; the quilting adds texture. Mary has proven herself to be especially creative in this area. From the first quilt she pieced, she always designed her own quilting patterns. When people talk of Mary's "style," they are speaking, in part, about her original quilting designs. As in her piecing and appliqué, the hallmark of her quilting designs is deceptive simplicity. Thirty-three of her original quilting designs are reproduced in 70 *Classic Quilting Patterns* (Marston and Cunningham 1987).

The two triangular designs shown here are typical of the shapes Mary favors. Depending on the size of the triangle to be filled, she adjusts these themes to fit the space, sometimes simplifying or elaborating on the basic design shape.

Original Schafer quilting designs

As mentioned before, Mary likes muslin. She has often used this neutral fabric as the ground in her appliqué blocks, for her plain blocks, and for the backing of her quilts. She likes the inherent simplicity of this most humble material. Influenced by appliqués from the nineteenth century, she followed suit in using white or muslin as a ground. The quilting stitch, as exemplified in Mary's quilts, seems to like muslin, too. She purposely leaves a lot of open space to be filled with elaborate quilting, and she knows that quilting shows up best on muslin. Her graceful, symmetrical designs fairly jump out at the viewer, giving her quilts a decidedly three-dimensional character. In quilting, as in piecing, Mary knows what notes her raw materials are capable of playing, and she plays every note to the max.

As Mary follows her artistic instincts in quilting, she also follows her own advice. While not shy about stating her personal views on the art of quilt making, she doesn't tell anyone else what to do. As the quilt world has changed around her, commercializing and reinventing the core elements of what makes a quilt, she doesn't object and never criticizes. Neither does she rush to embrace the changes. She has stayed with her own definitions of balance, size, color, and texture in quilts. She tries to understand the new art quilt movement but is not convinced.

In a phone conversation with Mary sometime in 1995, she offered a little advice on the subject of keeping one's own counsel: "Be cautious with advice. Wise men don't need it, and fools won't heed it." This is good counsel, and I wrote it down immediately. It's another thing that Mary Schafer taught me.

Finding a Home for the First Collection

A RECURRING THEME IN MY CONVERSATIONS WITH MARY since the time we met in 1977 centered on what would happen to her quilts. It was a great concern for Mary. As her friend, it became a central concern for me, too. I knew she would never relax about it until she was assured that her quilts would be taken care of, so I wanted to help her resolve this issue once and for all. I had enjoyed the privilege of getting to know and love Mary's quilts, and I wanted to help her find a good home for them because I felt so strongly that she had created a unique collection.

We began to explore possibilities for housing Mary's quilts permanently. Ideally, Mary wanted to find an institution that would keep all of her quilts together as an intellectual whole, preserving the selection decisions she had carefully made over the years as she developed her collection.

Mary had spent years carefully gathering quilts that represented the *whole* of quilt making. Her intent had been to build a collection that represented the major regional and historical styles of American quilts. Not only did she collect financially valuable and unique antique quilts, but she collected the kind of everyday quilts that represented what the majority of quilt makers produced. In fact, she worried most about what would happen to the simpler, cruder quilts. She told me it is like loving all your children but being most concerned for the one who is disadvantaged in some way: "They are like children. No matter how homely or naughty they are, they are still my children." What a tender way of looking at her collection.

Mary was sure that the beautifully made quilts would be valued and taken care of. She worried most about the simplest quilts, afraid they would not be understood and appreciated, afraid they would be turned out into the world to fend for themselves.

Having such regard for the quilters of the past, she knew that most of the quilts made by our grandmothers were humble quilts, not the grand master-pieces so often collected by museums and shown in quilt books. The majority of quilts were made to be used. Mary was interested in the complete history of quilt making, and she understood that simple utility quilts are the backbone of the history of American quilt making.

She hoped that her quilts could stay together as a historical resource. Together they had many stories and lessons to impart to future generations interested in American folk art and women's history. In addition to keeping the collection intact, she hoped that the quilts would be professionally cared for and preserved and that they would be made accessible to the public. For this, it seemed a museum would be best suited for the collection's permanent home.

After exploring a number of possibilities, the museum at Michigan State University seemed like the best option. Mary liked the idea of her quilts stay-ing in her state. Always concerned about raising the esteem of past quilters and about educating people about quilts, Mary was pleased that her quilts would be housed at a public institution where they would be made accessible to people now and in the future.

The curator of folk arts at the Michigan State University Museum, Marsha MacDowell, acknowledged the importance of the museum's acquisition of the Schafer collection and echoed Mary's enthusiasm about the educational possi-bilities: "With the main portion of the collection in an institution with a long history of quilt scholarship and public education, Mary Schafer's collection will continue to serve as an educational resource for generations to come."[1]

Despite these benefits, Mary had certain reservations about museum owner-ship in general and the terms offered by MSU. She knew that after the quilts left her hands she would not have control over them. She knew that museums change direction and can sell works within their collections. From the begin-ning, MSU would not agree to keep Mary's collection together, which is usual museum procedure. Knowing this, we still felt that it was the best option.

In determining what to sell to the Michigan State University Museum, Mary used the catalog *The Mary Schafer Quilt Collection* (Marston 1980). She con-sidered this body of work to be the "First Collection." While the catalog docu-ments 121 quilts, Mary sold only 118 of them to the museum. She kept 3 quilts for personal reasons. Yankee Puzzle was the first crib quilt Mary made, and it

RADICAL ROSE
80″ × 97″, 1965. Made by Mary Schafer specifically for her own bed. (Collection of Mary Schafer. Photo by Alan Zinn.)

was made for her granddaughter, Deborah. She kept RADICAL ROSE, which she had made especially for her bedroom, and the SHOO FLY quilt because it was Fred's favorite.

As negotiations inched slowly forward, Mary decided to have her quilts appraised. In June 1992, she hired Patricia Hubbel Boucher, a certified AQS appraiser, to appraise the first fifty quilts listed in *The Mary Schafer Quilt Collection.* Boucher appraised the quilts "evaluated as of today's date, and priced for the Michigan market and general population of the United States."[2]

The museum obtained a grant for twenty-five thousand dollars from the Ruth Mott Fund in Flint, Michigan, and began hosting fund-raising events mostly conducted by various supportive Michigan quilt guilds. Mary and I both helped raise funds for the acquisition of her quilts. In 1996, she donated a Maltese Cross quilt top to the museum as a fund-raiser for the purchase of her collection. The top was generously quilted by the Ann Arbor Quilt Guild. I had written an ABC book called *Q Is for Quilt.* Illustrated with appropriate quilt blocks, it is an early American history lesson for children. When I showed my story to Mary, she offered to help me make the blocks. Before I knew it, she had made all twenty-six. I gave both the quilt and the book to MSU to use as a fund-raiser for the acquisition of Mary's quilts.

Negotiations with the museum began in the early 1980s and ground slowly along due to the enormity of the task. Funds had to be raised to purchase the collection and secure proper housing for the quilts. The legalities of the arrangement had to be ironed out. Maneuvering through large bureaucracies tends to be cumbersome and slow, and universities are no different. In the spring of 1998, the Michigan State University Museum paid Mary one hundred thousand dollars and took possession of the First Collection.[3] It had taken more than twenty-one years to finalize a resting place for Mary's quilts.

Besides the quilts, another valuable part of the collection consists of her papers and other quilt-related materials. Mary was meticulous about keeping all of the letters she had received throughout the years. She saved all of her quilt magazines and, for that matter, everything that pertained to quilts. She also had an extensive collection of quilt patterns, quilt blocks she had made, antique blocks, and antique fabrics. She donated the majority of her papers and related items to the museum. The gift included, among other things, 252 quilt patterns, 208 quilt blocks, vintage fabrics, 30 ribbons she had won, periodicals, books, and most of her correspondence. Virginia Anderson helped Mary organize and document the related materials. Kitty Cole appraised the materials, and in appreciation of their efforts Mary made each of them a one-patch doll quilt.

In order to pay Mary in full for the collection, MSU had borrowed some of the money from another source. The museum decided it would be necessary to sell some of the quilts to private individuals in order to raise the money needed to repay the loan.

The museum determined that of the 118 Schafer quilts, it would sell all but 75. According to Marsha MacDowell, "The remaining quilts are to be periodically auctioned or raffled to raise funds to complete the purchase of the collection and to support the long-term care of the collection."[4] Mary's quilts, in essence, are buying Mary's quilts.

In October of 1998, the museum held the first auction. Mary was asked for her input on determining which quilts would be sold. She politely declined the offer, telling me it was just too hard to decide which quilts would have to go. Fifteen of Mary's quilts were auctioned at the Greater Ann Arbor Quilt Guild show in Ann Arbor. With this first auction, MSU raised more than eleven thousand dollars. An additional quilt was sold the following year.

In October 1999, the museum sold HOLLAND QUEEN, which had been begun by Betty Harriman around 1965 and finished by Mary in 1978. HOLLAND QUEEN was purchased by an anonymous buyer for an unknown sum and then given as a gift to the American Quilt Study Group to be used as a fund-raiser. The AQSG held its annual meeting in East Lansing in 1999, and, according to the program, "Our 1999 Opportunity Quilt, the gift of an anonymous donor, features nine 22-inch blocks made by Betty Harriman in 1965. . . . In the 1970's Mary Schafer completed HOLLAND QUEEN, adapting the block design and using Betty's fabric to create a border with swags, smaller tulips and diamond-shaped

HOLLAND QUEEN
83" × 99". Begun by Betty Harriman, 1965, completed by Mary Schafer, 1978. (Photo by Alan Zinn.)

leaves."[5] According to Betty's notes, the pattern had come from a quilt made in West Virginia around 1892.

In my view, the auction kicked the legs out from under the collection by selling some of its best and rarest quilts. When writing *Sets and Borders, American Beauties,* and *Mary Schafer and Her Quilts,* I naturally selected what I considered to be the most significant Schafer quilts to include in these publications. Of the sixteen quilts that were sold, fourteen were shown in one of these books. Fourteen important quilts were sold.

Three Harriman/Schafer quilts (WASHINGTON PLUME, ENGLISH PLUME, and HOLLAND QUEEN) were among those sold. Mary's great effort to complete the quilts begun by Betty makes it difficult to know that these particular quilts have lost sight of each other. Close friendships and collaborations are not news in the quilt world. However, two great quilt makers whose working relationship transcended death and culminated in a large body of technically demanding and artistically impressive work is. With these quilts now in private hands, the public has lost access to this unique story in its completeness; a story without rival and unlikely to be repeated.

The auction was sorely disappointing on another level. All the quilts were sold well below their market value. Seven of the fifteen quilts had been appraised seven years earlier and were sold well below the appraisal figures, which is questionable at best. In the seven years that had passed, quilts had risen in price, as they had in demand. Attic Window was appraised at $3,100 in 1992 and sold for $1,050 in 1998. Delectable Mountains was appraised at $3,100 and sold for $2,000. Fox and Geese was appraised at $3,000 and sold for $1,000. CHURN DASH was appraised at $1,060 and sold for $500. Fly Foot was appraised at $1,095 and sold for $450. ENGLISH PLUME appraised at $1,500 and sold for $900. Double Pyramid was appraised at $800 and sold for $500.

Quilts that had not been officially appraised were also sold at low prices. Mary's PINE TREE, dated 1884, sold for $300. The date was cleverly quilted into the quilt. Some of the green fabrics in the quilt had faded to blue, but other than that PINE TREE was in good condition. Classical feather wreaths graced the quilt, accompanied

PINE TREE
65" × 72", 1884. Dated quilt, Franklin County, Ohio. (Photo by Alan Zinn.)

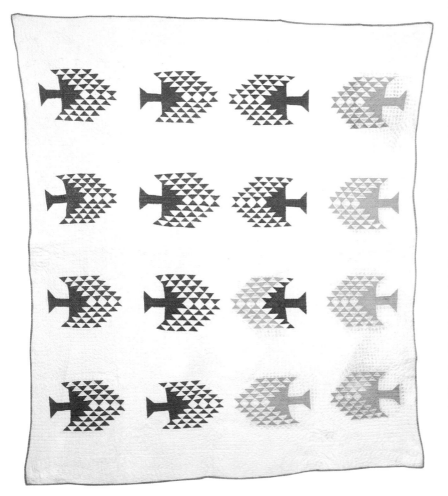

by a feathered vine. ROSE WREATH, circa 1850, sold for $225. While this quilt was worn, it was a beautiful example of early appliqué and had very close and elegant quilting. The old quilt was from Fayetteville, Pennsylvania. Mary admired this grand old appliqué so much that she made her own version of it. Copying old quilts was her way of learning what they had to teach and her way of preserving fine artistic ideas.

ENGLISH PLUME and TOBACCO LEAF are two unique quilts. They are both unusual old patterns that are seldom seen. In fact, in going through all of my books with photographs of antique quilts I've never run across one that even slightly resembles either of these.

ENGLISH PLUME was the last quilt Mary received from the Betty Harriman estate. She obtained this unfinished quilt in exchange for finishing another of Betty's starts for the Harriman sisters. The quilt she finished was Oriental Poppy, one of the most beautiful, as well as the most difficult, of appliqués. From Mary's snapshot of the quilt, it appears that Betty was making a near copy of the Rose Kretsinger Oriental Poppy shown in *The Romance of the Patchwork Quilt in America*.[6]

ENGLISH PLUME is perhaps the most outstanding of the Harriman and Schafer quilts. Betty began the quilt around 1967, and Mary finished it in 1972. The majority of the plume quilts have four blocks. This masterpiece has one large central plume measuring seventy inches across, making it even more dramatic. The fabric is a beautiful paisley print. The border's individual oak leaves float along as if the wind had tossed them there. The red veins on the plume and the red star in the center of the plume are worked in reverse appliqué. The red vines on the oak leaves on the border lie on top of the leaves, worked in regular appliqué. In my view, it is disappointing that the Michigan State University Museum did not retain this unique quilt.

Betty began WASHINGTON PLUME in 1965, and Mary completed it in 1980. Betty Harriman delighted in creating quilts in early historical styles. The red and green color scheme, three-sided border, and half blocks are reminiscent of the grand four-block quilts of the mid–nineteenth century.

ENGLISH PLUME
80½″ × 97″. Begun by Betty Harriman, 1967, finished by Mary Schafer, 1979. (Collection of Carol Spaly.)

ROSE OF SHARON
74″ × 79″, ca. 1875–1900. (Collection of Carol Spaly.)
(Photo by Alan Zinn.)

CHURN DASH
82″ × 92″, ca. 1915. Top. Mary added the outer border and completed the quilt. (Photo by Alan Zinn.)

ROSE OF SHARON, also sold by Michigan State University Museum, was a favorite of both Mary's and mine. While it shows wear, its primitive design qualities make it a charmer. As with other old appliqué quilts I've seen, the shapes are quilted around both the outside and the inside. This always amazed me, as the little leaves on the borders are only a quarter inch wide. The three-sided borders and the designs in the corner squares are another delightful feature.

Another quilt that was sold was CHURN DASH, an old top Mary found in Flint and finished. It's an interesting quilt because of its old-fashioned bar setting. The bars made up of pieced blocks are staggered; one bar begins with a pieced block, and the next begins with a plain block.

The Michigan State University Museum, as custodian of the Mary Schafer Collection, has been a mixed blessing in my view. Mary has found that in addition to worrying about the preservation of the more simple and primitive utility quilts in her collection she has reason to worry about the finer quilts, too. With more quilts yet to be sold for the purpose of paying back the loan taken out to purchase the collection, it seems irresponsible that the first sixteen quilts were sold below market value.

Mary's First Collection is rare in scope, containing quilts thoughtfully and knowledgeably gathered to represent the wide spectrum of quilts made in America. As a complete collection, it is an incredibly comprehensive source for study. To the extent that the collection is fragmented, it will become less useful for study. Selling additional Schafer quilts will further destroy the integrity and depth of the collection. I hope that given the museum's educational mission it will keep the remainder of the collection intact, but that is not likely.

Retaining the 102 quilts currently in the museum's possession, along with the archival materials Mary donated, would serve future quilt historians well in their quest to understand quilt history. The range of the quilts and the scope of the correspondence and related materials will give researchers an outstanding resource for learning about quilters, quilting, and some remarkable women of the nineteenth and twentieth centuries.

These are the fifteen quilts sold at the Ann Arbor auction. I list the 1998 selling price and the 1992 appraisal figure of those quilts that were appraised. Due to the cost, Mary did not have all of her quilts appraised. As many of these quilts have been pictured in various publications, I include that information as well.

Attic Window. 80″ × 100″, 1975. Made by Mary Schafer. Selling price: $1,050. Appraisal: $3,100. Shown in *Mary Schafer and Her Quilts*, 31, fig. 34.

CHURN DASH. 79½″ × 88½″, ca. 1915. Old top completed by Mary Schafer. Selling price: $500. Appraisal: $1,060. Shown in *Sets and Borders,* 26.

Delectable Mountains. 88″ × 100″, 1975. Made by Mary Schafer. Selling price: $2,000. Appraisal: $3,100. Cover quilt: *The Mary Schafer Quilt Collection.*

Delectable Mountains Variation. 100″ × 100″, ca. 1850. Bird-in-Hand, Pennsylvania. Selling price: $550.

Double Pyramid. 71″ × 83″, ca. 1850–75. Made by Martha Wade Sherwood, Holly, Michigan. Selling price: $500. Appraisal: $800. Shown in *Sets and Borders,* 27.

ENGLISH PLUME. 80½″ × 97″. Begun by Betty Harriman, 1967, completed by Mary Schafer, 1979. Selling price: $900. Appraisal: $1,500. Shown in *Sets and Borders,* 27; and *Mary Schafer and Her Quilts,* 29, fig. 31.

Fly Foot. 82″ × 96½″, ca. 1915. Made in Goderich, Ontario, Canada. Selling price: $450. Appraisal: $1,095.

Fox and Geese. 78″ × 90″, 1964. Made by Mary Schafer. Selling Price: $1,000. Appraisal: $3,000. Shown in *Sets and Borders,* 33; and *Mary Schafer and Her Quilts,* 14.

HOLLAND QUEEN. 83″ × 99″. Begun by Betty Harriman, ca. 1965, completed by Mary Schafer, 1978. Selling price: not known by author. Shown in *American Beauties,* 33, pl. 27.

ROSE OF SHARON. 74″ × 79″ ca. 1875–1900. Selling price: $500. Shown in *American Beauties: Rose and Tulip Quilts,* 26.

ROSE WREATH. 76″ × 76″, ca. 1850. Fayetteville, Pennsylvania. Selling price: $225. Shown in *American Beauties,* 27, pl. 16.

TOBACCO LEAF. 79½″ × 96½″, 1977. Made by Mary Schafer. Selling price: $1,200. Shown in *Sets and Borders,* 52; and *Mary Schafer and Her Quilts,* 39, fig. 46.

WASHINGTON PLUME. 88″ × 96″. Begun by Betty Harriman, ca. 1965, completed by Mary Schafer, 1980. Selling price: $1,100. Shown in *Sets and Borders,* 55.

Morning Star. 81″ × 101″, 1978. Made by Mary Schafer. Selling price: $600.

PINE TREE. 65″ × 72″, dated quilt, 1884. Franklin County, Ohio. Selling price: $300. Shown in *Mary Schafer and Her Quilts,* 36, fig. 42.

Rose and Hearts. 82½″ × 98″, 1963. Made by Ella McInturff, Mannington, West Virginia. Selling price: $600. Shown in *American Beauties,* 24, pl. 10.

The Second Collection

 WITH THE FIRST COLLECTION HOUSED, MARY WAS LEFT WITH what became known, by default, as the Second Collection. These 106 quilts are a testimony to the knowledge and skill gained through years of dedication to the study and making of quilts. Mary did the work, and the work speaks for itself. The majority of the full-size quilts in the Second Collection were made between 1980 and 1990.

The Second Collection is as impressive as the first in terms of the number of large quilts made by Mary and their artistry. In 1980, she made four spectacular medallion quilts. Her interest in early and unusual quilts continued. She also made simple pieced quilts in her effort to make quilts that would encourage and inspire new quilters and because she really liked them. And, as a mature and gifted quilter, she produced exquisite quilts that I would consider to be classical in style.

One of the main differences between the First and Second Collections is that Mary's collecting of antique quilts slowed dramatically after 1980. Although the First Collection has many grand antique quilts, in the Second Collection there are only two. She was still very involved with making quilts, but she felt she had already accumulated a significant number of antiques. She no longer felt the need to build a representative collection of American styles, having accomplished that goal in the First Collection.

Now she felt a new freedom to make the quilts she wanted to make for herself. Mary found new challenges in medallion quilts, Amish quilts, and small quilts. She continued her habit of finishing old tops and also kept working on the quilts her friend Betty Harriman had started. The Second Collection contains as many outstanding full-size quilts made by Mary Schafer as does the first.

I list 106 quilts in the Second Collection. This does not include unquilted tops or projects in progress.

MEDALLIONS

In 1980, Mary made four impressive medallion quilts. In our discussions about the early history of American quilts, medallions had come up frequently. I'd found some decorator prints reminiscent of early prints. I shared them with Mary, including a piece of fabric with a beautiful bird. Mary turned it into BIRD OF PARADISE.

Just as Mary couldn't stop with one challenge quilt, or one bicentennial quilt, once she became interested in medallions she wanted to explore them completely. Using a piece of Toile de Jouy fabric showing a scene with people harvesting grain as the center, Mary made THE HARVESTERS. What a wonderful quilt this is—border after border, all meticulously hand pieced! This was at a time when I saw Mary almost weekly. She pieced the entire quilt in ten days. It amazed me when I saw it.

Then came WELSH MEDALLION, inspired by an old Welsh quilt shown in *Lady's Circle Patchwork Quilts* (no. 24, winter 1981). The original quilt was brought to the United States in 1972 by Peggy Wanamaker of Annapolis, Maryland. The simplicity of the old quilt, coupled with the typical Welsh quilting designs, fascinated Mary. As with many accomplished artists, her sophisticated understanding of her medium drew her to quilts that were rare or unusual.

Her final medallion was COUNTRYSIDE. She found the inspiration for this quilt in Patsy and Myron Orlofsky's book *Quilts in America* (1974, 92). This old medallion was made in 1813 with English block-printed fabrics from the 1780s. In these last two quilts, Mary

BIRD OF PARADISE
84″ × 99″, 1980. Made by Mary Schafer. Mary says this quilt is "an original interpretation of a New England style medallion quilt."

THE HARVESTERS
82″ × 97¹/₂″, 1980. Made by Mary Schafer. Mary says that The Harvesters "is an original interpretation of a mid-American medallion."

WELSH MEDALLION
76″ × 85″, 1980. Made by Mary Schafer.

COUNTRYSIDE
80″ × 86″, 1980. Made by Mary Schafer. Mary says that "this is an adaptation of an 1813 quilt from Pennsylvania or Delaware and housed in the Winterthur Museum."

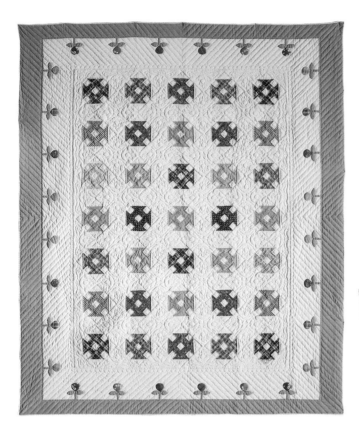

CHURN DASH
76″ × 79″, 1982. Made by Mary Schafer.

BEAR'S PAW
71″ × 85″, 1981. Made by Mary Schafer.

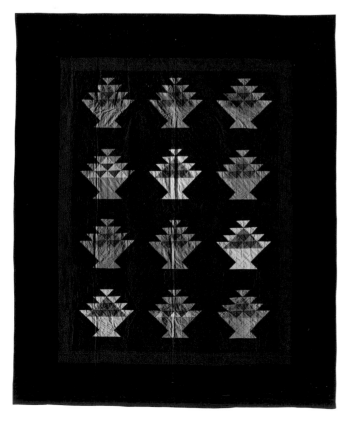

BASKETS
58″ × 71″, 1985. Made by Mary Schafer.

was reaching further back than she ever had. When she was working on her medallions, she told me that "it is easier for me to work backward in time than to work forward."

Mary continued to make simple, traditional quilts in classical styles such as her CHURN DASH. Made with a variety of blue prints, it has a delightful, fresh look. Mary used the same appliqué border motif she had used on another blue and white CHURN DASH, this one begun by Betty Harriman and finished by Mary.

Amish Quilts

Mary's interest in Amish quilts began in the 1970s. She made two full-size Lancaster County Amish quilts in 1976 and 1977, which are a part of the permanent collection at the Michigan State University Museum. Her Second Collection is peppered with Amish-style quilts. BEAR'S PAW is a reproduction of an Amish quilt from my collection. My quilt was made in Kansas in 1921 by Ida Bontrager. Mary was so fond of the Bontrager quilt that she borrowed it and made her own version. In 1985, she made BASKETS in the style of Midwest Amish quilts. She continued her adventure with Amish quilts, working in the small format of doll and crib quilts. The Second Collection contains fourteen crib quilts and four doll quilts in the Amish style.

Small Quilts

A marked difference between the First and Second Collections is that the First Collection has no doll or crib quilts and the Second Collection contains vast numbers of them, twenty-seven crib and thirty-four doll quilts. This is because the cutoff date for the First Collection was 1980 and Mary's fascination with doll and crib quilts didn't begin until 1981.

Until 1982, Mary almost exclusively made full-size quilts to fit beds. The only exception was a Yankee Puzzle crib quilt Mary made for a grandchild in 1965. Making small quilts had never occurred to her. All of that changed when Woodard and Greenstein published *Crib Quilts and Other Small Wonders* in 1981. This book gave credibility to the idea of making small quilts. Once Mary began making small quilts she couldn't quit because, as she said, making them "was as easy as eating candy."

Mary made her first doll quilt in 1982. She had found an old doll quilt at a local antique store. She called it MATERIAL PLEASURES, reflecting how she felt about this little charmer. It wasn't long before she was making her own version of the old quilt. Made that same year, HIT AND MISS was Mary's first effort to make what she considered to be a casual, primitive quilt.

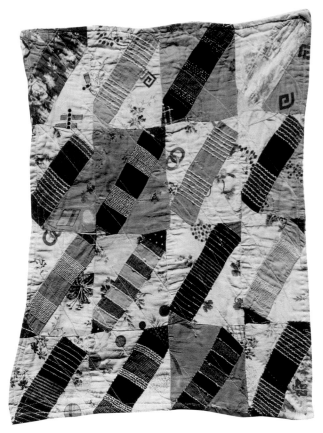

MATERIAL PLEASURES
12″ × 17³/₄″, date unknown. Antique quilt. (Collection of Mary Schafer.)

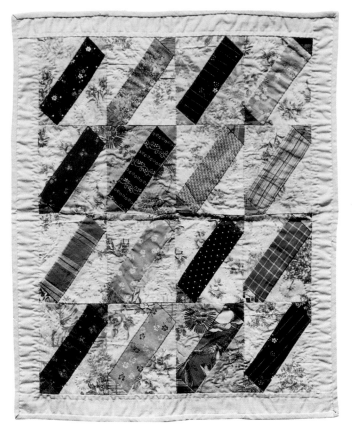

MATERIAL PLEASURES
15¹/₂″ × 19¹/₂″, 1982. Made by Mary Schafer.

HIT AND MISS
17¹/₄″ × 23¹/₄″, 1982. Made by Mary Schafer.

In making doll quilts, Mary took her cues from antiques. Most doll quilts from the nineteenth century were pieced, and most employed very simple, common patterns. Following this example, Mary drafted simple pieced, traditional patterns for these small wonders. These characteristics can be seen in HONEYCOMB and BOW TIE.

Mary enjoyed hand quilting her doll quilts and found that it was easiest to quilt them in her lap. With the majority of her doll quilts made between 1982 and 1986, her collection would eventually grow to thirty-four.

Mary began making crib quilts seriously at the same time. Early crib quilts were small versions of full-size quilts, just as children's clothing imitated adult apparel. Material goods designed with children in mind is a twentieth-century notion. Mary took her cues from the antique crib quilts she studied, and her crib quilts echoed the traditional designs of her full-size quilts.

PINWHEELS, made in 1982, was made in a classical style, composed of sixty little pinwheels and quilted handsomely with feather wreaths and fans. The scrappy CACTUS BASKET also fits the definition of a classical quilt.

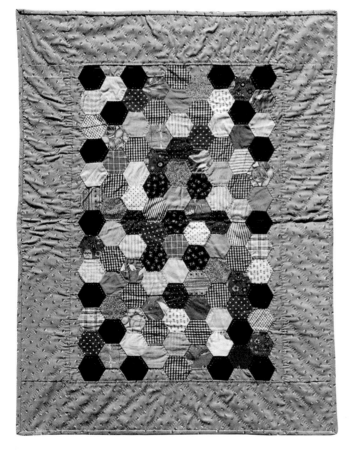

HONEYCOMB
20″ × 26¹/₂″, 1985. Made by Mary Schafer.

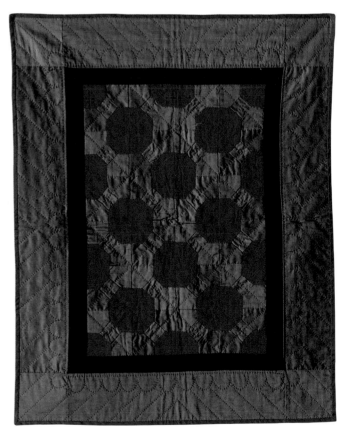

BOW TIE
18¹/₂″ × 24¹/₄″, 1982. Made by Mary Schafer.

PINWHEELS
42" × 51", 1982. Made by Mary Schafer.

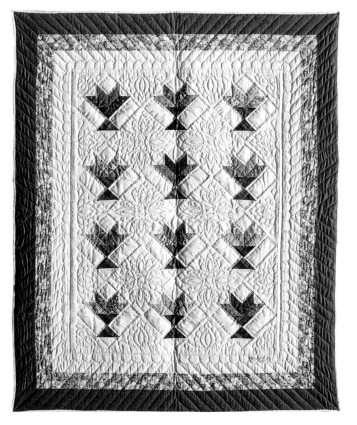

CACTUS BASKET
40" × 50½", 1983 or 1984. Made by Mary Schafer.

PENNSYLVANIA DUTCH
NINE-PATCH VARIATION
43" × 49", 1986. Made by Mary Schafer.

PENNSYLVANIA DUTCH NINE-PATCH VARIATION shows Mary's interest
in making quilts in historical styles by using an old traditional pieced pattern
and typical Pennsylvania Dutch colors.

Out of a total of twenty-seven crib quilts in Mary's Second Collection,
fourteen are quilts made in the Amish style. She made five quilts using
ideas from Woodard and Greenstein's *Crib Quilts and Other Small Wonders* (1981),
including OLD MAID'S PUZZLE and ONE PATCH, which Mary also calls
CHECKERBOARD.

For her next Amish-style quilt, Mary returned to an earlier publication by
Robert Bishop and Elizabeth Safanda called *A Gallery of Amish Quilts*, published
in 1976. Mary's BARS quilt is a small version of a Lancaster County quilt
shown on page 46, number 59, of the book. She described the quilting to me in
a letter:

> *The wide outer border is lavender with purple corners, binding intense green.
> Quilted—cross hatch over bars, pumpkin seed blossoms in border diamonds, rose motif
> in corners. Outer border quilted with wavy feathers and a tri-foil design.*[1]

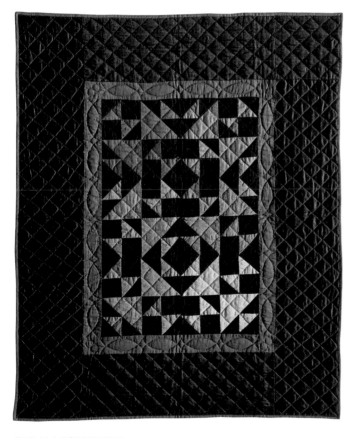

OLD MAID'S PUZZLE
33¼" × 42", 1982. Made by Mary Schafer.

ONE PATCH
43" × 43", 1983. Made by Mary Schafer.
Mary has also referred to this quilt as CHECKERBOARD.

BARS
$46^{1}/_{4}'' \times 46^{1}/_{4}''$, 1984. Made by Mary Schafer.

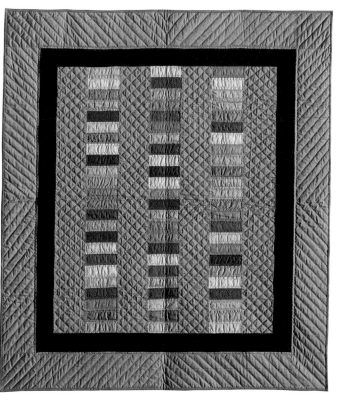

CHINESE COINS
$42'' \times 49''$, 1985. Made by Mary Schafer.

BRICKS
$33'' \times 38^{1}/_{2}''$, 1985. Made by Mary Schafer.

Mary's bisque doll, given to her by her husband Fred

Other books with photographs of Amish quilts began to appear on the market. In 1985, *Amish Crib Quilts,* by Rachel and Kenneth Pellman, was published. CHINESE COINS and BRICKS were inspired by quilts shown in the Pellman book. Mary drafted her patterns from the photographs and came within a few inches of the original sizes.

I think Mary took such great pleasure in making doll and crib quilts in part because they seemed childlike and playful. Mary had to grow up quickly. By the time she was ten years old, she was already in charge of the household. She grew up never owning a doll. Knowing this, sometime in the early 1960s, her husband Fred gave her a bisque doll. Fred's thoughtfulness meant a great deal to Mary. She made an old-fashioned outfit for her new doll. When I asked her if she had ever given the doll a name, she said she hadn't. "I just called it my bisque doll from Fred," she said.

Soon after Fred gave Mary the doll, they took a road trip through the Smoky Mountains. They found someone who was making and selling chairs, and they bought one. Mary describes it as a Tennessee-style chair. Ever since I've known Mary, her bisque doll from Fred has sat on the Tennessee-style chair by the fireplace.

BETTY HARRIMAN STARTS

Persistence is the key word here. Between 1972 and 1980, Mary completed seventeen quilts begun by her friend Betty Harriman. Since 1980, she has finished five more Harriman starts and one antique top from the Harriman estate. Tucked away in boxes, Mary has other unfinished Harriman starts and antique blocks and fabrics from Betty's estate. At this point in her life, Mary is content to have finished a total of twenty-three of the quilts begun by her friend.

One of Betty's starts was DEMO-CRATIC ROSE. Betty had acquired the

DEMOCRATIC ROSE
80″ × 95″. Begun by Betty Harriman, ca. 1960, finished by Mary Schafer, 1981.

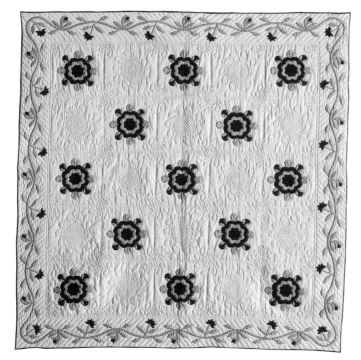

WASHINGTON ROSE
90½″ × 92″. Begun by Betty Harriman, 1969, finished by Mary Schafer, 1984.

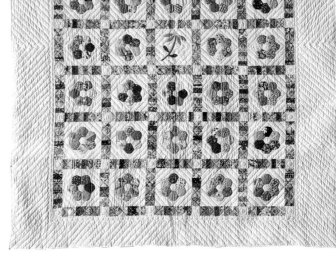

JOSEPH'S COAT
79″ × 93″. Begun by Betty Harriman, ca. 1960, finished by Mary Schafer, 1984.

DRESDEN PLATE
80″ × 97″. Begun by Betty Harriman, 1969, finished by Mary Schafer, 1986.

pattern for this grand four-block quilt from an antique block. Mary received the old block and the four blocks Betty had appliquéd along with some extra fabric. She set Betty's blocks together and designed the center motif and the swag border. I'm sure Betty would approve.

By 1984, Mary had completed WASHINGTON ROSE, JOSEPH'S COAT, and DRESDEN PLATE. Mary had sent Betty the pattern for WASHINGTON ROSE, which I discuss at length in "The Schafer and Harriman Collaboration." Betty was so fond of this pattern that she completed one quilt and had begun a second. This quilt arrived with the blocks completely appliquéd. Mary set the blocks together and appliquéd the borders.

Betty had all of the patches cut out for JOSEPH'S COAT and had started the blocks. Mary finished the blocks, pieced the sashing, and put the quilt together. DRESDEN PLATE came with most of the rings pieced. Mary finished them and appliquéd them on the background. These quilts are similar in that the patches are pieced together and then appliquéd to the background block. Both are also nice examples of quilts made in the 1930s. Mary made the majority of the blocks, put the quilts together, and once again designed flawless borders for both of these quilts.

Betty had pieced all the blue and white blocks for CHURN DASH. Mary put them together, designed and stitched the sweet appliqué border, and designed

CHURN DASH
78″ × 95″. Begun by Betty Harriman, finished by Mary Schafer in 1983.

FRAMED NINE PATCH
87″ × 93″, date unknown. Antique top from the Harriman estate. Mary finished this quilt in 1986.

the quilting patterns. This quilt has a sense of restfulness coming from its simple but solid design elements and the use of blue and white. It is a reminder that sometimes less is more and simple is good.

In 1986, Mary finished an antique top from the Harriman estate, FRAMED NINE PATCH.

ANTIQUE QUILTS

Antique quilts continued to interest Mary, but she bought only two after 1980. When she found a Midwest Amish quilt, she couldn't refuse it. Mary thought CUPS AND SAUCERS typified the Midwest Amish style. Always interested in Michigan quilts, she bought a Star of Bethlehem made in the vicinity of Flushing, Michigan.

FINISHING OLD TOPS

Mary continued to finish old tops, as she had done from the beginning. And she still enjoyed adding examples of different types of quilts to her collection. She bought a cross-stitched top made by Helen Day in Flint, Michigan. Helen had bought the kit through *Better Homes and Gardens* magazine around 1950. She worked at an automotive supply factory, and she told Mary that she bought the quilt so she would have something to work on during her lunch breaks. Helen finished the top in 1952 and then lost interest in it. She didn't want to do the quilting, and the top lay around until Mary came along. Mary bought the top and finished Cross-Stitch Rose in 1986.

Mary bought the ROSE WREATH top in an antique store near her home. She was always diligent in collecting any and all information about a quilt. The dealer told her that the quilt had been found in Shipshewana, Indiana. What Mary liked about the wreath quilt was the angular seven-sided flowers and the wide inner border.

Besides Mary's quilts, she also has quilt-related items in her Second Collection: an antique C-clamp, a unique thimble, and the sewing bird that

ROSE WREATH
78" × 96½", ca. 1930. Quilt top from Shipshewana, Indiana. Completed by Mary Schafer in 1985.

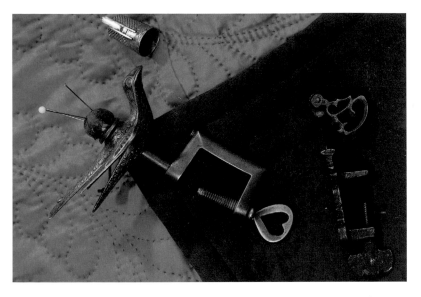

Antique sewing bird and thimble with attachment for cutting thread. (Mary Schafer Collection.)

Mary's friend Robert May had given her. The sewing bird is a beautiful and useful tool that was common in homes in the nineteenth century. The head of the bird is a clamp. The bird has a heart-shaped turning screw used to attach the clamp to the quilting frame. A pincushion on top of the bird's back keeps needles and pins conveniently close by. It is spring loaded so that when you squeeze the tail the beak opens and when the tail is released, the beak snaps shut. Mary tells me the beak worked like a third hand. When the bird was clamped to the edge of a table, the beak would hold one end of cloth tightly and straight while the seamstress stitched.

The antique thimble was a gift from Ruth Parr, the woman from Mississippi with whom Mary corresponded for a number of years. Mary says she has never seen another thimble like it and doesn't know how old it is. She explains, "It has a little attachment that can cut thread and still doesn't interfere with the use of the thimble at all."

Losing your mother as a child is not an easy thing to forget, and Mary never

JULIANNA
79" × 94", 1985. Made by Mary Schafer.

did. She made JULIANNA in memory of her mother, Julianna Zelko Vida, who died of consumption (tuberculosis) at the age of twenty-six. Mary attached a label to this quilt, which reads as follows.

*Julianna Quilt
Cotton 79" × 99", 1984
Made in memory of my mother
Julianna (Zelko) Vida
By
Mary (Vida) Schafer*

Mary made the quilts in her Second Collection for no other reason than that she wanted to make them. By 1980, she had already amassed a body of work representing the major styles of American quilts and had selected a permanent home for the First Collection. She now felt free to pursue whatever struck her fancy. Even so, the quilts she produced after 1980 do pay homage to past quilt makers, a goal of which she never lost sight. The Second Collection personifies the work of a gifted and mature quilt maker. Nice going, Mary.

$\mathcal{M}$otivation

One day I was having a conversation about mary with an artist friend who is not a quilter. She asked me a simple question: why did Mary make quilts? It was a good question, but it caught me by surprise. Usually I can field just about any question I am asked about Mary and her quilts. But this one stopped me cold: I did not have a ready reply.

As a daughter and later as a wife, Mary's life was almost completely defined by the men in her life. As a daughter, her father decided what was best for her. Her married life was shaped by Old World sensibilities. The majority of women who married in the 1920s and 1930s, for the most part, accepted the norm that their husbands made the critical decisions. In those times, the roles of husbands and wives were pretty clearly defined. People expected the husband to be the primary breadwinner, and he was considered to be the head of the family. The wife took care of the house and family.

I never heard Mary complain about her role as a homemaker. Fred was a good husband, and Mary liked taking care of her house and garden.

Still, as a young homemaker, Mary was the kind of woman who needed something else to challenge her. She was smart, capable, and full of energy and had an extremely inquisitive mind. She was also very creative.

Mary found her niche in quilts. Here she had her own identity. She was not someone's daughter, wife, or mother. She created a world all her own, full of challenge and adventure. In this world, she made all the decisions. Within the boundaries of her life as a homemaker, Mary found an acceptable way to express her thoughts and feelings. Now she had something she could really sink her teeth into. Not only could she apply her needlework skills, but she could use her mind. The opportunity for study and discovery thrilled her. It was perfect timing for Mary, as the quilt world she walked into was abuzz with the gathering of quilt history.

From the confines of her home, Mary's world enlarged through correspondence with quilters all over the country. Now she was a part of a new circle of women who shared a common interest. Even more important were the friendships that grew and developed into a support group. For women who were fairly isolated in their homes, this was a true blessing of real importance. As she embraced this new world, it opened itself to her in ways she couldn't have envisioned. Quilts enriched her life. This is a byproduct of quilting that is as true for today's quilters as it was in Mary's time.

I think Mary loved *everything* about the quilt world. She thoroughly enjoyed making quilts, drafting complicated patterns, and creating original designs. She had always enjoyed handwork. She could satisfy her curiosity by researching quilt history. She put her organizational skills to work when documenting her growing pattern collection and other archival materials. She could quench her thirst for learning as she preceded each quilt with investigations into the origin and historical context of the pattern. There was always some new discovery around the corner. Mary loved American history and discovered how closely it was wedded to quilt history. She fairly hurled herself into those bicentennial quilts. The shoe fit.

Mary found satisfaction in bringing esteem to unknown quilt makers of the past. She never lost sight of this. If I heard her talk about this once, I heard her talk about it one hundred times. One means she found of honoring past quilters was to finish old tops and make reproductions of old, worn quilts.

COUNTRY HOME
77″ × 96″, 1986. Made by Mary Schafer.

In addition, Mary always found it rewarding to educate and inspire new quilters and quilt admirers. She took this responsibility so seriously that it altered the course of her own quilt making. She shifted direction in 1977. I remember talking to her on numerous occasions about a profound insight she had regarding the impact of her work on others. While she was pleased with people's admiration for her complicated and exquisitely executed quilts, she detected something in their response that bothered her. She was dismayed to notice that these quilts often intimidated new quilters. Concerned that she might discourage new quilters, she determined to stop making elaborate quilts and return to simple pieced patterns. She wanted to make quilts that would be accessible to as many quilters as possible.

This calculated and truly remarkable decision clearly reveals that her motivation for making quilts was never selfish or designed to bring her personal acclaim. Rather, it was always simply about the quilts.

YARMOUTH SQUARE
78½″ × 96½″, 1984. Made by Mary Schafer.

This change in philosophy resulted in quilts such as COUNTRY HOME, YARMOUTH SQUARE, and PINWHEEL. Of the latter, Mary says, "This simple design would be a good one for a beginning quilter. Also a good 'rest' design—to rest while making, or in between more involved piecing or appliqué, or when a simple design would be more appropriate."[1]

Taking a simple pattern and treating it seriously results in quilts like COUNTRY HOME and YARMOUTH SQUARE. The name YARMOUTH SQUARE came from an untitled quilt Mary saw in a picture in *Country Living* magazine. The illustration showed the quilt on a bed in a Yarmouth, Massachusetts, home on Cape Cod.

While obviously capable of piecing the most complex of patterns, Mary had a special affection for simple pieced patterns. These were, she knew, at the very heart of the American quilting experience, as the vast majority of quilts were made from common, simple patterns. Her repeated return to this humble style shows her love of quilts over personal acclaim. Mary was confident in her quilt making and in herself. She had nothing to prove to anyone. This is a wonderful, freeing attitude to hold—and a refreshing attitude to behold.

When Mary decided to make simple quilts that would encourage and inspire new quilters, she wanted to demonstrate that simple quilts can also be artistically successful. A good example is ONE AND FOUR SQUARE, an extremely basic pattern made of squares. Yet under Mary's direction this quilt is a beautiful example of strong graphic design. She described this quilt, saying, "this simple block pattern is given interest by the pieced lattice strips."

CHURN DASH is another simple quilt. Made with a variety of blue prints, it has a delightful, fresh look. Mary used the same appliqué border motif she had used on the blue and white CHURN DASH, which Betty Harriman started and Mary finished.

I remember being awestruck by Mary's decision to focus on simple quilts in order to promote quilt making in general. For Mary, it was always about quilts, just about quilts. I love her for it.

Mary's motivation came from a deeply rooted love of quilts. This was true for other quilt enthusiasts of the time. Although comparatively small, the quilt world in the 1950s and 1960s was hardcore. While it was not as visible as it is today, it was intense.

In Mary's heyday, commercialization had little influence on quilt making. People neither spent money nor made money on quilts as they do today. No one got rich or had "careers" making and selling new quilts, collecting and studying quilts, or writing and lecturing about quilts. Antique quilts and blocks could be bought at reasonable prices. Women such as Florence Peto and Lenice Bacon, both highly respected lecturers, made little if any money. Dolores Hinson began lecturing sometime around 1955, and she lectured "for nothing but thanks at that time."[2] When Mary began giving some lectures in the 1970s, she was content with a ten dollar fee. Interest and personal satisfaction, certainly not financial reward, motivated the scholars, quilt makers, and collectors of that time.

In the first quarter of the twentieth century, Marie Webster did get a successful commercial enterprise off the

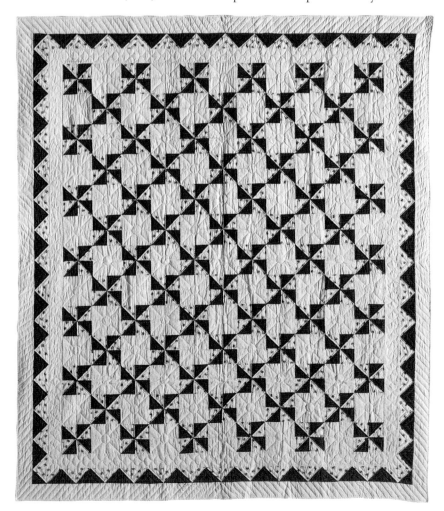

PINWHEEL
85" × 97", 1980. Made by Mary Schafer.

ONE AND FOUR SQUARE
83″ × 96¹/₂″, 1981. Made by Mary Schafer.

MOURNING QUILT
80″ × 94″, ca.1875–1900. Top made by Eliza Fairchilds, East Jordan, Michigan.
Completed by Mary Schafer in 1983.

ground. She sold her own original patterns, kits, and quilts. Still, her efforts pale in comparison with modern commercial ventures.

Before the mid-1970s, there was not yet a strong audience of quilt "consumers" to support quilt businesses. Quilt makers were still content with making quilts primarily from scraps, and they accomplished the task with basic sewing tools. Fabric made specifically for quilters did not exist, nor did tools made specifically for quilters. I doubt that anyone even thought of opening a "quilt shop" to sell supplies to "quilters."

The rewards for excellence in quilt making were modest by today's standards. Regional and state fairs gave women avenues to show their work and be recognized, but prize ribbons were the reward and fame stayed on a local level. Mary almost always won ribbons at such events, and I imagine such validation gave her satisfaction. Still, for Mary it was about quilts, not winning. As she encouraged others to enter shows, she purposely avoided entering in the same category in case she might take a ribbon away from a friend. She talked me into entering my second quilt (a red and white Irish Chain) in the Saginaw Fair in either 1978 or 1979. I won a blue ribbon, and my prize was a Mountain Mist quilt batt.

In the years since then, there have been dramatic changes. Quilt competitions began to offer larger and ever larger cash prizes. With well-organized quilt guilds and more quilting magazines spreading the word, excellent quilters might hope to fatten their wallets and gain national attention. The stakes are much higher.

As described in earlier chapters, uncovering quilt history was the primary driving force quilt enthusiasts shared in the early years. Continuing her quest to collect quilt history continues to motivate Mary. Always fascinated with the unusual, when she found the MOURNING QUILT she was glad to add it to her collection. Mary thinks this quilt, with its simple design and somber color, may be a traditional funeral cover. Her note attached to the quilt reads as follows.

*"Mourning Quilt Top made by Eliza Andrews Fairchilds, East Jordan, MI.
c. 1875–1900. Assembled and completed by MVS, Flushing June 3, 1983."*

While it was certainly complex and manifested in many disciplines—sewing, history, organization, and teaching—at the core of Mary's motivation was an abiding love of quilts.

The Quilts in the First Collection

 MARY SCHAFER'S FIRST COLLECTION OF QUILTS NUMBERED 118: 63 antique quilts, 38 full-size quilts made by Mary Schafer, and 17 of the Harriman/Schafer collaborations. Within the classification of quilts made solely by Mary Schafer are the acclaimed challenge and bicentennial quilts.

The 118 quilts that originally comprised Mary's First Collection were collected and/or made prior to 1980. The First Collection was acquired by the Michigan State University Museum in 1998. It plans to sell all but 75 of the quilts. As of this writing, the museum has sold 16. Quilts that are no longer in the collection are marked with an asterisk.

Mary often said that her quilts spoke for her. If you know how to read them, they tell the Mary Schafer story. The first quilts Mary made were kit quilts.

Poppy Wreath. 78″ × 93″, 1953.

For her first pieced quilt, Mary copied from an old, unnamed quilt. In making this quilt, she formulated the defining characteristics from which her mature work evolved. This was the quilt that captured Mary's heart and mind and turned her into a quilter.

Linden Mill. 80″ × 94″, 1956.

Mary made her second pieced quilt from an old pattern.

*Fox and Geese. 78″ × 90″, 1964.

The next quilt was made from antique blocks.

Star and Cross. 82″ × 100″, 1964.

In 1966, Mary set a challenge for herself: To make a series of tribute quilts for those who had inspired her and whom she admired. This culminated in seven spectacular quilts. CLAMSHELL, made to honor Ruth Finley, won Best Pieced and Viewers' Choice at the first National Quilt Association Contest in 1970. In 1968, Mary made Coxcomb for Glenna Boyd, HONEY BEE for Ruby McKim, and WASHINGTON PLUME for Betty Harriman. In 1969, Mary made LOBSTER for Florence Peto and OAK LEAF AND CHERRIES for Rose Wilder Lane. She completed the series with SAVANNAH STAR, paying homage to unknown quilt makers. These seven ambitious challenge quilts demonstrate Mary's technical expertise, artistic vision, and dedication to honoring women.

Clamshell. 79″ × 97½″, 1966.
Coxcomb. 84½″ × 98″, 1968.
Honey Bee. 79″ × 95″, 1968.
Washington Plume. 93″ × 93″, 1968.
Lobster. 80″ × 94″, 1969.
Oak Leaf and Cherries. 80″ × 100″, 1969.
Savannah Star. 76½″ × 97″, 1970.

Considering that Mary sews completely by hand, the challenge quilts represent an impressive output, but at that time she was in full gear. During the challenge period, she also snuck in a few other quilts:

Variable Star. 84″ × 95″, 1967.
Eisenhower. 56″ × 102″, 1968.
North Carolina Lily. 79″ × 96″, 1971.
October Foliage. 84½″ × 94″, 1971.

In 1972, Mary made her Lee's Rose and Buds from a pattern Betty Harriman sent. The pattern is attributed to the Robert E. Lee home.

Lee's Rose and Buds. 81″ × 99½″, 1972.

Her interest in historical quilts and traditional patterns prompted Pineapples, inspired by a quilt in the Shelburne Museum, and Variable Star, a copy of an old quilt from Wiscassett, Maine.

Pineapples. 82″ × 100″, 1973.
Variable Star. 82″ × 99″, 1973.
Wild Goose Chase. 84″ × 101″, 1973.
Single Chain and Knot. 87″ × 99″, 1974.

Mary celebrated the bicentennial by making five new quilts with patriotic themes. She included WASHINGTON PLUME (a copy of a quilt at Mount Vernon made as a tribute to Betty Harriman) to bring the series to six outstanding quilts.

Queen Charlotte's Crown. 76″ × 98″, 1973.
Burgoyne Surrounded. 84″ × 103½″, 1974.
Lafayette Orange Peel. 85″ × 100″, 1974.
Spirit of '76. 82½″ × 100½″, 1974.
Molly Pitcher. 78½″ × 106″, 1975.

As she rushed to complete her ambitious bicentennial series, Mary somehow found time to hand piece three more quilts:

Hidden Star. 80½″ × 99″, 1974.
*Attic Window. 80″ × 100″, 1975.
*Delectable Mountains. 88″ × 100″, 1975.

Her interest in quilts with historical themes did not cease at the conclusion of the bicentennial celebrations. Double Hour Glass is a copy of one of her antique Michigan-made quilts. Dutchman's Puzzle is made from fabrics dating from the early 1900s. It won a blue ribbon for "best pieced quilt from old fabrics" at the 1978 Festival of Quilts Contest in Santa Rosa, California. TOBACCO LEAF is an example of Mary's approach to research and design in her work. As mentioned before, she learned that before the cultivation of tobacco by white settlers Jamestown was a virtual prison camp riddled with disease and on the edge of failure. After the natives introduced tobacco to the settlers, it became the first commercial crop harvested in America. Tobacco was the salvation of the new settlement. The quilt is green and brown to suggest the tobacco leaf. Mary designed a pieced border using a traditional pattern called Tree of Life, reminiscent of native design.

Double Hour Glass. 81″ × 98″, 1976.
Dutchman's Puzzle. 80″ × 98″, 1976.
Georgetown Circle. 83½″ × 98″, 1977.
*Tobacco Leaf. 79½″ × 96½″, 1977.

During the same period, Mary became interested in Amish quilts and made two classical Lancaster County Amish-style quilts.

Bars. 75″ × 83½″, 1976.
Sunshine and Shadow. 83″ × 83″, 1977.

Later pieced quilts include the following.

String Star. 81″ × 97″, 1977.
*Morning Star. 81″ × 101″, 1978.
Black Elegance. 82½″ × 99″, 1980.

Mary completed two antique tops from Michigan in 1980. Three Sisters was collected in Michigan and Pyramid was made by Matilda Vary of Ceresco, Michigan. She finished 1980 with a variation of the Mariner's Compass block that shows Mary's ability to draft and make complicated patterns.

Three Sisters. 85″ × 100″, ca. 1918. Top, completed 1980.
Pyramid. 83″ × 98″, ca. 1876. Top, completed 1980.
Sunburst. 80″ × 97″, 1980.

The Harriman/Schafer Quilts

The Betty Harriman/Mary Schafer tale is one of the most remarkable and heartfelt stories in quilt literature. A deep love and respect had grown between these two women as they corresponded over many years. They never met face to face. When Betty died in 1971, Mary acquired all of her unfinished work sight unseen. Betty had been a prolific quilt maker. She had many ambitious works in progress, of which Mary eventually completed twenty quilts begun by Betty and three antique tops from the Harriman estate. As some of the quilts were started in the 1920s, they span sixty years in the making. The First Collection contains seventeen Harriman/Schafer quilts, fifteen begun by Betty and two antique tops that she collected.

The first quilt Mary finished was a copy of a Robert E. Lee quilt that Betty and Mary were both making versions of when Betty died.

Lee's Rose and Buds. 84″ × 101″. Begun 1969, finished 1972.

Next came a complex Marie Webster pattern. Betty hadn't started this quilt. Mary received the pattern and fabric only.

Grapes and Vines. 83½″ × 97″, 1972.

Two more appliqués followed.

Missouri Rose Tree. 89″ × 92″. Begun 1966, finished 1973.
Pennsylvania Dutch Flower Garden. 81″ × 103″. Beginning date
    unknown, finished 1973.

Mary took time out from the Harriman quilt project to prepare for the bicentennial. After the celebration was over, she returned to the Harriman quilts with a vengeance. Between 1977 and 1980, she completed thirteen more of Betty's "starts," as she called them.

Star of Bethlehem. 79½″ × 96″, ca. 1940–50. Top, finished 1977.
Colonial Basket. 83½″ × 96″. Beginning date unknown, finished 1978.
Drunkard's Path. 84″ × 97″. Begun 1937, finished 1980.

Among the quilts were two WASHINGTON PLUMEs. Mary wasn't surprised. Betty was related to our first president through marriage and had a passion for American history.

Washington Plume. 90″ × 96″. Top ca. 1965, finished 1978.
*Washington Plume. 88″ × 96″. Top ca. 1965, finished 1980.

Mary worked like a woman on a hallowed quest. Five appliqués were finished in 1978 and 1979 and the last in 1980. FLOWERING ALMOND, a popular motif in the nineteenth century, has a most unusual border treatment. ENGLISH PLUME is the last Harriman quilt Mary would receive from Betty's estate. It is unusual in color and scale, with the center plume measuring seventy inches across. According to Betty, it is a copy of an Ohio quilt made in the late 1800s.

*Holland Queen. 83″ × 99″. Begun ca. 1965, finished 1978.
Alice Blue Wreath. 90″ × 93″. Begun ca. 1966, finished 1979.
Democratic Rose. 83″ × 101″. Begun 1923, finished 1979.
Flowering Almond. 85″ × 99″. Begun ca. 1968, finished 1979.
*English Plume. 82″ × 98½″. Begun 1967, finished 1979.
York County. 92″ × 92″. Begun ca. 1963, finished 1980.

Mary also finished two antique tops that she had received from the Harriman estate.

Boxes. 89″ × 99″. Top ca. 1900, finished 1980.

Eight-Pointed Star. 85″ × 100″. Top ca. 1850, finished 1980.

When Mary was asked why she had taken on the enormous task of finishing so many elaborate quilts, she answered, "because she was my friend."

ANTIQUE QUILTS

The First Collection is noteworthy because of its sixty-three antique quilts, which fall into three categories: thirty-six antique quilts, seven old tops or blocks finished into quilts, and twenty documented Michigan-made quilts.

The first quilt Mary collected was Feather-Edged Star. Album is a dated quilt in exceptionally fine condition. Mary bought five outstanding antique quilts from Betty Harriman: Sunburst, Four Patch, Mariner's Compass, Framed Square, and an all white stuffed quilt. Other enduring favorites include Love Apple, three Whig Rose quilts and a second all white quilt.

This collection is unique in that all the quilts were selected to constitute a survey of quilt making in America.

THIRTY-SIX ANTIQUE QUILTS

1. Album. 85″ × 92″, dated 1856. Bird-in-Hand, Pennsylvania.
2. Bars. 77″ × 87″, ca. 1876. Pennsylvania Amish quilt.
3. Cracker. 70″ × 84″, ca. 1900. Michiana, Indiana.
*4. Delectable Mountains Variation. 100″ × 100″, ca. 1850. Bird-in-Hand, Pennsylvania.
5. Dutch Iris. 94″ × 96″, ca. 1900–1910. Westchester, Pennsylvania.
6. Feather-Edged Star. 74″ × 90″, ca. 1850. Ora Brown, Monroeville, Indiana.
*7. Fly Foot. 82″ × 96½″, ca. 1915. Goderich, Ontario, Canada.
8. Four Patch. 99½″ × 104″, ca. 1800–1825. Harriman.
9. Framed Square. 97″ × 102″, ca. 1800–1825. Quilt has cutout corners. Harriman.
10. Linden Mill. 68″ × 76″, ca. 1900. Michigan.
11. Love Apple. 94″ × 96″, ca. 1850. Signed quilt: Susannah Allen, Gettysburg, Pennsylvania.
12. Mariner's Compass. 97″ × 100″, ca. 1830–50. Harriman.
13. Mrs. Ewer's Tulip. 85″ × 86″, ca. 1850–75. Signed quilt: Ellie.
14. Nine-Patch Variation. 92″ × 92″, ca. 1800–25.
15. North Carolina Lily. 82″ × 83″, ca. 1920. Breezewood, Pennsylvania.
16. North Carolina Lily. 77″ × 93″, ca. 1925. Collected in Flint, Michigan.
17. Path through the Woods. 71″ × 83″, ca. 1900. Collected in Flint, Michigan.

*18. Pine Tree. 65″ × 72″, 1886. Dated quilt, Franklin County, Ohio.

19. Poppy. 82″ × 82″, ca. 1850–75. West Chester, Pennsylvania.

*20. Rose and Hearts. 82½″ × 98″, 1963. Made by Ella McInturff, Mannington, West Virginia.

*21. Rose of Sharon. 74″ × 79″, ca. 1875–1900.

*22. Rose Wreath. 76½″ × 78″, ca. 1850. Fayetteville, Pennsylvania.

23. Savannah Star. 81″ × 81″, ca. 1910–20. Collected in Flint, Michigan.

24. Single Tulip. 69″ × 97″, ca. 1860. Collected in Salem, Michigan.

25. Single Tulip. 82″ × 82″, ca. 1850. Lintner family, Hamilton, Ohio.

26. Single Wedding Ring. 81″ × 81″, ca. 1900–1915. Collected in Flint, Michigan.

27. Snowball. 82″ × 85″, ca. 1900. Mt. Morris, Michigan.

28. Sunburst. 86″ × 86″, ca. 1825. New England. Harriman.

29. Sunflower or Sunburst. 79½″ × 96″, ca. 1875. Macomb County, Michigan.

30. Valley Star. 86″ × 88″, ca. 1900–1910. Collected in Flint, Michigan.

31. Whig Rose. 104″ × 106″, ca. 1834. Greenfield, Massachusetts.

32. Whig Rose. 89″ × 90″, ca. 1850. West Chester, Pennsylvania (on white print ground).

33. Whig Rose. 89″ × 90″, ca. 1850. West Chester, Pennsylvania (on mustard yellow print ground).

34. White Quilt. 82″ × 83″, 1837. Signed and dated: "Theresa M. Hamilton, October 8, 1837, Harpersfield." Stuffed and trapunto quilt.

35. White Quilt. 78″ × 88″, ca. 1800–1810. Stuffed and trapunto quilt. Harriman.

36. White Quilt. 75″ × 85″, ca. 1950. Fayetteville, Pennsylvania.

Mary rescued antique tops and bought old blocks when she found them. When she finished an old top, she often added a border before sending it out for quilting. She has made a number of quilts from antique blocks, including Star and Cross and Hazel Hanks' Star, which was said to have been made by a relative of Nancy Hanks, Abraham Lincoln's mother.

Seven Old Tops or Blocks
Finished by Mary Schafer

*1. Churn Dash. 82″ × 92″, ca. 1915. Top collected in Flint, Michigan. Mary added the border and completed the quilt.

2. Good Fortune. 81½″ × 93″, ca. 1915–20. Top collected in Flint, Michigan, completed by Mary Schafer.

3. Hazel Hanks' Star. 76″ × 94″, ca. 1926. Blocks said to be made by Hazel Hanks, Springfield, Illinois, descendant of Nancy Hanks, Abraham Lincoln's mother.

4. Path through the Woods Variation. 82″ × 98″, ca. 1935. Top collected in Flint, Michigan. Mary added the border and completed the quilt.

5. Star and Cross. 82″ × 100″, ca. 1860. Mary bought the blocks and made the quilt in 1964.

6. Three Sisters. 85″ × 100″, ca. 1918. Top collected in Flushing, Michigan. Mary added the border and completed the quilt in 1980.

7. Turkey Tracks. 82″ × 101″, ca. 1910. Tied quilt bought in poor condition. Mary took it apart, repaired the top, added the border, and completed the quilt in 1968.

Always careful to document the quilts she collected as thoroughly as possible, Mary accumulated twenty Michigan-made antique quilts. She wanted them to stay in the state where they originated. Sunrise is notable because of its fine workmanship. Full Blown Tulip, Odd-Fellows Patch, and Strips of Triangles are particularly appealing samples of regional folk art. Eight of these quilts were tops Mary collected and finished.

Twenty Documented Michigan-Made Antique Quilts

1. Album. 85″ × 96″, ca. 1900. DesJardin family, Essexville, Michigan.

2. Bear's Paw. 86″ × 94″, ca. 1890–1910. Adella Penoyer, Flushing, Michigan. Mary added the border and completed the quilt.

3. Chimney Sweep. 80½″ × 98½″, ca. 1923. Emma Catherine Zink Frey, Flint, Michigan.

4. Courthouse Steps. 75″ × 87″, ca. 1926. Top by Clara Bloss, Swartz Creek, Michigan. Completed by Mary Schafer.

5. Diamond in a Square. 79″ × 96½″, ca. 1890. Top by Eliza Andrews Fairchilds, East Jordan, Michigan. Mary added the border and completed the quilt.

6. Double Hour Glass. 77½″ × 86½″, ca. 1910–15. James Pollack family, Genesee County, Michigan.

*7. Double Pyramid. 71″ × 83″, ca. 1850–75. Martha Wade Sherwood, Holly, Michigan.

8. Drunkard's Path. 85″ × 98″, ca. 1887. Top by Martha Wade Sherwood, Holly, Michigan. Completed by Mary Schafer.

9. Drunkard's Path Variation. 79″ × 88″, ca. 1850. Top by Israel Parshall family, Saginaw County, Michigan. Completed by Mary Schafer.

10. Full Blown Tulip. 72″ × 87″, ca. 1850. Israel Parshall family, Saginaw County, Michigan.

11. Log Cabin, Barn Raising. 88″ × 100″, ca. 1915–20. DesJardin family, Essexville, Michigan.

12. Log Cabin, Sun and Shadow. 66″ × 77½″, ca. 1875. Taylor family, Flint, Michigan.

13. London Stairs. 78½″ × 97½″, ca. 1895. Top by Eliza Andrews Fairchilds, East Jordan, Michigan. Mary added the border and completed the quilt.

14. Ocean Waves. 72″ × 72″, ca. 1900. Ralph Bartholomew family, Clio, Michigan.

15. Odd-Fellows Patch. 76″ × 84″, ca. 1870–80. Matilda Vary, Ceresco, Michigan.

16. Pyramid. 83″ × 98″, ca. 1876. Top by Matilda Vary, Ceresco, Michigan.

17. Sawtooth. 82″ × 98½″, ca. 1876. Top by Matilda Vary, Ceresco, Michigan. Mary added the border and completed the quilt.

18. Strips of Triangles. 68″ × 76″, ca. 1910–15. Anna Rolf, Flushing, Michigan.

19. Sunrise. 68″ × 101″, ca. 1863. Susan Brown, Owosso, Michigan.

20. Thousand Pyramids. 84″ × 100″, ca. 1890. DesJardin family, Essexville, Michigan.

The Quilts in the Second Collection

MARY HAD A BIG YEAR IN 1980. IT WAS THE YEAR THAT determined which quilts would comprise the First Collection and which would make up the second. And it was Mary's most prolific year. A total of twenty full-size quilts passed through her hands that year. The nine quilts that were completed in time to be listed in *The Mary Schafer Quilt Collection* catalog (Marston 1980) became part of the First Collection, and the other eleven became part of the second. Refer to the "Mary Schafer Timeline" for a list of these twenty quilts.

The Second Collection contains 106 quilts. It features 33 full-size quilts made by Mary. It contains 61 small quilts, of which all but 4 were made by Mary. It includes 6 more Harriman/Schafer quilts, 4 antique tops Mary finished, and 2 antique quilts she purchased. Working as a mature quilt maker and for her own pleasure, the quilts Mary made from 1980 onward are as exciting as those housed in the First Collection.

FULL-SIZE QUILTS

The Second Collection contains thirty-three full-size bed quilts made by Mary. The year 1980 was one of her most prolific. It was the year she became interested in early-style medallion quilts and produced a series of four spectacular quilts.

Bird of Paradise. 84″ × 99″, 1980.
Countryside. 80″ × 86″, 1980.
The Harvesters. 82″ × 95½″, 1980.
Welsh Medallion. 76″ × 85″, 1980.

While working on the medallion series, Mary found time to make GIANT TULIP, a reproduction of a nineteenth-century appliqué, and two fine pieced scrap quilts.

Giant Tulip. 75″ × 86″, 1980.
Grandmother's Pride. 79″ × 99″, 1980.
Flower Pot. 79″ × 99″, 1980.

At the same time, she was working on a series of simple quilts as a way to encourage new quilters. She feared that her more ambitious works intimidated new prospects, and she determined to make quilts that would invite recruits not frighten them away.

Ebb Tide. 72″ × 96½″, 1980.
Kaleidoscope. 79″ × 100″, 1980.
Pinwheel. 81″ × 96″, 1980.

Mary ended the year by returning to LINDEN MILL. She made a second version, this time in blue and white.

Linden Mill. 81″ × 96″, 1980.

Mary's interest in Amish quilts continued. BEAR'S PAW, made in 1981, was a copy of a Midwest Amish quilt in the Marston collection. BASKETS (1985) was also made in the Midwest Amish style.

Bear's Paw. 71″ × 85″, 1981.
Baskets. 58″ × 71″, 1985.

Rebecca Merritt, made in 1981, was a copy of an original made in New York State around 1800.

Rebecca Merritt. 76″ × 97″, 1981.

From 1981 to 1983, she continued her efforts to make simple quilts, hoping to encourage newcomers to the craft. She was also beginning to shift her attention to doll quilts, beginning in 1982, leaving fewer hours in the day to make large quilts.

One and Four Square. 83″ × 96½″, 1981.
Scallops. 77″ × 95″, 1982.
Churn Dash. 76″ × 79″, 1982.
Evening Star. 78″ × 93″, 1982.
Spring Woodland. 78″ × 95″, 1983.
Variable Star. 77″ × 87″, 1983.

Over the next several years, Mary made fewer full-size quilts as she concentrated on small quilts. YARMOUTH SQUARE, based on the traditional Nine Patch, is another of her simple quilts. During this period, she also made the incredibly beautiful and technically demanding Feather-Edged Star and PRAIRIE QUEEN, which delights everyone who has seen it. Mary also decided to make a quilt in memory of her mother, Julianna Zelko Vida, who died when Mary was only five years old.

Yarmouth Square. 78½″ × 96½″, 1984.
Feather-Edged Star. 77″ × 97″, 1984.
Spools. 76½″ × 95″, 1985.
Prairie Queen. 82″ × 97″, 1985.
Julianna. 79″ × 94″, 1985.

CUPS AND SAUCERS demonstrates Mary's understanding of how to make traditional patterns her own. This beautiful pieced quilt in blue and white features a perfectly engineered sawtooth border and her exquisite quilting designs. In 1990, she made two classical appliqués, ROSE WREATH and POMEGRANATE, and in 1991 she made FRIENDSHIP STAR, another scrappy pieced quilt in her typical style.

MONTEREY NINE PATCH is a reminder of Mary's ability to work with simple patterns and in a nineteenth-century style. With this quilt, she returned to the very roots of American quilt making. It is fitting that her last full-size quilt would be a Nine Patch. While she was capable of making elegant and formal quilts such as ROSE WREATH and POMEGRANATE, she always had a fondness for the simple designs familiar to so many quilters of the past.

Cups and Saucers. 80½″ × 95½″, 1989.
Rose Wreath. 82″ × 82″, 1990.
Pomegranate. 82″ × 94″, 1990.
Friendship Star. 78″ × 91″, 1991.
Monterey Nine Patch. 76″ × 90″, 1992.

All the quilts in the Second Collection, with the exception of two, were made in 1980 or later. These were originally part of the First Collection, but

Mary didn't want to part with them for personal reasons. She made RADICAL ROSE specifically for her bedroom, and she wanted to keep SHOO FLY because it was her husband's favorite quilt.

Radical Rose. 80″ × 97″, 1965.
Shoo Fly. 81″ × 98″, 1977.

HARRIMAN/SCHAFER QUILTS

Periodically Mary would complete another Harriman quilt. Six are included in the Second Collection. The Framed Nine Patch is an antique top from the Harriman estate that Mary had quilted.

Churn Dash. 78″ × 95″. 1983.
Democratic Rose. 80″ × 95″. Begun ca. 1960, finished 1981.
Dresden Plate. 80″ × 97″. Finished 1986.
Joseph's Coat. 79″ × 93″. Begun ca. 1960, finished 1984.
Washington Rose. 90½″ × 92″. Begun 1969, finished 1984.
Framed Nine Patch. 87″ × 93″. Antique top from Harriman estate, completed 1986.

DOLL QUILTS

The majority of Mary's thirty-four doll quilts were made between 1982 and 1985. Mary made all but four quilts in this collection. She found working on a small scale delightful. It allowed for experimentation not possible in large, hand-stitched quilts.

All quilts listed here were made by Mary with the exception of two antique quilts (numbers 10 and 17) and two quilts given to Mary by her friend Hildegard Hoag (numbers 6 and 18).

1. Amish Sunshine and Shadow. 21½″ × 21½″, 1982.
2. Birds in Flight. 18¾″ × 22¼″, 1984.
3. Bow Tie. 21″ × 27″, 1982. Amish.
4. Bow Tie. 18½″ × 24¼″, 1982.
5. Churn Dash. 19¼″ × 25″.
6. Clamshell. 20″ × 23″. Gift to Mary from Hildegard Hoag.
7. Dear Hearts. 19″ × 23½″, 1985.
8. Hit and Miss. 17¼″ × 23¼″, 1982.
9. Honeycomb. 20″ × 26½″, 1985.
10. Material Pleasures. 12″ × 17¾″. Antique quilt, date unknown.
11. Material Pleasures. 15½″ × 19½″, 1982.

12. One and Four Square. 19″ × 23″.

13. One and Four Square. 12¼″ × 15¼″.

14. One and Four Square. 14¼″ × 14¼″, 1986.

15. One and Four Square. 17¾″ × 21¼″, 1982.

16. One Patch. 15¼″ × 18″, 1982.

17. One Patch. 17½″ × 24½″. Antique.

18. One Patch. 20¼″ × 29″. Hildegard's gift.

19. One-Patch Floral, Nine-Patch Center. 15¼″ × 18¼″.

20. One-Patch Raffle Quilt. 16″ × 18″.

21. Peach and Rose. 18½″ × 22″.

22. Persian Pear. 22″ × 22½″.

23. Pieced-Look Print with Church Print Border. 18½″ × 22¾″.

24. Pink Print and Plain. 18¾″ × 23¼″.

25. Pinwheel. 15½″ × 15½″.

26. Puss in a Corner. 17¾″ × 19¼″.

27. Pyramid. 18¼″ × 21¾″, 1982.

28. Sunshine and Shadow. 21¾″ × 22½″, 1982.

29. Surfer's Wave. 19¾″ × 20″, 1982.

30. Thirty-six Small Hearts. 19½″ × 20¾″.

31. Tumbler. 20½″ × 23½″, 1982.

32. Vera Town Nine Patch. 12¾″ × 17″.

33. Vertical Stripes. 16¾″ × 21¼″, 1982.

34. Yellow Nine Patch. 16¼″ × 21″, 1982.

Twenty-seven Crib Quilts Made by Mary

1. Attic Window. 29½″ × 38″, 1984 or 1985.

2. Cactus Basket. 40″ × 50½″, 1983 or 1984.

3. Cherry Basket. 39¾″ × 47″, 1985.

4. Dear Hearts. 38″ × 43″, 1986.

5. India, Clamshell. 36″ × 43½″, 1984 or 1985.

6. Painted Circle. 40¼″ × 40¾″, 1982.

7. Pennsylvania Dutch Nine-Patch Variation. 43″ × 49″, 1986.

8. Periwinkle. 36¾″ × 44¾″, 1983 or 1984.

9. Pinwheels. 42″ × 51″, 1982.

10. Roses and Hearts. 43½″ × 43½″, 1982.

11. Sixteen Patch. 38″ × 47″, 1983 or 1984.

12. Sun Bonnet Babies. 36½″ × 45″, 1984 or 1985.

13. Yankee Puzzle. 26½″ × 45″, 1965. Mary's first crib quilt.

14. Album. 37″ × 37½″, 1985.
15. Bars. 46¼″ × 46¼″, 1984.
16. Bow Tie. 32″ × 41½″, 1982.
17. Bricks. 33″ × 38½″, 1985.
18. Carolina Lily. 33″ × 50″, 1982.
19. Chinese Coins. 42″ × 49″, 1985.
20. Old Maid's Puzzle. 33¼″ × 42″, 1982.
21. One Patch. 38″ × 50″, 1982.
22. One Patch. 43″ × 43″, 1983. Also called Checkerboard.
23. Roman Stripe. 35″ × 43½″, 1982.
24. Sunshine and Shadow. 39″ × 39″, 1983.
25. Sunshine and Shadow. 47½″ × 47½″, 1982.
26. Sunshine and Shadow. 46″ × 47″, 1984.
27. Sunshine and Shadow. 49″ × 49″, 1984.

Two Antique Quilts
Mary Purchased after 1980

1. Cups and Saucers. 69″ × 80¼″, ca. 1920–30. Midwest Amish.
2. Star of Bethlehem. 71″ × 87″, ca. 1930. Stiffel family quilt purchased in Flushing, Michigan.

Four Quilt Tops Finished by Mary

1. Cross-Stitch Rose. 83″ × 97″. Completed in 1986.
2. Monticello. 76″ × 94″, ca. 1920. All white top completed in 1981. Quilted by Mary Ann Miller.
3. Mourning Quilt. 80″ × 94″. Top ca. 1875–1900. Top made by Eliza Andrews Fairchilds, East Jordan, Michigan. Completed in 1983.
4. Rose Wreath. 78″ × 96½″, ca. 1930, Shipshewana, Indiana. Completed in 1985.

Mary still has quite a number of unfinished works. Quilt makers don't just stop making quilts one day, but they slow down when they reach ninety-two years of age. In a letter to Gwen Marston dated February 5, 2002, Mary reminded Gwen that "I'm still interested in quilts but don't do much sewing. I do what I can—and thankful I can."

Ten Mary Schafer Quilt Patterns

FLOWER POT

PRAIRIE QUEEN

GRANDMOTHER'S PRIDE

CHURN DASH

BASKETS

BEAR'S PAW

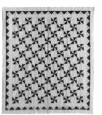
PINWHEEL

WASHINGTON ROSE

LINDEN MILL

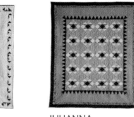
JULIANNA

FLOWER POT
$7^3/_4'' \times 7^3/_4''$
Add $^1/_4''$ seam allowance to each pattern piece.

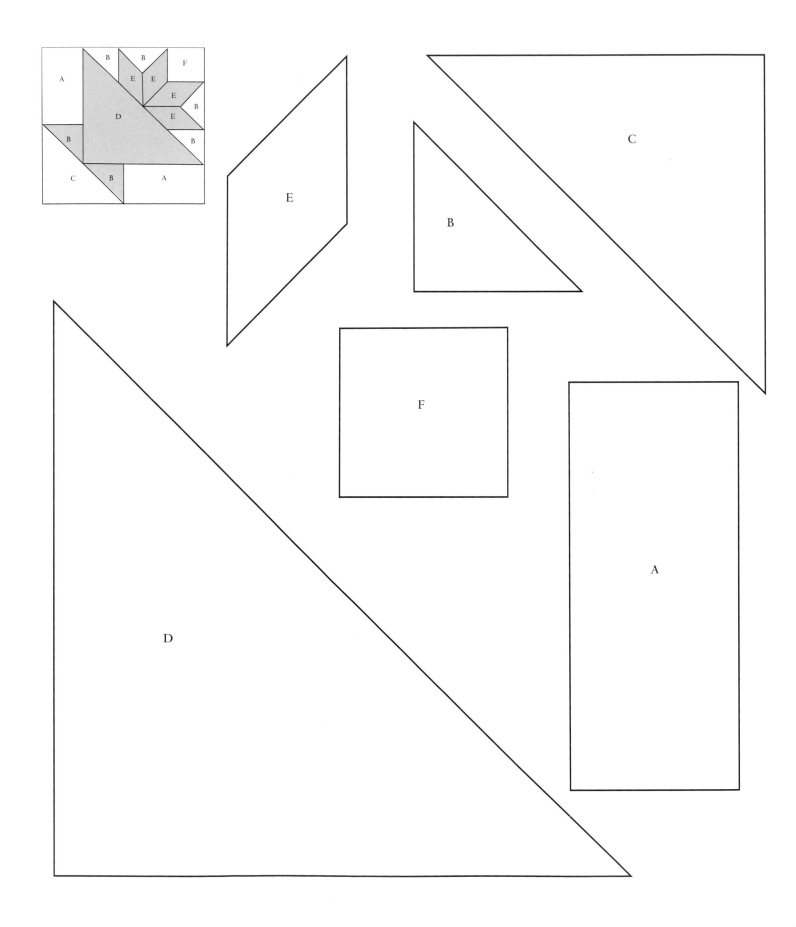

PRAIRIE QUEEN
9″ × 9″
Add ¼″ seam allowance to each pattern piece.

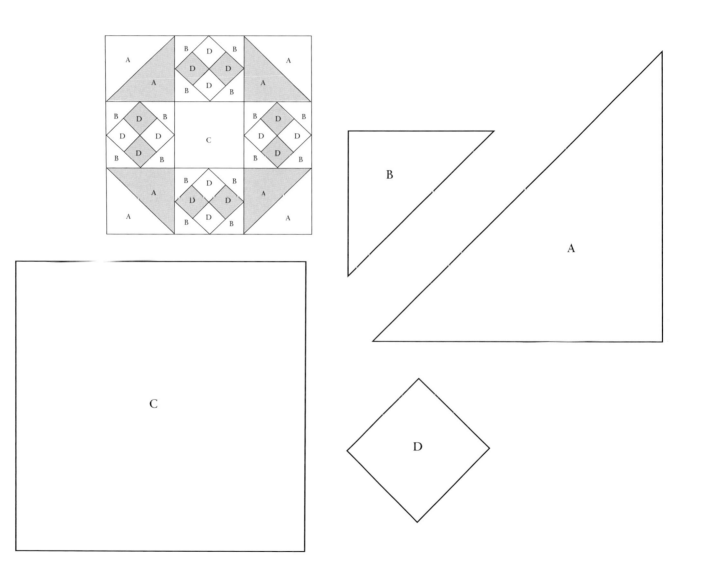

GRANDMOTHER'S PRIDE
9″ × 9″
Add ¹⁄₄″ seam allowance to each pattern piece.

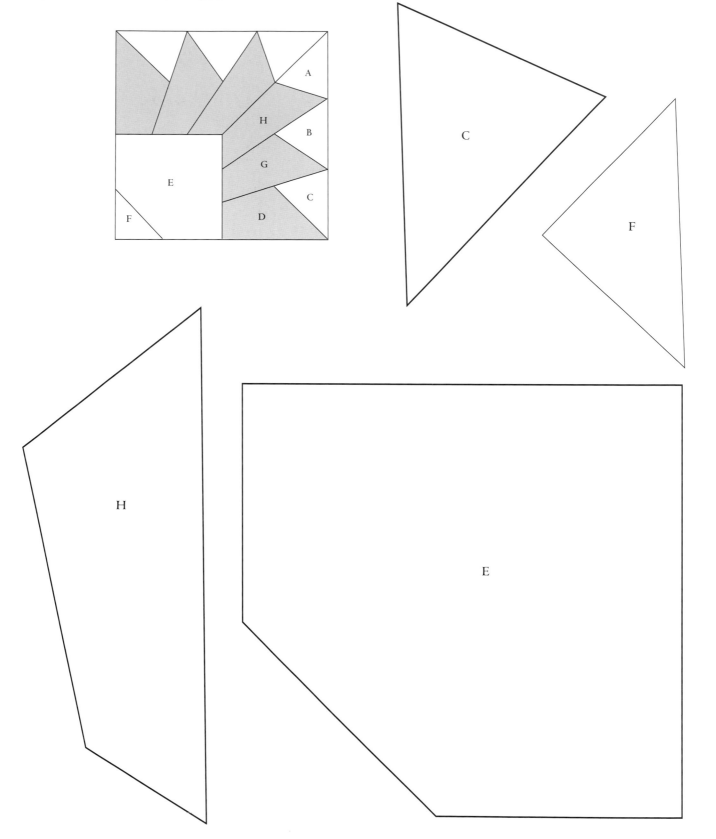

Reverse pattern pieces for the opposite side.

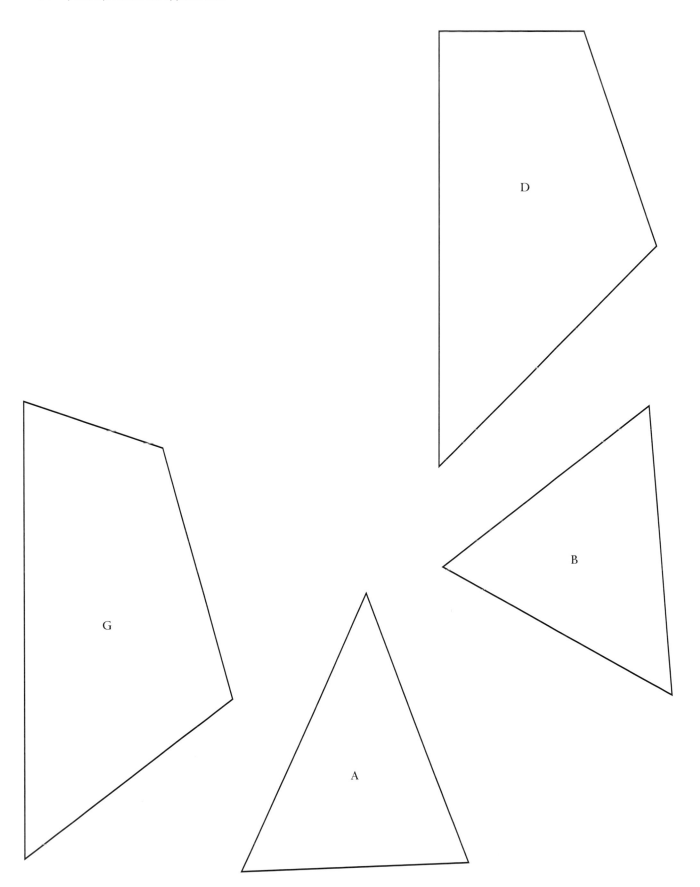

CHURN DASH
$7^1/_2'' \times 7^1/_2''$
Add $^1/_4''$ seam allowance to each pattern piece.

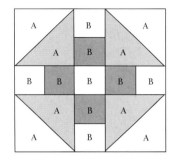

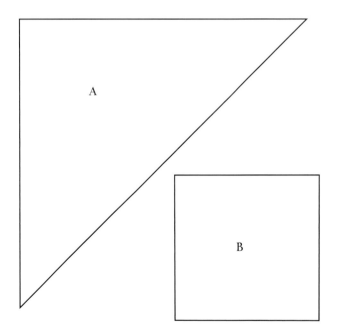

CHURN DASH appliqué

BASKETS
9″ × 9″
Add ¼″ seam allowance to each pattern piece.

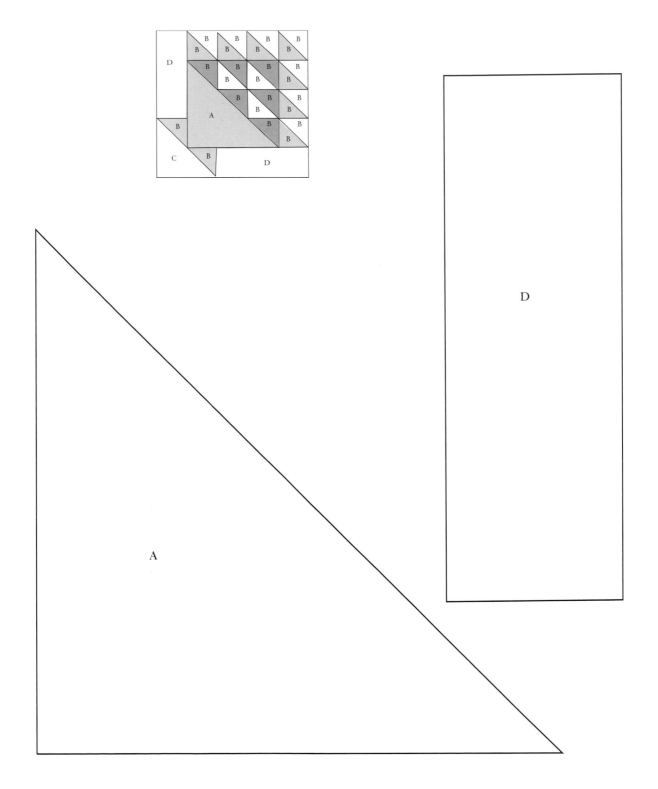

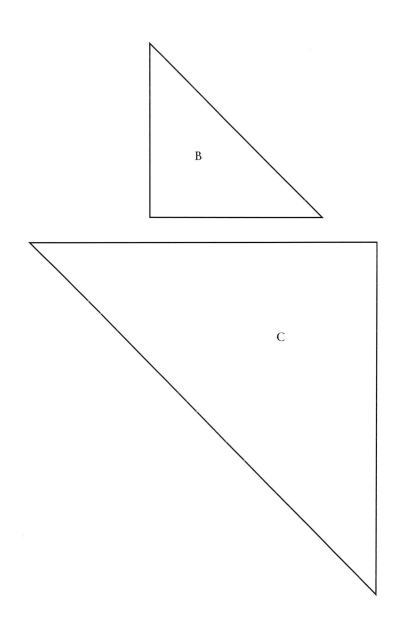

BEAR'S PAW

9″ × 9″

Add ¼″ seam allowance to each pattern piece.

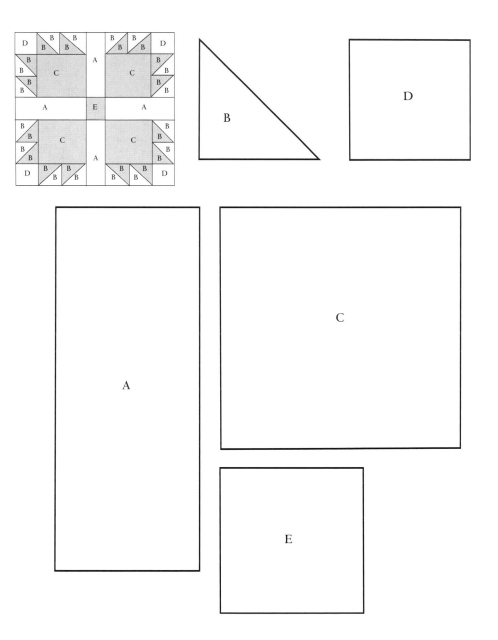

PINWHEEL
6″ × 6″
Add ¼″ seam allowance to each pattern piece.

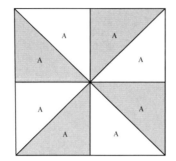

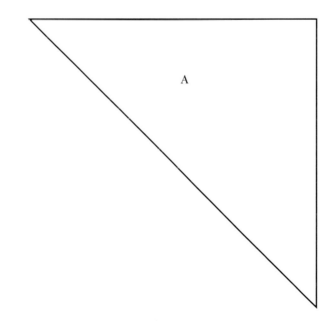

A

WASHINGTON ROSE
15″ × 15″
Add ¼″ seam allowance to each pattern piece.

LINDEN MILL
10″ × 10″
Add ¼″ seam allowance to each pattern piece.

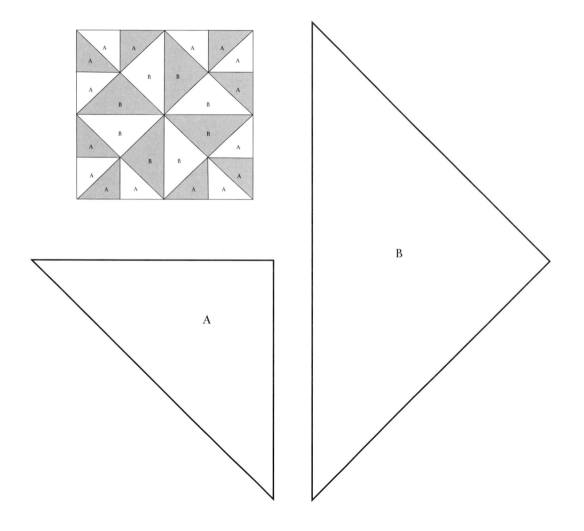

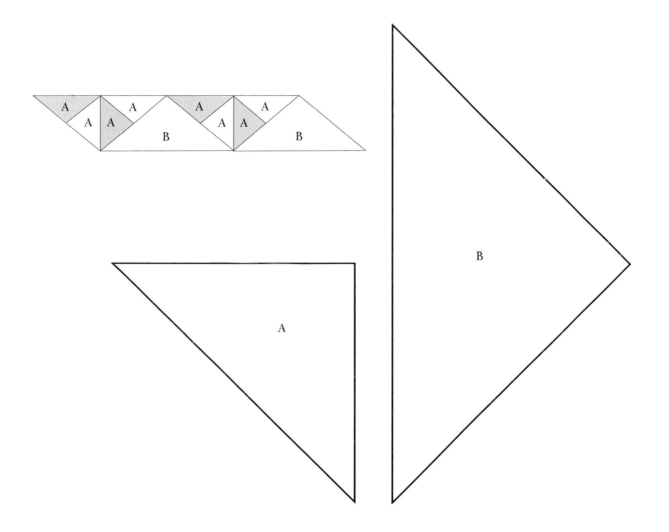

JULIANNA
9″ × 9″
Add ¼″ seam allowance to each pattern piece.

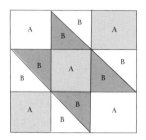

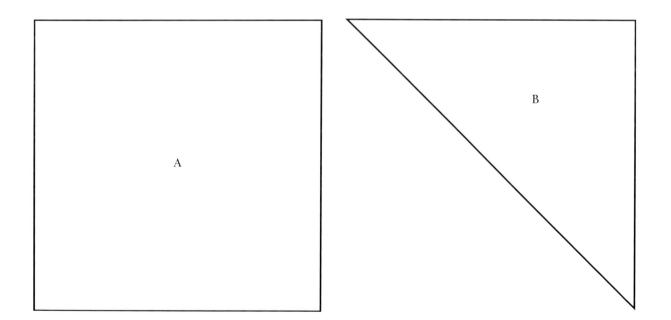

JULIANNA border

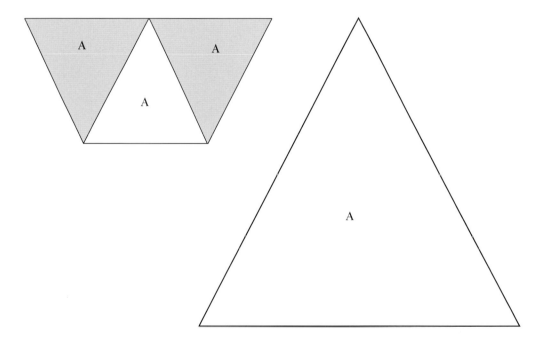

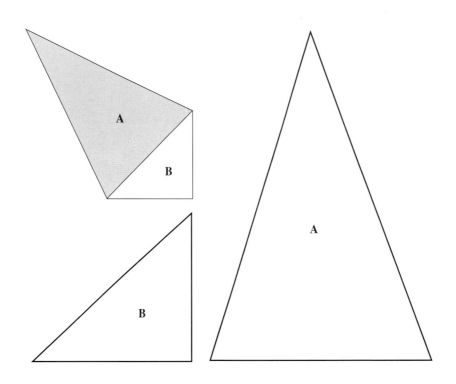

Complete Inventory of Mary Schafer Quilts

TRYING TO KEEP TRACK OF MARY AND HER QUILTS IS A BIG JOB. The total number of quilts is 290. This list was compiled from my personal records and Mary's records. Even then, I am sure some quilts have fallen through the cracks. This list does not include Mary's unfinished tops. In a visit with Mary in 2002, she showed me 21 unquilted doll quilts, 7 unquilted crib quilts, and 4 unquilted full-size quilts, which are not included in this list.

The quilts are divided into Mary's First and Second Collections. Within each, they are grouped into major categories. Quite a few of Mary's quilts, including those now housed permanently at the Michigan State University Museum in East Lansing and those that have been sold by the museum, have been shown in various publications. I have included these sources with the following reference codes.

S&B: *Sets and Borders* (Marston and Cunningham 1987)
AB: *American Beauties: Rose and Tulip Quilts* (Marston and Cunningham 1988)
MSHQ: *Mary Schafer and Her Quilts* (Marston and Cunningham 1990)
MQ: *Michigan Quilts: 150 Years of a Textile Tradition* (MacDowell and Fitzgerald 1987)
GLGQ: *Great Lakes, Great Quilts* (MacDowell 2001)

As of this writing, sixteen quilts in the First Collection have been sold by the Michigan State University Museum. These quilts are indicated with an asterisk. The selling price is given in parentheses.

Because of Mary's careful documentation and because she signed and dated her quilts, I have accurate dates for most of them. The exceptions are Mary's doll and crib quilts in the Second Collection and the quilts she gave as gifts. For many of these, I can only estimate. I do know that Mary began making doll and crib quilts in 1981. Once she began making small quilts, her enthusiasm drove her to make a lot of them in a short period of time. The majority were made between 1982 and 1985.

FIRST COLLECTION: PERMANENT COLLECTION OF THE MICHIGAN STATE UNIVERSITY MUSEUM (118 QUILTS)

The original collection that the museum purchased from Mary consisted of 118 quilts.

Thirty-six Antique Quilts

1. Album. 85″ × 92″, dated 1856. Bird-in-Hand, Pennsylvania. MSHQ.
2. Bars. 77″ × 87″, ca. 1876. Pennsylvania Amish quilt.
3. Cracker. 70″ × 84″, ca. 1900. Michiana, Indiana.
*4. Delectable Mountains Variation. 100″ × 100″, ca. 1850. Bird-in-Hand, Pennsylvania. ($550)
5. Dutch Iris. 94″ × 96″, ca. 1900–1910. Westchester, Pennsylvania.
6. Feather-Edged Star. 74″ × 90″, ca. 1850. Ora Brown, Monroeville, Indiana. First antique quilt Mary purchased. MSHQ.
*7. Fly Foot. 82″ × 96½″, ca. 1915. Goderich, Ontario, Canada. ($450)
8. Four Patch. 99½″ × 104″, ca. 1800–1825. Purchased from Betty Harriman.
9. Framed Square. 97″ × 102″, ca. 1800–1825. Purchased from Betty Harriman. MSHQ.
10. Linden Mill. 68″ × 76″, ca. 1900, Michigan. MSHQ.
11. Love Apple. 94″ × 96″, ca. 1850. Gettysburg, Pennsylvania. Signed quilt: Susannah Allen.
12. Mariner's Compass. 97″ × 100″, ca. 1830–50. Purchased from Betty Harriman. MSHQ.
13. Mrs. Ewer's Tulip. 85″ × 86″, ca. 1850–75. Signed quilt: Ellie. AB.
14. Nine-Patch Variation. 92″ × 92″, ca. 1800–25.
15. North Carolina Lily. 82″ × 83″, ca. 1920. Breezewood, Pennsylvania.
16. North Carolina Lily. 77″ × 93″, ca. 1925. Collected in Flint, Michigan. MSHQ.
17. Path through the Woods. 71″ × 83″, ca. 1900. Collected in Flint, Michigan.

*18. Pine Tree. 65″ × 72″, 1884. Dated quilt, Franklin County, Ohio. MSHQ. ($300)

19. Poppy. 82″ × 82″, ca. 1850–75. West Chester, Pennsylvania.

*20. Rose and Hearts. 82½″ × 98″, 1963. Made by Ella McInturff, Mannington, West Virginia. ($600) AB.

*21. Rose of Sharon. 74″ × 79″, ca. 1875–1900. ($500) AB.

*22. Rose Wreath. 76″ × 76″, ca. 1850. Fayetteville, Pennsylvania. ($225). AB.

23. Savannah Star. 81″ × 81″, ca. 1910–1920. Collected in Flint, Michigan. S&B, MSHQ.

24. Single Tulip. 69″ × 97″, ca. 1860. Collected in Salem, Michigan. AB.

25. Single Tulip. 82″ × 82″, ca. 1850. Lintner family, Hamilton, Ohio. AB.

26. Single Wedding Ring. 81″ × 81″, ca. 1900–1915. Collected in Flint, Michigan. MSHQ.

27. Snowball. 82″ × 85″, ca. 1900. Mt. Morris, Michigan. MSHQ.

28. Sunburst. 86″ × 86″, ca. 1825. New England. Purchased from Betty Harriman. MSHQ.

29. Sunflower or Sunburst. 79½″ × 96″, ca. 1875. Macomb County, Michigan. S&B.

30. Valley Star. 86″ × 88″, ca. 1900–1910. Collected in Flint, Michigan. MSHQ.

31. Whig Rose. 104″ × 106″, ca. 1834. Greenfield, Massachusetts. AB.

32. Whig Rose. 89″ × 90″, ca. 1850. West Chester, Pennsylvania (on white print ground). AB.

33. Whig Rose. 89″ × 90″, ca. 1850. West Chester, Pennsylvania (on mustard yellow print ground). AB, GLGQ.

34. White Quilt. 82″ × 83″, 1837. Signed and dated: "Theresa M. Hamilton. October 8, 1837. Harpersfield." Stuffed and trapunto quilt. GLGQ

35. White Quilt. 78″ × 88″, ca. 1800–1810. Stuffed and trapunto quilt. Purchased from Betty Harriman.

36. White Quilt. 75″ × 85″, ca. 1950. Fayetteville, Pennsylvania.

Seven Old Tops or Blocks Finished by Mary Schafer

*1. Churn Dash. 97½″ × 88½″, ca. 1915. Collected in Flint, Michigan. Mary added the border and completed the quilt. ($500) S&B.

2. Good Fortune. 81½″ × 93″, ca. 1915–20. Top collected in Flint, Michigan. Mary completed the quilt.

3. Hazel Hanks' Star. 76″ × 94″, blocks ca. 1926. Blocks were said to be made by Hazel Hanks, Springfield, Illinois, a descendant of Nancy Hanks, Abraham Lincoln's mother. MSHQ.

4. Path through the Woods Variation. 82″ × 98″, ca. 1935. Top collected in Flint, Michigan. Mary added the border and completed the quilt.

5. Star and Cross. 82″ × 100″, blocks ca. 1860. Mary bought the blocks and made the quilt in 1964. MSHQ.

6. Three Sisters. 85″ × 100″, ca. 1918. Top from Flushing, Michigan. Mary added the border and completed the quilt in 1980. MSHQ.

7. Turkey Tracks. 82″ × 101″, ca. 1910. Tied quilt bought in poor condition. Mary took it apart, repaired the top, added the border, and completed the quilt in 1967.

Twenty Documented Michigan-Made Antique Quilts

1. Album. 85″ × 96″, ca. 1900. DesJardin family, Essexville, Michigan.

2. Bear's Paw. 86″ × 94″, ca. 1890–1910. Adella Penoyer, Flushing, Michigan. Mary added the border and completed the quilt. MQ.

3. Chimney Sweep. 80½″ × 98½″, ca. 1923. Emma Catherine Zink Frey, Flint, Michigan.

4. Courthouse Steps. 75″ × 87″, ca. 1926. Top by Clara Bloss, Swartz Creek, Michigan. Completed by Mary Schafer.

5. Diamond in a Square. 79″ × 96½″, ca. 1890. Top by Eliza Andrews Fairchilds, East Jordan, Michigan. Mary added the border and completed the quilt.

6. Double Hour Glass. 77½″ × 86½″, ca. 1910–1915. James Pollack family, Genesee County, Michigan.

*7. Double Pyramid. 71″ × 83″, ca. 1850–75. Martha Wade Sherwood, Holly, Michigan. ($500) S&B.

8. Drunkard's Path. 85″ × 98″, ca. 1887. Top by Martha Wade Sherwood, Holly, Michigan. Completed by Mary Schafer. MQ.

9. Drunkard's Path Variation. 79″ × 88″, ca. 1850. Top by Israel Parshall family, Saginaw County, Michigan. Completed by Mary Schafer.

10. Full Blown Tulip. 72″ × 87″, ca. 1850. Israel Parshall family, Saginaw County, Michigan. AB.

11. Log Cabin, Barn Raising. 88″ × 100″, ca. 1915–20. DesJardin family, Essexville, Michigan.

12. Log Cabin, Sun and Shadow. 66″ × 77½″, ca. 1875. Taylor family, Flint, Michigan.

13. London Stairs. 78½″ × 97½″, ca. 1895. Top by Eliza Andrews Fairchilds, East Jordan, Michigan. Mary added the border and completed the quilt.

14. Ocean Waves. 72″ × 72″, ca. 1900. Ralph Bartholomew family, Clio, Michigan.

15. Odd-Fellows Patch. 76″ × 84″, ca. 1870–80. Matilda Vary, Ceresco, Michigan. MSHQ.

16. Pyramid. 83″ × 98″, ca. 1876. Top by Matilda Vary, Ceresco, Michigan. Mary added the border and completed the quilt in 1980. MSHQ.

17. Sawtooth. 82″ × 98½″, ca. 1876. Top by Matilda Vary, Ceresco, Michigan. Mary added the border and completed the quilt.

18. Strips of Triangles. 68″ × 76″, ca. 1910–15. Anna Rolf, Flushing, Michigan.

19. Sunrise. 68″ × 101″, ca. 1863. Susan Brown, Owosso, Michigan. MSHQ.

20. Thousand Pyramids. 84″ × 100″, ca. 1890. DesJardin family, Essexville, Michigan.

Seventeen Quilts Begun by Betty Harriman and Finished by Mary Schafer

Mary knows when Betty started some of these quilts due to their correspondence. For other quilts, she knows approximately when Betty started them. For the remainder, she doesn't know at all.

1. Alice Blue Wreath. 90″ × 93″. Begun ca. 1966, finished 1979.

2. Boxes. 89″ × 99″, ca. 1900. Top, finished 1980.

3. Colonial Basket. 83½″ × 96″. Beginning date unknown, finished 1978.

4. Democratic Rose. 83″ × 101″. Begun 1923, finished 1979. AB.

5. Drunkard's Path. 84″ × 97″. Begun 1937, finished 1980.

6. Eight-Pointed Star. 85″ × 100″, ca. 1850. Top, finished 1980. MSHQ.

*7. English Plume. 82″ × 98½″. Begun 1967, finished 1979. ($900) S&B, MSHQ.

8. Flowering Almond. 85″ × 99″. Begun ca. 1968, finished 1979. S&B, GLGQ.

9. Grapes and Vines. 83½″ × 97″. Mary received Betty's pattern and fabric only. She made the quilt in 1972. S&B, MSHQ.

*10. Holland Queen. 83″ × 99″. Begun ca. 1965, finished 1978. (Price unknown) AB.

11. Lee's Rose and Buds. 84″ × 101″. Begun 1969, finished 1972. AB, MSHQ.

12. Missouri Rose Tree. 89″ × 92″. Begun 1966, finished 1973. AB.

13. Pennsylvania Dutch Flower Garden. 81″ × 103″. Beginning date unknown, finished 1973. AB.

14. Star of Bethlehem. 79½″ × 96″, ca. 1940–50. Top, finished 1977.

*15. Washington Plume. 88″ × 96″, ca. 1965. Top, finished 1980. ($1,100) S&B.

16. Washington Plume. 90″ × 96″, ca. 1965. Top, finished 1978. MSHQ.

17. York County. 92″ × 92″. Begun ca. 1963, finished 1980.

Thirty-eight Full-Size Quilts Made by Mary

*1. Attic Window. 80″ × 100″, 1975. ($1,050) MSHQ.

2. Bars. 75″ × 83½″, 1976. Copy of an old-fashioned Lancaster County Amish quilt. MSHQ.

3. Black Elegance. 82½″ × 99″, 1980. S&B.

4. Burgoyne Surrounded. 84″ × 103½″, 1974. Bicentennial quilt. MSHQ.

5. Clamshell. 79″ × 97½″, 1966. Challenge quilt. Won two blue ribbons at the National Quilt Association show in 1970. S&B, MSHQ.

6. Coxcomb. 84½″ × 98″, 1968. Challenge quilt.

*7. Delectable Mountains. 88″ × 100″, 1975. ($2000)

8. Double Hour Glass. 81″ × 98″, 1976. Copy of the Pollack family Double Hour Glass listed under "Twenty Documented Michigan-Made Antique Quilts." MSHQ.

9. Dutchman's Puzzle. 80″ × 98″, 1976. Made from fabrics dating from the early 1900s. Won a blue ribbon for the best pieced quilt from old fabrics at the 1978 Festival of Quilts Contest in Santa Rosa, California.

10. Eisenhower. 56″ × 102″, 1968. Shown in 20th Century Quilts, 1900–1970: Women Make Their Mark, Museum of the American Quilter's Society, Paducah, Kentucky, 1997. MSHQ.

*11. Fox and Geese. 78″ × 90″, 1964. ($1,000) S&B, MSHQ.

12. Georgetown Circle. 83½″ × 98″, 1977.

13. Hidden Star. 80½″ × 99″, 1974.

14. Honey Bee. 79″ × 95″, 1968. Challenge quilt. Original border. MSHQ.

15. Lafayette Orange Peel. 85″ × 100″, 1974. Bicentennial quilt. MSHQ.

16. Lee's Rose and Buds. 81″ × 99½″, 1972. Pattern copied from Betty Harriman's quilt of the same name. Original pattern from the Robert E. Lee home. AB.

17. Linden Mill. 80″ × 94″, 1956. Mary's first pieced quilt. Original border. MSHQ.

18. Lobster. 77″ × 93″, 1969. Challenge pattern from Florence Peto's book *Historic Quilts* (1939). S&B, MSHQ.

19. Molly Pitcher. 78½″ × 106″, 1975. MSHQ.

*20. Morning Star. 81″ × 101″, 1978. ($600)

21. North Carolina Lily. 78″ × 94″, 1971. Original border. S&B, MSHQ.

22. Oak Leaf and Cherries. 80″ × 100″, 1969. Challenge quilt. Original border. S&B, MSHQ.

23. October Foliage. 84½″ × 94″, 1971. Original border.

24. Pineapples. 82″ × 100″, 1973. Inspired by a quilt in the Shelburne Museum, Shelburne, Vermont.

25. Poppy Wreath. 78″ × 93″, 1953. Mary's second appliqué quilt. MSHQ.

26. Queen Charlotte's Crown. 76″ × 98″, 1973. Bicentennial quilt. S&B, MSHQ.

27. Rhododendron. 81″ × 99″, 1952. Mary's first quilt. MSHQ.

28. Savannah Star. 76½″ × 97″, 1970. Challenge quilt. Original border. S&B, MSHQ.

29. Single Chain and Knot. 87″ × 99″, 1974.

30. Spirit of '76. 82½″ × 100½″, 1974. Bicentennial quilt. MSHQ.

31. String Star. 81″ × 97″, 1977.

32. Sunburst. 80″ × 97″, 1980. Original border. S&B.

33. Sunshine and Shadow. 83″ × 83″, 1977. Copy of Lancaster County, Pennsylvania, Amish quilt.

*34. Tobacco Leaf. 79½″ × 96½″, 1977. ($1,200) S&B, MSHQ.

35. Variable Star. 82″ × 99″, 1973. Copy of an old quilt from Wiscassett, Maine.

36. Variable Star. 84″ × 95″, 1967.

37. Washington Plume. 93″ × 93″, 1968. Challenge and Bicentennial quilt. S&B, MSHQ.

38. Wild Goose Chase. 84″ × 101″, 1973.

SECOND COLLECTION: MARY SCHAFER COLLECTION (106 QUILTS)

The quilts in the Second Collection remain in Mary's possession.

Thirty-three Full-Size Quilts Made by Mary

1. Baskets. 58″ × 71″, 1985. Midwest Amish.

2. Bear's Paw. 71″ × 85″, 1981. Midwest Amish.

3. Bird of Paradise. 84″ × 99″, 1980. Medallion.

4. Churn Dash. 76″ × 79″, 1982.

5. Country Home. 77″ × 96″, 1986.

6. Countryside. 80″ × 86″, 1980. Medallion.

7. Cups and Saucers. 80½″ × 95½″, 1989.

8. Ebb Tide. 72″ × 96½″, 1980.

9. Evening Star. 78″ × 93″, 1982.

10. Feather-Edged Star. 77″ × 97″, 1984.

11. Flower Pot. 79″ × 99″, 1980.

12. Friendship Star. 78″ × 91″, 1991.

13. Giant Tulip. 75″ × 86″, 1980.

14. Grandmother's Pride. 79″ × 99″, 1980.

15. The Harvesters. 82″ × 97½″, 1980. Medallion.

16. Julianna. 79″ × 94″, 1985.

17. Kaleidoscope. 79″ × 100″, 1980.

18. Linden Mill. 81″ × 96″, 1980. Mary's second Linden Mill.

19. Monterey Nine Patch. 76″ × 90″, 1992.

20. One and Four Square. 83″ × 96½″, 1981.

21. Pinwheel. 85″ × 97″, 1980.

22. Pomegranate. 82″ × 94″, 1990.

23. Prairie Queen. 82″ × 97″, 1984. Quilted by Jacqueline Flick.
24. Radical Rose. 80″ × 97″, 1965. Original border. Mary made this specifically for her bed. She made two more Radical Rose quilts as well (listed under "Mary's Quilts Made for Others").
25. Rebecca Merritt. 76″ × 97″, 1981.
26. Rose Wreath. 82″ × 82″, 1990.
27. Scallops. 77″ × 95″, 1982.
28. Shoo Fly. 81″ × 98″, 1977. Fred's favorite quilt.
29. Spools. 76½″ × 95″, 1985.
30. Spring Woodland. 78″ × 95″, 1983.
31. Variable Star. 77″ × 87″, 1983.
32. Welsh Medallion. 76″ × 85″, 1980. Medallion.
33. Yarmouth Square. 78½″ × 96½″, 1984.

Six Betty Harriman and Mary Schafer Quilts

1. Churn Dash. 78″ × 95″. Beginning date unknown, finished 1985–90.
2. Democratic Rose. 80″ × 95″. Begun ca. 1960, finished 1981. AB.
3. Dresden Plate. 80″ × 97″. Beginning date unknown, finished 1986.
4. Framed Nine Patch. 87″ × 93″. Antique top, Harriman estate, finished 1986.
5. Joseph's Coat. 79″ × 93″. Begun ca. 1960, finished 1984.
6. Washington Rose. 90½″ × 92″. Begun 1969, finished 1984. MSHQ, AB.

Thirty-four Mary Schafer Doll Quilts

Mary made all but four quilts in this group. Numbers 10 and 17 are antique quilts, and numbers 6 and 18 were gifts to Mary from her friend Hildegard Hoag. Completion dates for some of Mary's doll quilts were never recorded and this information is lost. However, these thirty-four quilts were all made between 1982 and 1986.

1. Amish Sunshine and Shadow. 21½″ × 21½″, 1982.
2. Birds in Flight. 18¾″ × 22¼″, 1984.
3. Bow Tie. 21″ × 27″, 1982. Amish quilt.
4. Bow Tie. 18½″ × 24¼″, 1982.
5. Churn Dash. 19¼″ × 25″.
6. Clamshell. 20″ × 23″. Gift from Hildegard Hoag. The top is made of cheater's cloth.
7. Dear Hearts. 19″ × 23½″, 1985.

8. Hit and Miss. 17¼″ × 23¼″, 1982.

9. Honeycomb. 20″ × 26½″, 1985.

10. Material Pleasures. 12″ × 17¾″. Antique quilt, date unknown.

11. Material Pleasures. 15½″ × 19½″, 1982.

12. One and Four Square. 19″ × 23″.

13. One and Four Square. 12¼″ × 15¼″.

14. One and Four Square. 14¼″ × 14¼″, 1986.

15. One and Four Square. 17¾″ × 21¼″, 1982.

16. One Patch. 15¼″ × 18″, 1982.

17. One Patch. 17½″ × 24½″. Antique quilt.

18. One Patch. 20¼″ × 29″. Gift from Hildegard Hoag.

19. One-Patch Floral, Nine-Patch Center. 15¼″ × 18¼″.

20. One-Patch Raffle Quilt. 16″ × 18″.

21. Peach and Rose. 18½″ × 22″.

22. Persian Pear. 22″ × 22½″.

23. Pieced-Look Print with Church Print Border. 18½″ × 22¾″.

24. Pink Print and Plain. 18¾″ × 23¼″.

25. Pinwheel. 15½″ × 15½″.

26. Puss in a Corner. 17¾″ × 19¼″.

27. Pyramid. 18¼″ × 21¾″, 1982.

28. Sunshine and Shadow. 21¾″ × 22½″, 1982.

29. Surfer's Wave. 19¾″ × 20″, 1982.

30. Thirty-six Small Hearts. 19½″ × 20¾″.

31. Tumbler. 20½″ × 23½″, 1982.

32. Vera Town Nine Patch. 12¾″ × 17″.

33. Vertical Stripes. 16¾″ × 21¼″, 1982.

34. Yellow Nine Patch. 16¼″ × 21″, 1982.

Twenty-seven Crib Quilts Made by Mary

1. Attic Window. 29½″ × 38″, 1984 or 1985.

2. Cactus Basket. 40″ × 50½″, 1983 or 1984.

3. Cherry Basket. 39¾″ × 47″, 1985.

4. Dear Hearts. 38″ × 43″, 1986.

5. India, Clamshell. 36″ × 43½″, 1984 or 1985.

6. Painted Circle. 40¼″ × 40¾″, 1982.

7. Pennsylvania Dutch Nine-Patch Variation. 43″ × 49″, 1986.

8. Periwinkle. 36¾″ × 44¾″, 1983 or 1984.

9. Pinwheels. 42″ × 51″, 1982.

10. Roses and Hearts. 43½″ × 43½″, 1982.

11. Sixteen Patch. 38″ × 47″, 1983 or 1984.

12. Sun Bonnet Babies. 36½″ × 45″, 1984 or 1985.

13. Yankee Puzzle. 26½″ × 45″, 1965. Mary's first crib quilt.

Mary's Amish-Style Crib Quilts

14. Album. 37″ × 37½″, 1985.
15. Bars. 46¼″ × 46¼″, 1984.
16. Bow Tie. 32″ × 41½″ ,1982.
17. Bricks. 33″ × 38½″, 1985.
18. Carolina Lily. 33″ × 50″, 1982.
19. Chinese Coins, 42″ × 49″, 1985.
20. Old Maid's Puzzle. 33¼″ × 42″, 1982.
21. One Patch. 38″ × 50″, 1982.
22. One Patch. 43″ × 43″, 1983. Also called Checkerboard.
23. Roman Stripe. 35″ × 43½″, 1982.
24. Sunshine and Shadow. 39″ × 39″, 1983.
25. Sunshine and Shadow. 47½″ × 47½″, 1982.
26. Sunshine and Shadow. 46″ × 47″, 1984.
27. Sunshine and Shadow. 49″ × 49″, 1984.

Two Antique Quilts Purchased after 1980

1. Cups and Saucers. 69″ × 80¼″, ca. 1920–30. Midwest Amish quilt.
2. Star of Bethlehem. 71″ × 87″, ca. 1930. Stiffel family quilt purchased in Flushing, Michigan.

Four Quilt Tops Finished by Mary

1. Cross-Stitch Rose. 83″ × 97″. Completed in 1986.
2. Rose Wreath. 78″ × 96½″, ca. 1930. Shipshewana, Indiana. Completed in 1985.
3. Monticello. 76″ × 94″, ca. 1920. All white top completed in 1981. Quilted by Mary Ann Miller.
4. Mourning Quilt. 80″ × 94″, ca. 1875–1900. Eliza Andrews Fairchilds, East Jordan, Michigan. Completed in 1983.

MARY'S QUILTS MADE FOR OTHERS (SIXTY-SIX QUILTS)

These are full-size quilts unless noted. Completion dates for some of these quilts were never recorded.

1. Attic Window. Crib quilt. Made for Steven Joseph Kamorny, grandson of Mary's neighbors, Hazel and Bill Gillanders.
2. Dear Hearts. 1995. Doll quilt. Gift for Jessi McConnell, Fenton, Michigan.
3. Ebb Tide. 1980. Gift for Joe Cunningham.
4. Feather-Edged Star. 75″ × 96″, 1993. Gift for Hazel and Bill Gillanders, Mary's neighbors and friends.
5. Fox and Geese. Made for the Buzzell House, a restored historical house in Flint, Michigan.
6. Hearts. Crib quilt. Gift for Heather M. Gillanders, granddaughter of Mary's neighbors, Hazel and Bill Gillanders.
7. Horn of Plenty. Made for Barbara Bannister in exchange for a Paragon kit, American Glory, no. 01147.
8. Malinda's Princess Plumes. Commissioned quilt for Ruth Parr, Meridian, Mississippi.
9. Megan's One Patch. 18″ × 21″, 1989. Doll quilt. Gift for Megan Ballard.
10. Nine-Patch Variation. Gift for Charles and Joyce Johnson, Mary's neighbors.
11. One Patch. Doll quilt. Gift for Kathleen Zintsmarter, a neighbor's child.
12. One Patch. Doll quilt. Gift for Virginia Anderson, Flushing, Michigan.
13. One Patch. Doll quilt. Made for Kitty Cole, Milford, Michigan.
14. Oriental Poppy. Made for Betty Harriman's sister Marcia in exchange for the English Plume.
15. Radical Rose. Made for Ida Pullman. This and the following quilt were made for Ida's two sons in exchange for quilting.
16. Radical Rose.
17. Tea Leaves. Gift for Sophie Ignotov, Mary's childhood friend.

Four Commissioned Quilts

Exact dates are unavailable but the commission quilts were made in the 1980s.

1. Dutchman's Puzzle. Quilt top sold to Mary Gleason, Mount Rose, Michigan.
2. Pineapples. Commission for Dr. Raymond Hagan, Mary's dentist, Flushing, Michigan
3. Pumpkin Vine. Crib quilt. Commission for Robert May, Detroit, Michigan.
4. Tea Leaves. Commission for Robert May, Detroit, Michigan.

Gwen Marston's Schafer Quilts (Fourteen Quilts)

1. Bow Tie. 20⅔″ × 26¼″, 1982.
2. Four-Patch Variation. 41″ × 41″, 1995.

3. Four Patch. 36″ × 48″, 1986.
4. Hit and Miss. 17¼″ × 24″, 1982.
5. Hole in the Barn Door Variation. 44½″ × 44½″, 1991.
6. Honeycomb. 19¾″ × 26¼″, 1988.
7. Improved Nine Patch. 17¾″ × 19½″, 1996.
8. Nine Patch. 17″ × 21″, 1982.
9. Rose of Sharon. 77″ × 93″, 1979.
10. Roses, 42″ × 42″, 1987.
11. Shoo Fly. 42″ × 42″, 1993.
12. Streak o'Lightning. 30″ × 36″, 1983.
13. Sunshine and Shadow. 21″ × 21″, 1998.
14. Linden Mill. 17″ × 19″, 1996.

Gifts for Mary's Family (Twenty-two Quilts)

The dimensions and year of completion for many of these quilts were never recorded.

1. Blazing Star. Gift for Joseph G. Vida, Mary's brother.
2. Country Home. Gift for Fred's brother, Alex Schafer, and his wife Mary.
3. Dear Hearts. Crib quilt. Gift for Fred's sister Molly's son, Charles Hilgendorf.
4. Evening Star. Crib quilt. Gift for Kaylee, granddaughter of Edward Hilgendorf.
5. Linden Mill. 1991. Gift for Mary's son Ronald.
6. Little Skipper. Crib quilt. Gift for Jared, son of Edward Hilgendorf, Molly's son.
7. Little Skipper. 35″ × 46″, 1984. Gift for Mary's great-grandson, Samuel J. Schmondiuk.
8. Pansy. Gift for Mary's son Ronald and his wife Esther.
9. Pinwheel. Doll quilt. Gift for Charles Hilgendorf.
10. Pinwheel. Gift for Mary's grandson Carey.
11. Sampler Quilt. Gift for Kort, son of Charles Hilgendorf.
12. Savannah Star. 40½″ × 50½″, 1983 or 1984. Gift for Natalie Schmondiuk, Mary's granddaughter.
13. Shoo Fly. Crib quilt. Gift for Garette, grandson of Edward Hilgendorf.
14. Single Wedding Ring. Gift for Edward Hilgendorf.
15. Star Quilt. Gift for Brian, son of Charles Hilgendorf.
16. Sunshine and Shadow. Gift for a nephew.
17. Tea Leaves. Gift for Mary's granddaughter Jennifer.
18. Tea Leaves. 2000. Gift for Fred's sister Ann.
19. Tea Leaves. Made for Molly Schafer Hilgendorf, Fred's sister.

20. Teddy Bear. Gift for Robert Hilgendorf.
21. Ten Hearts. Crib quilt. Gift for Heidi, granddaughter of Edward Hilgendorf.
22. Tulip. Gift for Mary's granddaughter Deborah.

Nine Benefits Quilts

1. Broken Dishes. Donated to the Whaley Historical House for raffle, 1980.
2. Churn Dash. Given to the Genesee Star Quilters Guild for their auction.
3. Hands All Around. Donated to the Whaley Historical House for raffle, 1979.
4. Maltese Cross. Quilt top donated to Michigan State University for raffle to raise money for purchase of the Mary Schafer Collection.
5. Nine-Patch Variation. Donated to the Whaley Historical House for raffle, 1981.
6. Railroad Crossing. Quilt top donated to the Flushing Area Historical Society.
7. Roman Stripe. Donated to the Whaley Historical House for raffle, 1983. (This quilt was made by Mary Schafer and Gwen Marston).
8. Sunshine and Shadow. Crib quilt. Given to Planned Parenthood for auction, ca. 1990.
9. Tea Leaves. Donated to the Whaley Historical House for raffle, 1982.

Mary Schafer Timeline

 INCLUDED IN THE TIMELINE ARE THE FULL-SIZE QUILTS MADE by Mary Schafer. I included the Harriman/Schafer quilts when I know the dates of completion. Key events in Mary's life appear in italic type.

1952	Rhododendron
1953	Poppy Wreath
1956	Linden Mill
1964	Fox and Geese
1964	Star and Cross (quilt made from antique blocks)
1965	Radical Rose
1965	Yankee Puzzle (crib quilt)
1966–70:	*Challenge Period*
1966	Clamshell
1967	Variable Star (blue and white)
1967	Turkey Tracks
1968	Eisenhower
1968	Coxcomb
1968	Washington Plume (Mount Vernon)
1968	Honey Bee

❄

1969	Lobster
1969	Oak Leaf and Cherries
1970	*Mary wins two blue ribbons at the first Natonal Quilting Association show*
1970	Savannah Star
1971	*Betty Harriman dies, June 21*
1971	North Carolina Lily
1971	October Foliage
1972	*Fred retires in October*
1972	Lee's Rose and Buds
1972	Lee's Rose and Buds (Harriman/Schafer)
1972	Grapes and Vines (Harriman/Schafer)
1973	Wild Goose Chase
1973	Pineapples
1973	Queen Charlotte's Crown
1973	Variable Star (Wiscasset, Maine, copy)
1973	Missouri Rose Tree (Harriman/Schafer)
1973	Pennsylvania Dutch Flower Garden (Harriman/Schafer)
1974	Single Chain and Knot
1974	Burgoyne Surrounded
1974	Hidden Star
1974	Lafayette Orange Peel
1974	Spirit of '76
1975	Attic Window
1975	Delectable Mountains
1975	Molly Pitcher
1976	Double Hour Glass
1976	Dutchman's Puzzle
1976	Bars
1977	*Gwen Meets Mary*
1977	Georgetown Circle
1977	Shoo Fly
1977	Sunshine and Shadow
1977	Tobacco Leaf
1977	Star of Bethlehem (Harriman/Schafer)
1977	String Star
1978	*Mary's Dutchman's Puzzle wins blue ribbon for "best pieced quilt from old fabrics" at the 1978 Festival of Quilts Contest in Santa Rosa, California*
1978	*First of six Mary Schafer exhibits at the Whaley Historical House, Flint, Michigan*
1978	Morning Star
1978	Colonial Basket (Harriman/Schafer)
1978	Holland Queen

1978	Washington Plume (Harriman/Schafer)
1979	Alice Blue Wreath (Harriman/Schafer)
1979	Democratic Rose (Harriman/Schafer)
1979	English Plume (Harriman/Schafer)
1979	Flowering Almond (Harriman/Schafer)
1979	Rose of Sharon
1980	*Publication of Marston's* The Mary Schafer Collection
1980	Black Elegance
1980	Sunburst
1980	Washington Plume (Harriman/Schafer)
1980	Pyramid (old top completed)
1980	Three Sisters (old top completed)
1980	Eight-Pointed Star (Harriman/Schafer)
1980	Boxes (Harriman/Schafer)
1980	Drunkard's Path (Harriman/Schafer)
1980	York County (Harriman/Schafer)
	Cutoff for First Collection
1980	Bird of Paradise (medallion)
1980	The Harvesters (medallion)
1980	Countryside (medallion)
1980	Welsh Medallion
1980	Ebb Tide
1980	Flower Pot
1980	Giant Tulip
1980	Grandmother's Pride
1980	Kaleidoscope
1980	Pinwheel
1980	Linden Mill
1981	Bear's Paw (Amish)
1981	One and Four Square
1981	Rebecca Merritt
1981	York County (Harriman/Schafer)
1981	Democratic Rose (Harriman/Schafer)
1981	Monticello
1982	Churn Dash
1982	Scallops
1982	Evening Star
1983	*Small Quilts Exhibit, Flint, Michigan*
1983	Mourning Quilt
1983	Rose Wreath (Shipshewana, Indiana)
1983	Spring Woodland
1983	Variable Star

1984	Feather-Edged Star
1984	Yarmouth Square
1984	Joseph's Coat (Harriman/Schafer)
1984	Washington Rose (Harriman/Schafer)
1985	Baskets (Amish)
1985	Julianna
1985	Prairie Queen
1985	Spools
1986	*Now and Then Exhibit, Birmingham Bloomfield Art Association, Birmingham, Michigan. Exhibit traveled to Cazenovia, New York; Winfield, Kansas; and the Jesse Besser Museum, Alpena, Michigan.*
1986	*Michigan State Senate Resolution honoring Mary's contributions*
1986	Country Home
1986	Dresden Plate
1987	*Publication of Marston and Cunningham's* Sets and Borders, *featuring thirty-one Mary Schafer quilts*
1987	*Publication of Marston's* Q Is for Quilt. *Gwen wrote the book, Mary made the blocks.*
1987	*Publication of Marston and Cunningham's* 70 Classic Quilting Patterns, *featuring eighteen original Mary Schafer quilting designs and six Betty Harriman quilting designs*
1987	*Reflections on American History: Quilts from the Mary Schafer Collection exhibit, American Museum of Quilts, San Jose, California, November 3 through December 5, 1987*
1988	*Fred Schafer dies on December 8*
1988	*Mary buys her first car, takes driving lessons, and gets her license*
1988	*Mary honored by the Michigan Women's Foundation for contributions to the arts*
1988	*Publication of Marston and Cunningham's* American Beauties: Rose and Tulip Quilts, *featuring seven blocks and twenty-four quilts by Mary Schafer*
1989	*Mary Schafer and Her Quilts: A Retrospective, New England Quilt Museum, Lowell, Massachusetts*
1989	Cups and Saucers
1990	*Publication of Marston and Cunningham's* Mary Schafer and Her Quilts
1990	*American Lung Association uses Mary's quilt blocks for regional fund-raising stickers*
1990	Pomegranate
1990	Rose Wreath
1991	*Mary Schafer Quilts exhibit, Museum of the American Quilter's Society, Paducah, Kentucky*
1991	Friendship Star
1991	Linden Mill (for son Ron)
1992	Monterey Nine Patch

1993:   Feather-Edged Star (for Hazel and Bill Gillanders)

1995   *The Mary Schafer Retrospective, Crossroads Village Open Air Museum, Flint, Michigan*

1995   Dear Hearts (doll quilt for Jessi McConnell)

1997   *Mary chosen to participate in 20th Century Quilts, 1900–1970: Women Make Their Mark exhibit, Museum of the American Quilter's Society, Paducah, Kentucky*

1998   *Michigan State University Museum acquires Mary's First Collection*

1999   *Selections from the Michigan State University Museum's Mary Schafer Quilt Collection exhibit, Michigan State University Museum, East Lansing, Michigan, October 15–17*

1999–2001   *Mary participates in The Red Beret Exhibit, traveling show honoring the Emergency Women's Brigade of the Great Sit-Down Strike at Flint, 1936–37*

2001   *The Mary Schafer Collection: A Legacy of Quilt History exhibit, Michigan State University Museum, East Lansing, Michigan, July 29–December 31*

2002   *Michigan Heritage Award presented by the Michigan State University Museum*

Mary Schafer Résumé

 MARY SCHAFER, BORN IN 1910, HAS BEEN ACTIVELY INVOLVED in making, collecting, and studying quilts since 1952. She is a quilter of uncommon breadth whose artistic achievements include re-creations of antique quilts and original work. A substantial amount of her work is now housed permanently at the Michigan State University Museum in East Lansing, Michigan.

MARY SCHAFER HONORS

The first National Quilting Association exhibit, September 1970. Won blue ribbons for Best Pieced and Viewers' Choice for her CLAMSHELL quilt.

State of Michigan proclamation honoring Mary for her contribution to quilt making, Senate Resolution 605, September 9, 1986.

Michigan Women's Foundation award for outstanding contributions to the arts, May 25, 1988.

Permanent Mary Schafer Collection housed at Michigan State University Museum, East Lansing, Michigan. Acquired in 1998.

Michigan Heritage Award presented by the Michigan State University Museum, 2002.

Solo Exhibits

Annual Whaley House exhibits, Flint, Michigan, 1978–83, Gwen Marston, curator.

Small Quilts exhibit, Citizens Bank, Flint, Michigan, May 1983, Gwen Marston, curator.

Mary Schafer Quilts at the Sloan Museum, Flint, Michigan, August 1985.

Reflections on American History: Quilts from the Mary Schafer Collection, American Museum of Quilts, San Jose, California, November 3 through December 5, 1987, Gwen Marston, curator.

Mary Schafer and Her Quilts: A Retrospective, New England Quilt Museum, Lowell, Massachusetts, March 20–May 7, 1989, Gwen Marston and Joe Cunningham, curators.

Mary Schafer Quilts, Museum of the American Quilter's Society, Paducah, Kentucky, April 25–June 1, 1991, Gwen Marston and Joe Cunningham, curators. This first exhibition at the MAQS featured forty-four quilts from Mary's collection.

The Mary Schafer Retrospective, Crossroads Village Open Air Museum, Flint, Michigan, September 1995, Valerie Clarke and Ken Hannon, organizers.

The Mary Schafer Collection: A Legacy of Quilt History, Michigan State University, East Lansing, Michigan, July 29–December 31, 2001.

Group Exhibits

Festival of Quilts Contest, Santa Rosa, California, April 21–23, 1978.

World of Quilts, Meadowbrook Hall, Rochester, Michigan, 1983.

Now and Then, Birmingham Bloomfield Art Association, Birmingham, Michigan, September–October, 1986, Merry Silber, curator. Exhibit traveled to Cazenovia, New York; Winfield, Kansas; and the Jesse Besser Museum, Alpena, Michigan, in 1987.

Reunion, Art Source Gallery, Flint, Michigan, July 29–August 26, 1988.

Michigan Directions: Flint Area Artists, Flint Institute of Arts, Flint, Michigan, November 27, 1994–January 15, 1995, Christopher R. Young, curator.

20th Century Quilts, 1900–1970: Women Make Their Mark, Museum of the American Quilter's Society, Paducah, Kentucky, March 22–June 29, 1997, Joyce Gross and Cuesta Benberry, curators.

The Red Beret Exhibit, traveling show honoring the Emergency Women's Brigade of the Great Sit-Down Strike at Flint, 1936–37, 1999–2001, Valerie Clarke, organizer.

Selections from the Michigan State University Museum's Mary Schafer Quilt Collection, Michigan State University Museum, East Lansing, Michigan, October 15–17, 1999.

Genesee Star Quilters Guild Show and Exhibition, Flushing, Michigan, September 27–29, 2002. The exhibit featured forty-three Schafer quilts.

Publications

Clarke, Valerie. "A Quiltmaker's Quiltmaker: Mary Schafer," *Lady's Circle Patchwork Quilts* 110 (February 1996): 5–11.

Cunningham, Joe. "Fourteen Quilts Begun by One Woman and Finished by Another." In *Uncoverings 1986*. Mill Valley, CA: American Quilt Study Group, 1987.

Gross, Joyce. "Mary Schafer." *Quilters' Journal* 1, no. 3 (1978): 3–4.

MacDowell, Marsha, ed. *Great Lakes, Great Quilts: From the Michigan State University Museum*. Lafayette, CA: C&T Publishing, 2001.

Marston, Gwen. *The Mary Schafer Quilt Collection*. Flint, MI: 1980.

———. "The Meetin' Place." *Quilter's Newsletter Magazine* 158 (January 1984): 40–42.

———. *Q Is for Quilt*. East Lansing: Michigan State University Museum, 1987.

Marston, Gwen, and Joe Cunningham. *Amish Quilting Patterns*. New York: Dover, 1987.

———. *70 Classic Quilting Patterns*. New York: Dover, 1987.

———. *Sets and Borders*. Paducah, KY: American Quilter's Society, 1987.

———. *American Beauties: Rose and Tulip Quilts*. Paducah, KY: American Quilter's Society, 1988.

———. *Mary Schafer and Her Quilts*. East Lansing: Michigan State University Museum, 1990.

Notes

PREFACE

1. See "Finding a Home for the First Collection" for more about the placement of the Schafer Collection at Michigan State University.
2. See Gwen Marston and Joe Cunningham, *Sets and Borders* (Paducah: American Quilter's Society, 1987), 45.

PART I. LAYING THE GROUNDWORK

1. Roderick Kiracofe, *The American Quilt* (New York: Clarkson Potter, 1993), 210.
2. Merikay Waldvogel, *Soft Covers For Hard Times: Quiltmaking and the Great Depression* (Nashville: Rutledge Hill Press, 1990), 40.
3. Kiracofe 1993, 216.
4. Mary Katherine Jarrell, "Three Historic Quilts," in *Uncoverings 1981* (Mill Valley, CA: American Quilt Study Group, 1982), 97–104.
5. Marsha MacDowell, ed. *Great Lakes, Great Quilts: From the Michigan State University Museum* (Lafayette, CA.: C&T Publishing, 2001), 5.

INFLUENCES

1. Joyce Gross, "Cuesta Ray Benberry," *Quilters' Journal* 23 (1984): 4.
2. Mary Schafer, "100 Years of the North Carolina Lily," *Nimble Needle Treasures*, fall 1972, 4.
3. Joyce Gross, "Bonnie Leman," *Quilters' Journal* 20 (1982): 3.
4. Bonnie Leman, Heirloom Plastics Catalog, 1971.

QUILT STUDY

1. Gwen Marston and Joe Cunningham, *Mary Schafer and Her Quilts* (East Lansing: Michigan State University Museum, 1990), 55.

2. Ibid., 11, 12, 45, 45, 55.

3. Joy Craddock to Mary Schafer, February 17, 1965.

4. Dolores Hinson to Gwen Marston, February 2000.

5. Maxine Teele, "Crazy Like a Fox," *Nimble Needle Treasures*, fall 1973, 6.

6. Ibid., 6, 7.

7. Dolores Hinson to Gwen Marston, February 2000.

8. Quoted in Gwen Marston and Joe Cunningham, *American Beauties: Rose and Tulip Quilts* (Paducah: American Quilter's Society, 1988), 89; and Cuesta Benberry, "A Quiet Pattern Collector's Project: State Rose Quilt Patterns," *Nimble Needle Treasures*, spring 1974, 7.

9. Marston and Cunningham 1990, iii.

10. Maxine Teele, "Quilting Is Her Hobby," *Nimble Needle Treasures*, summer 1973, 23.

11. Mary Schafer to Gwen Marston, December 1986.

12. Joyce Gross and Cuesta Benberry, *20th Century Quilts, 1900–1970: Women Make Their Mark* (Paducah: American Quilter's Society, 1997), 6.

MARY'S CORRESPONDENCE

1. Mary Schafer to round robin participants, October 29, 1964.

2. Barbara Bannister and Edna Ford, *The United States Patchwork Pattern Book: 50 Quilt Blocks for 50 States from "Hearth & Home" Magazine* (New York: Dover, 1976).

3. Barbara Bannister and Edna Ford, *State Capitals Quilt Blocks: 50 Patchwork Patterns from "Hearth & Home" Magazine* (New York: Dover, 1977).

4. Barbara Bannister to Mary Schafer, November 8, 1964.

5. Mary Schafer to Gwen Marston, February 2000.

6. Cuesta Benberry to Gwen Marston, January 14, 2000.

7. Cuesta Benberry, "The Face behind the Familiar Name: Barbara Bannister," *Quilter's Newsletter Magazine* 200 (March 1988): 26.

8. Cuesta Benberry, *Always There: The African-American Presence in American Quilts* (Louisville: Kentucky Quilt Project, 1992), 116 and *Quilters' Journal* 23 (1984): 12; Jane Benson and Nancy Olsen, *The Power of Cloth: Political Quilts, 1845–1986* (Cupertino, CA: De Anza College and the Euphrat Gallery, 1987), 33.

9. Cuesta Benberry to Gwen Marston, June 15, 1985.

10. Cuesta Benberry, Christmas letter, December 16, 1996.

11. Cuesta Benberry to Gwen Marston, February 11, 1985.

12. Celia Y. Oliver, ed. *55 Famous Quilts from the Shelburne Museum* (New York: Dover, 1990), 24, 42, 43.

13. Phillip H. Curtis, *American Quilts in the Newark Museum Collection*, vol. 25 (Newark, NJ: Newark Museum, 1973), 21, 60.

14. Gross and Benberry 1997, 25, 26.

15. Maxine Teele, "In Partial Payment," *Nimble Needles Treasures*, winter 1973, 9.

16. Ibid.

17. *Muscatine Iowa Journal*, October 31, 1967.

18. *Sunday Register* (Des Moines), April 6, 1975, 5.

19. Ibid.

20. Maxine Teele, "Hit and Miss," *Nimble Needle Treasures*, winter 1974, 8.

21. Teele 1973, 23.

22. Lenice Bacon, *American Patchwork Quilts* (New York: William Morrow, 1973), 25.

23. Ibid., dust jacket.

24. Gross 1984, 12.

25. Dolores Hinson, phone conversation with Gwen Marston, March 2000.

26. Ibid.

27. Mary Schafer to Ruth Parr, January 26, 1973.

28. Mary Schafer to Ruth Parr, April 13, 1973.

THE SCHAFER AND HARRIMAN COLLABORATION

1. Suellen Meyer, "Betty Harned Harriman." *Quilters' Journal* 18 (1982): 3–6, 17.

2. Ibid., 6.

3. Ibid., 5.

4. Betty Harriman to Mary Schafer, November 18, 1969.

5. Jesse F. Seay to Betty Harriman, February 17, 1970.

6. Jesse F. Seay to Betty Harriman, November 30, 1970.

7. Ann White, "Skill of Long-Ago Eras in Quilts," *Kansas City Star*, ca. 1950.

8. Marston and Cunningham 1990, 10, fig. 10.

9. Ibid., 11, fig. 11.

10. Ibid., 14, fig. 12.

11. Ibid., 55, fig. 76.

12. Ibid., 56, fig. 78.

13. Meyer 1982, 17.

14. Phone conversation with Mary Schafer, November 29, 2002.

15. Thomas K. Woodward and Blanche Greenstein, *Twentieth Century Quilts, 1900–1950* (New York: E. P. Dutton, 1988), 19, pls. 13, 14, 15.

16. Carrie Hall and Rose Kretsinger, *The Romance of the Patchwork Quilt in America* (Caldwell, ID: Caxton, 1935), 241; Helen Foresman Spencer Museum of Art, *Quilter's Choice* (Lawrence, KS: University of Kansas, Lawrence, 1978), 60; Barbara Brackman, *American Patchwork Quilt: Quilts from the Spencer Museum* (Tokyo: Kokusai Art, 1987), 44.

COMING TO AMERICA

1. Mary Schafer to Gwen Marston, December 27, 1999.

MARY'S EARLY QUILTS

1. Marston and Cunningham 1990, 4, fig. 4.

PATTERN COLLECTING

1. Barbara Brackman, *An Encyclopedia of Pieced Quilt Patterns* (Lawrence, KS: Prairie Flower Publishing, 1979), 603.

2. Mary Schafer to round robin participants, February 8, 1966.

3. Cuesta Benberry, *Quilters' Journal* 23 (1984): 12.

4. Joy Craddock to Mary Schafer, undated.

5. Mary Schafer to round robin participants, 1964.

6. Mary Schafer to round robin participants, October 29, 1964.

7. Carol Lynch to Mary Schafer, February 26, 1965.

8. Mary Schafer to round robin participants, February 8, 1966.

9. Barbara Bannister to Mary Schafer, November 8, 1964.

10. Mary Schafer to Joan Kaim, October 1, 1965.

11. Dolores Hinson to Gwen Marston, April 10, 2000.

MARY MAKES QUILT BLOCKS

1. Gross 1984, 12.
2. Dolores Hinson to Gwen Marston, February 2000.
3. Dolores Hinson to Gwen Marston, April 10, 2000.
4. Dolores A. Hinson, "Quilters' Catalogs," *Antiques Journal* 25, no. 9 (September 1970): 12–14.
5. Wilene Smith, "Quilt Blocks? Or Quilt Patterns?" in *Uncoverings 1986* (Mill Valley, CA: American Quilt Study Group, 1987), 101–14.
6. Laurel Horton, ed., *Quiltmaking in America: Beyond the Myths* (Nashville: Rutledge Hill Press, 1994), 30–39.
7. Hall and Kretsinger 1935, 7.
8. Benberry 1984, 13.
9. Cuesta Benberry, Christmas letter, December 16, 1996.

THE CHALLENGE PERIOD

1. Marie Webster, *Quilts: Their Story and How to Make Them* (Garden City, NY: Doubleday, Page and Company, 1915), xvii–xviii.
2. Ruth E. Finley, *Old Patchwork Quilts and the Women Who Made Them* (Philadelphia: Lippincott, 1929), 62–63.
3. *Nimble Needle Treasures*, spring 1971, 23.
4. Florence Peto to Mary Schafer, February 7, 1969.
5. Marston and Cunningham 1987, 44; Marston and Cunningham 1990, 22, fig. 22.
6. Marston and Cunningham 1987, 47; and Marston and Cunningham 1990, 23, fig. 23, and 24, fig. 24.
7. Marston and Cunningham 1990, 17, fig. 17; Gross and Benberry 1997.
8. Marston and Cunningham 1987, 43; Marston and Cunningham 1990, 25, fig. 25.

THE BICENTENNIAL QUILT REVIVAL

1. Mary Schafer to Ruth Parr, March 1973.
2. Webster 1915, xviii.
3. Dolores A. Hinson, "The Spirit of '76," *Nimble Needle Treasures*, fall 1970, 2.
4. Cuesta Benberry, "Victory Quilts," *Nimble Needle Treasures*, winter 1970, 4.
5. Cuesta Benberry, "More Patriotic Quilts of the World War II Era," *Nimble Needle Treasures*, winter 1970, 4.
6. Finley 1929, 79.
7. Samuel Eliot Morison, *Oxford History of the American People* (New York: Oxford University Press, 1965), 226.
8. Dolores A. Hinson, *A Quilter's Companion* (New York: Arco, 1973), 76.

MARY'S QUILTS FOR OTHERS

1. Hazel Gillanders to Gwen Marston, October 15, 1999.
2. Cyril Nelson, ed., *The Quilt Engagement Calendar* (New York: E. P. Dutton, 1988), pl. 41.
3. Phone conversation with Mary Schafer, April 28, 2000.
4. Mary Schafer to Gwen Marston, December 3, 1988.
5. *Flushing Observer*, August 11, 1985, A3.
6. Cuesta Benberry, Christmas letter, December 16, 1996.

1. Mary donated thirty ribbons to the Michigan State University Museum as part of her archival materials.
2. Pat Almy, "First Quilter's Show Is a Big Success," *Nimble Needles Treasures*, spring 1971, 23.
3. Bonnie Lehman, ed., "Quilt Show Review," *Quilter's Newsletter Magazine* 80 (January 1979): 8–9.
4. Michigan State Senate Resolution 605, September 9, 1986.
5. Joyce Gross and Cuesta Benberry, 1997.
6. *Flushing Observer*, September 29, 2002.
7. Ibid.

MARY, 1990 TO THE PRESENT

1. Webster 1915, xviii.
2. Mary Schafer to Gwen Marston, December 16, 1996.
3. Meyer 1982, 5.
4. Mary Schafer to Gwen Marston, September 20, 1999.

MARY'S TECHNIQUE

1. Mary Schafer to Gwen Marston, February 23, 1985.
2. Kiracofe 1993, 243.
3. Hall and Kretsinger 1935, 263.
4. Ibid., 46.
5. Woodard and Greenstein 1988, 25.
6. Kiracofe 1993, 329.
7. Cuesta Benberry, "The Superb Mrs. Stenge," *Nimble Needle Treasures*, summer 1971, 4.
8. Mary Schafer to Ruth Parr, February 23, 1973.
9. Leman 1979, 9.

ARTISTIC CHARACTERISTICS

1. Mary Schafer to Ruth Parr, January 14, 1973.
2. Cuesta Benberry to Gwen Marston, 1983.

FINDING A HOME FOR THE FIRST COLLECTION

1. American Quilt Study Group, *Blanket Statements*, winter 1989–90, 7.
2. Patricia Hubbel Boucher, appraisal statement, June 11, 1992.
3. Mary Schafer to Gwen Marston, March 2000.
4. American Quilt Study Group 1989–90, 7.
5. American Quilt Study Group Twentieth Annual Seminar program, October 1999.
6. Hall and Kretsinger 1935, 241, pl. CIV; Brackman 1987, pl. 44.

THE SECOND COLLECTION

1. Mary Schafer to Gwen Marston, April 1985.

MOTIVATION

1. Mary Schafer notes to Gwen Marston, April 1985.
2. Dolores Hinson to Gwen Marston, February 2000.

Bibliography

Almy, Pat. "First Quilter's Show Is a Big Success." *Nimble Needle Treasures*, spring 1971, 23.

———. "Quilting Is Her Hobby: Maxine Teele." *Nimble Needle Treasures*, summer 1973.

———. "Preparations for the Bicentennial." *Nimble Needle Treasures*, spring 1975.

American Quilt Study Group. *Blanket Statements*, winter 1989–90.

Avery, Virginia. "Florence Peto: Renaissance Woman of Mid Century." *Quilter's Newsletter Magazine* 118 (January 1980).

Bacon, Lenice. *American Patchwork Quilts.* New York: William Morrow, 1973.

Bannister, Barbara. *Doll Quilts.* Alanson, MI: Needlecraft Books, 1976.

Bannister, Barbara, and Edna Ford. *The United States Patchwork Pattern Book: 50 Quilt Blocks for 50 States from "Hearth & Home" Magazine.* New York: Dover, 1976.

———. *State Capitals Quilt Blocks: 50 Patchwork Patterns from "Hearth & Home" Magazine.* New York: Dover, 1977.

Benberry, Cuesta. "More Patriotic Quilts of the World War II Era." *Nimble Needle Treasures,* winter 1970.

———. "Victory Quilts." *Nimble Needle Treasures,* fall 1970.

———. "The Superb Mrs. Stenge." *Nimble Needle Treasures,* summer 1971, 4.

———. "A Quilt Pattern Collector's Project: State Rose Quilt Patterns." *Nimble Needle Treasures,* spring 1974.

———. "The 20th Century's First Quilt Revival." *Quilters Newsletter Magazine* 114 (July–August 1979): 20–22; 115 (September 1979): 25, 26, 29.

———. "Afro-American Women and Quilts." In *Uncoverings 1980.* Mill Valley, CA: American Quilt Study Group, 1981.

———. "White Perspectives of Blacks in Quilts and Related Media." In *Uncoverings 1983.* Mill Valley, CA: American Quilt Study Group, 1984.

———. *Quilters' Journal* 23 (1984).

———. "The Face behind the Familiar Name: Barbara Bannister." *Quilter's Newsletter Magazine* 200 (March 1988): 26.

———. "Marie D. Webster: A Major Influence on Quilt Design in the 20th Century." *Quilter's Newsletter Magazine*, July–August 1990.

———. *Always There: The African-American Presence in American Quilts*. Louisville: Kentucky Quilt Project, 1992.

Benson, Jane, and Nancy Olsen. *The Power of Cloth: Political Quilts 1845–1986*. Cupertino, CA: De Anza College and the Euphrat Gallery, 1987.

Bishop, Robert, and Elizabeth Safanda. *A Gallery of Amish Quilts*. New York: E. P. Dutton, 1976.

Bishop, Robert. *New Discoveries in American Quilts*. New York: E. P. Dutton, 1975.

Brackman, Barbara. *An Encyclopedia of Pieced Quilt Patterns*. Lawrence, KS: Prairie Flower Publishing, 1979.

———. *American Patchwork Quilt: Quilts from the Spencer Museum*. Tokyo: Kokusai Art, 1987.

Brackman, Barbara, Jennie A. Chinn, Gayle R. Davis, Terry Thompson, Sara Reimer Farley, and Nancy Hornback. *Kansas Quilts and Quilters*. Lawrence, KS: University Press of Kansas, 1993.

Broude, Norma, and Mary D. Garrard. *Feminism and Art History: Questioning the Litany*, New York: Harper and Row, 1982.

Clarke, Valerie. *Mary Schafer Retrospective*. Flint: Greater Flint Arts Council, 1995.

———. "A Quiltmaker's Quiltmaker: Mary Schafer," *Lady's Circle Patchwork Quilts* 110 (February 1996): 5–11.

Cunningham, Joe. "Fourteen Quilts Begun by One Woman and Finished by Another." In *Uncoverings 1986*. Mill Valley, CA: American Quilt Study Group, 1987.

Curtis, Phillip H. *American Quilts in the Newark Museum Collection*. Vol. 25. Newark, NJ: Newark Museum, 1973.

Dunton, William Rush, Jr. *Old Quilts*. Catonsville, MD: William Rush Dunton Jr., 1946.

Finley, Ruth E. *Old Patchwork Quilts and the Women Who Made Them*. Philadelphia: Lippincott, 1929.

Gross, Joyce. "Betty Harriman." *Quilters' Journal* 1, no. 6 (1978).

———. "Mary Schafer." *Quilters' Journal* 1, no. 3 (1978).

———. "Florence Peto." *Quilters' Journal* 2, no. 4 (1979).

———. "Florence Peto and *Woman's Day*." *Quilters' Journal* 3, no. 2 (1980).

———. "Bonnie Leman." *Quilters' Journal* 20 (1982).

———. "Cuesta Ray Benberry." *Quilters' Journal* 23 (1984).

Gross, Joyce, and Cuesta Benberry. *20th Century Quilts, 1900–1970: Women Make Their Mark*. Paducah: American Quilter's Society, 1997.

Hall, Carrie A., and Rose Kretsinger. *The Romance of the Patchwork Quilt in America*. Caldwell, ID: Caxton, 1935.

Hansen, Klaudeen, and Annette Riddle, eds. *Quilt Art Engagement Calendar '92*. Paducah: American Quilter's Society, 1991.

Helen Foresman Spencer Museum of Art. *Quilter's Choice*. Lawrence, KS: University of Kansas, Lawrence, 1978.

Hinson, Dolores A. "Quilters' Catalogs." *Antiques Journal* 25, no. 9 (September 1970).

———. *Quilting Manual*. Knoxville: Hearthside Press, 1970.

———. "The Spirit of '76." *Nimble Needle Treasures*, fall 1970.

———. *A Quilter's Companion*. New York: Arco, 1973.

Holstein, Jonathan. *The Pieced Quilt: An American Design Tradition*. Boston: New York Graphic Society, 1973.